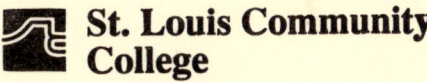

COMPLYING WITH THE AMERICANS WITH DISABILITIES ACT

Complying with the Americans with Disabilities ———Act———

A GUIDEBOOK FOR MANAGEMENT AND PEOPLE WITH DISABILITIES

Don Fersh and Peter W. Thomas, Esq.

Foreword by
Senator J. Robert Kerrey

QUORUM BOOKS
Westport, Connecticut
London

Library of Congress Cataloging-in-Publication Data

Fersh, Don.
 Complying with the Americans with Disabilities Act : a guidebook
for management and people with disabilities / Don Fersh and Peter W.
Thomas ; foreword by J. Robert Kerrey.
  p. cm.
 Includes bibliographical references and index.
 ISBN 0–89930–714–0 (alk. paper)
 1. Handicapped—Employment—Law and legislation—United States.
2. Discrimination against the handicapped—Law and legislation—
United States. 3. Handicapped—Legal status, laws, etc.—United
States. I. Thomas, Peter W. II. Title.
KF3469.F47 1993
344.73′01133—dc20
[347.3041133] 92–28478

British Library Cataloguing in Publication Data is available.

Library of Congress Catalog Card Number: 92–28478
ISBN: 0–89930–714–0

First published in 1993

Quorum Books, 88 Post Road West, Westport, Connecticut 06881
An imprint of Greenwood Publishing Group, Inc.

Printed in the United States of America

The paper used in this book complies with the
Permanent Paper Standard issued by the National
Information Standards Organization (Z39.48–1984).

10 9 8 7 6 5 4 3 2 1

Copyright Acknowledgments

The author and publisher gratefully acknowledge permission to use the
following:

Abeson, Alan. "Workers with Mental Retardation and Title I of the Americans
with Disabilities Act." Arlington, Tex.: The Arc.

Hanson, Thor, and Nancy Law. "The Impact of Title I of the Americans with
Disabilities Act on People with Multiple Sclerosis." New York: National
Multiple Sclerosis Society.

Jordan, I. King. "The ADA and the Person." Speech given at Lenoir-Rhyne
College, Hickory, North Carolina, January 9, 1992.

To my parents, Harriett and Sy
Don Fersh

In memory of my little brother, Eric
Peter W. Thomas

It is as old as scriptures and is as clear as the American Constitution. The heart of the question is whether all Americans are to be afforded equal rights and equal opportunities, whether we are going to treat our fellow Americans as we want to be treated.

President John F. Kennedy
June 11, 1963, civil rights address

Contents

Tables

Foreword

Senator J. Robert Kerrey

It is an honor for me to contribute to this guidebook. The Americans with Disabilities Act (ADA) is landmark legislation, particularly for the approximately 43 million Americans living with disabilities. This law reaffirms our undying commitment to the words of the statement declaring our independence: "We hold these truths to be self-evident, that all men are created equal, that they are endowed by their Creator with certain inalienable Rights, that among these are Life, Liberty and the pursuit of Happiness."

For the first 25 years of my life, I was temporarily able bodied. I had the strength and the physical ability to do everything on my own, to survive completely on my own, and to live completely on my own.

Then, in March of 1969, I was seriously wounded in Vietnam and found myself helpless, lying on my back in the Philadelphia Naval Hospital. When I wanted to move a few feet away, I had to ask someone for help. I went from being perfectly able—being able to run, swim, and hike—to spending every waking moment learning how to walk.

I was fortunate. I had excellent care through the Veterans Administration. I had supportive family and friends and, with time, I was able to get back to doing many of the things I had done prior to being wounded.

I had opportunity and the assistance and support I needed to pursue my career and personal goals. This is what all Americans, including all disabled Americans, deserve. The ADA represents a commitment to making impossible dreams possible for countless disabled Americans.

Indeed, the ADA is a legislative policy whose goals are ambitious. But it is critical that we do not let the greatness of the task deter us. We must begin to focus our attention and our efforts on people—on what they are capable of doing, not on their disabilities or what they cannot do.

Passage of the ADA is an excellent beginning toward addressing the needs of persons with all types of disabilities. As a partner in a chain of restaurants, I share the concerns of other small business owners about the impact of the ADA on business. While the ADA does pose certain requirements on business, it also provides these businesses with the opportunity to serve millions of potential new customers. Similarly, people with disabilities will benefit from increased opportunities to patronize those businesses.

This guidebook is designed to address the interests of people with disabilities, the concerns of business, and the questions of the general public about the ADA. It is a useful book because it is written in non-legal terms and is designed to be easily understood by anyone with an interest in the legislation.

It is imperative that we recognize that it is the spirit in each of us that moves us to achieve the impossible. Franklin Roosevelt said it very eloquently in this third inaugural address. Comparing a nation with a person, he said:

A person, has something deeper, something more permanent, something larger than the sum of all its parts. It is that something which matters most to its future— which calls forth the most sacred guarding of its present. It is a thing for which we find it difficult—even impossible—to hit upon a single, simple word. And yet we all understand what it is—the spirit.

The ADA will live on in the spirit in which it was passed: providing disabled Americans with the opportunity to achieve the goals to which we all aspire regardless of our abilities or disabilities.

Acknowledgments

This book was developed with the generous assistance of a great number of people including Bernard Posner, Ph.D., a consultant to the National Organization on Disability and former executive director of the President's Committee on Employment of People with Disabilities, who provided both initial enthusiasm and continuing encouragement throughout the writing of the manuscript. Our very special thanks to Paul G. Hearne, president of the Dole Foundation for Employment of People with Disabilities, who requested that the book be written. We would especially like to thank Senator J. Robert Kerrey (D-Nebraska) for writing the foreword, and in so doing, sharing his personal insights on the Americans with Disabilities Act based on his experience as a Vietnam veteran, a businessman, and as an individual who has overcome disability. We deeply appreciate the assistance of Chai R. Feldblum, visiting professor of law, Georgetown University Law Center; Robert L. Burgdorf, Jr., professor, District of Columbia School of Law; and Lex Frieden, senior vice president, The Institute for Rehabilitation Research; all of whom with Paul Hearne, drafted the Americans with Disabilities Act.

We very much appreciate the contribution of articles in the book by I. King Jordan, Ph.D., president of Gallaudet University; Alan Abeson, Ed.D., executive director, The Arc; and Vice Admiral Thor Hanson, USN (Ret.), president and CEO, and Nancy Law, LSW, program and development manager, National Multiple Sclerosis Society. We would very much like to thank Bill Schutz, public inquiries manager, who provided an enormous amount of research, and Roland Fagan, Theresa Craig, and Mark Odum, also of the National Rehabilitation Information Center (NARIC). We would especially like to thank the individuals who wrote us letters endorsing the concept of this book in 1990: Dr. Leonard Perlman, Ed.D., a consultant in rehabilitation psychology; former Congressman Paul G. Rogers, partner, Hogan & Hartson; Douglas K. Volmer, associate executive director, government relations, Paralyzed Veterans of America; Robert E. Brabham, Ph.D., former executive director, National Rehabilitation Association; Michael Ailsworth, vice president, government relations, Sandoz Corporation; and Michael S. Levy, former executive director, Epilepsy Foundation for the National Capital Area.

We deeply appreciate the assistance and contributions of author Hugh Gregory Gallagher; Mark L. Goldfarb, executive assistant to the president, Gallaudet University; Cynthia Lehman, director, legal advocacy, Epilepsy Foundation of America; Arney Rosenblat, director of public affairs, National Multiple Sclerosis Society; Brenda Bell, director, program marketing, National Alliance of Business; Susan R. Meisinger, SPHR, vice president, government and public affairs, Society for Human Resource Management; and Mary Nathan and Ray Schmitt. A number of persons in the federal government provided us with interviews and research materials, including, from the Equal Employment Opportunity Commission, Chairman Evan J. Kemp, Jr.; Howard Moses, deputy director, Technical Assistance Training Institute; and Cristopher Bell, attorney-advisor to the chairman. Barney Singer, Tom Gray, and Julie Weeks of the Small Business Administration were also extremely helpful.

Don Fersh thanks all of his family, sisters, Susan and Maryl, and especially his father for providing an interest in writing, semantics, the social sciences, fairness, and part of a childhood filled with Kipling-like adventures in India. My deepest thanks to the teachers who have been supportive and provided inspiration along the way. Thanks to Lynn Boze at the Cleveland Park Library, Washington, D.C., for research assistance and to Stanley Krippner, Ph.D., former president, Association for Humanistic Psychology, for helping me get started in writing. My heartfelt thanks to Ruth Wreshner, our agent, who helped make this book possible. My very special thanks to Eric Valentine, publisher, Quorum Books; Denise Van Acker, senior product manager, marketing; Ann E. LeStrange, assistant manager and bibliography developmental editor; and Mark Kane, production editor, all of the Greenwood Publishing Group, Inc. My deepest appreciation also goes to all of the people in the business community and disability community who were kind enough to contribute their time and energies.

Photographs have been graciously provided by the The Arc, Xerox Imaging Systems, Inc., Sabolich Prosthetic & Research Center, the Franklin D. Roosevelt Library, the National Multiple Sclerosis Society, Gallaudet University, and the National Easter Seal Society.

Peter Thomas extends his profound gratitude to his parents, Bill and Anita Thomas, for their continuing support and love through the years, his sister, Kathy, her husband, Gene, and their new sons, Brian and Robert, and his grandparents, Nana, and entire family. With gratitude for the gift of knowledge, thanks to my teachers, both formal and informal, from

Steven Porter to Peter White to the late Joseph Latino, and the omnipotent George DePontis. My heartfelt appreciation for the consistent generosity of my good friend George Breece, who defines savvy, and to all of my good friends in Northport, Boston, and in Washington, D.C. Special thanks to Elizabeth "Tess" Redshaw for her loving support and encouragement. My genuine thanks to Richard E. Verville and my law firm, White, Verville, Fulton and Saner, the American State of the Art Prosthetic Association, and the Amputee Coalition of America. Also, thanks to John Kemp, executive director, United Cerebral Palsy Associations, Inc., and to Bill Shore of Share Our Strength.

Don Fersh
Peter W. Thomas, Esq.

COMPLYING WITH THE AMERICANS WITH DISABILITIES ACT

CHAPTER 1

The Disabled Become Enabled

America and its history have been influenced by citizens with disabilities, from presidents, generals, and architects to inventors, physicists, and novelists. George Washington had failing vision as president. Stephen Hopkins, who had a form of palsy, declared after signing the Declaration of Independence, "My hand trembles, but my heart does not!"[1] A freed slave who ran the underground railroad, Harriet Tubman, had narcolepsy. The chief engineer of the Brooklyn Bridge, Washington Roebling, could not use his legs due to paralysis. Thomas Alva Edison, one of America's most inventive minds, had a learning disability and was deaf at the age of twelve.[2] President Franklin Delano Roosevelt stood during all his speeches with the aid of braces, having been paralyzed by polio eleven years before entering the White House. Their place in history is secure, not because they had a disability but because they had ability.

But despite these examples, the historical record indicates that people with disabilities, with few exceptions, have not been a part of the American mainstream. People with disabilities are still excluded from full participation in American society. Millions are seeking employment to earn a living and to become socially and economically independent. "The cost to the nation of two-thirds of working age people with disabilities not in the work force," according to Justin Dart, chairman of the President's Committee on Employment of People with Disabilities, "is $300 billion per year in welfare programs including lost taxes and productivity."[3]

There are 43 million people with disabilities in the United States, which includes a working-age (ages 16–64) population of 22.7 million, according to a 1986 report by the National Council on Disability, an independent federal agency.[4] The report found that 32 percent were employed, approximately 7.3 million, and 15.4 million were either unemployed or out of the work force.[5] Civilians are classified as unemployed if they are available for work, have sought employment during the last four weeks, or were waiting to be called back to a job, or start a job. Not in the labor force includes those civilians who are not actively seeking jobs. A 1986 Louis Harris and Associates, Inc. survey confirmed that two-thirds of people with disabilities are unemployed or out of the work force and found that 66 percent who are not working want to get a job.[6]

President Harry S. Truman, emphasizing the important role of rehabilitation after World War II, said, "Thousands of men and women annually apply to the rehabilitation service for help. . . . The restoration of disabled men and women is paying dividends, not only in humanitarian terms but in dollars and cents. . . . No longer are they tax consumers, they are taxpayers."[7] But fifty years later and despite advances in rehabilitation, millions are still tax consumers. According to a 1989 Senate report, these government benefits exceed $60 billion annually. The 1986 Louis Harris and Associates, Inc. survey found only one in four persons with a disability had a full-time job and concludes, "Not working is perhaps the truest definition of what it means to be disabled in this country. . . . Furthermore, unemployment among persons with disabilities as a group is a bigger problem than among any other demographic group of working-age Americans."[8] Three major barriers exist for working-age people with disabilities: discrimination, lack of employment opportunities, and in many cases, the need for a reasonably accommodated workplace.

People with disabilities and their numerous supporters in Congress in the late 1980s began to see a convergence between the employment and self-sufficiency needs and objectives of people with disabilities and the economic needs of business and government. In an age when the national economy is burdened by growing government deficits, both business and government began to recognize the importance of providing people with disabilities with greater independence through expanded opportunities in employment. Managers of businesses were beginning to see the productive potential of people with disabilities as a relatively untapped labor resource.

Why should tax dollars be spent to support people with disabilities when business and industry need a larger work force and the vast majority of people with disabilities want to work? President George Bush answered that question when he said, "The United States is now beginning to face labor shortages as the baby boomers move through the work force. The disabled offer a pool of talented workers whom we simply cannot afford to ignore, especially in connection with the high-tech growth industries of the future."[9]

The federal government, which is fighting a staggering deficit, would prefer to control billion-dollar program spending that frequently is a disincentive for people with disabilities in finding self-sustaining employment. Justin Dart said, "We are already paying unaffordable and rapidly escalating billions in public and private funds to maintain ever-increasing millions of potentially productive Americans in unjust, unwanted dependency."[10]

In meeting the needs of government and business, to provide employment opportunities for people with disabilities and to improve American productivity, Congress overwhelmingly passed, and President Bush signed, a new disability rights law—the Americans with Disabilities Act (ADA) on 26 July 1990. The new law expands equal employment opportunity laws for people with disabilities from the federal government and federally funded and awarded programs and contracts to the much wider sphere of small business, companies, nonprofit associations, state and local governments, labor unions, employment agencies, and joint labor management committees.

The ADA provides new employment rights and opportunities for people with disabilities and mandates that workplaces be accessible and usable. The first phase of the employment provisions of the new law for businesses was implemented on 26 July 1992. The public accommodation section of the ADA began on 26 January 1992. A 1989 Senate report recommending the passage of the ADA states, "The purpose of the ADA is to provide a clear and comprehensive national mandate to end discrimination against individuals with disabilities and to bring persons with disabilities into the economic and social mainstream of American life."[11] The law states that the nation's proper goals for people with disabilities "are to assure equality of opportunity, full participation, independent living, and economic self-sufficiency."[12] The law emphasizes that without the opportunity of people with disabilities to compete on an equal basis, it "costs the United States billions of dollars in unnecessary expenses resulting from dependency and non-productivity."[13]

AN EMANCIPATION PROCLAMATION

Members of Congress have described the Americans with Disabilities Act as an "emancipation proclamation" and as "simple justice" for people with disabilities. President Bush called the ADA "one of the most important pieces of legislation to ever reach Capitol Hill."[14] President Bush said, prior to the passage of the ADA:

More than two-thirds of our fellow citizens with disabilities of working age are, indeed, unemployed; and that is intolerable. And much of that unemployment stems from lack of opportunity. And ADA, that Act, will firm the foundation for policies and programs that can create opportunities for Americans to find and hold jobs, and to enjoy the income and satisfaction that productive participation in society brings to us all. And no longer can we allow ignorance or prejudice to deny opportunities to millions of Americans with disabilities.[15]

The ADA is the rare product of bipartisan support among the president and members of Congress to create new legislation encompassing social, economic, and civil rights issues. The ADA had the support of a large constituency, including conservatives and liberals. The landmark legislation provides for comprehensive civil rights protections to individuals with disabilities in the important areas of employment, public accommodations, state and local government services, transportation, and telecommunications. After one Senate and five House of Representatives committees held hearings over a two-year period, the ADA passed the House of Representatives by a margin of 377 to 28 on 12 July 1990. A day later the Senate passed the ADA by an overwhelming margin of 91 to 6. The ADA became law when it was signed by President Bush, in front of an audience of three thousand guests, most of whom had been advocates of the historic legislation, on the White House South Lawn on 26 July 1990.

Senator Tom Harkin (D-Iowa), whose brother is deaf, and who sponsored the legislation in the Senate, said:

The ADA is the twentieth century emancipation proclamation for people with disabilities. For millions of Americans with disabilities, segregation, isolation, and inequality are over. Today, our nation says "no" to second class citizenship for people with disabilities; "no" to patronizing attitudes. Today, our nation says "yes" to treating people with disabilities with dignity and respect; and "yes" to judging people with disabilities on the basis of ability and not on the basis of fear, ignorance, and prejudice. . . . This is the proudest day of my fifteen years in Congress because today 43 million Americans are finally written into our Constitution.[16]

When the landmark legislation was signed into law, Senator Robert J. Dole (R-Kansas), founder of the Dole Foundation for Employment of People with Disabilities, and who has a disability from a World War II injury, said, "1990 is a historic year and the beginning of a promising decade in completing civil rights mandates for all Americans. For too long Americans with disabilities had to face subtle and pervasive discrimination."[17] Another leading member of the Senate, Orrin Hatch (R-Utah), said, "The Americans with Disabilities Act is the most sweeping piece of civil rights legislation since the Civil War era. Persons with disabilities, through their hard work and self-determination, have already made great advances and successfully destroyed many of the stereotypes which have been used to deny them equal opportunities in the past. More can still be done."[18]

Connecticut Governor Lowell P. Weicker, Jr., who as senator introduced the original ADA legislation in 1988, said:

I believe that the Americans with Disabilities Act completes the work begun in 1973 [the Rehabilitation Act] to secure the rights of all Americans with disabilities. It provides a place in society for everyone. It does not guarantee you a job—it guarantees that you will not be denied a job on the basis of a disability. This law looks to the future, not to punish society for the sins of the past. . . . Not only is this an appropriate step in the national quest for equality, the ADA makes good economic sense as well. Right now, we have a system that is based on dependence, with over $57 billion a year in federal funds going for social insurance benefits for disabled persons. The economic return to society when people with disabilities are able to work cannot be overstated.[19]

In addition to the overwhelming support voiced by Congress and the White House, large segments of the American business community have taken a new look at the final legislation. Frank Sloan, Jr., former president and CEO of the National Federation of Independent Business, representing more than a half million small business owners, said, "The good will that can be generated by business sensitive to the needs of the disabled will result in the employment of loyal, dedicated workers, strengthening the competitive position of small firms."[20]

Also representing the business community, William H. Kolberg, president and CEO of the National Alliance of Business, said, "The Americans with Disabilities Act has helped focus the attention of the business community on the benefits of hiring people with disabilities. Businesses that are in need of highly skilled, competent, and motivated individuals should take full advantage of the talents of people with disabilities."[21] The National Alliance of Business represents 2,700 member companies, ranging from small businesses to large corporations.

The U.S. Chamber of Commerce stated, "For the first time, the federal government has placed its full power behind efforts to prevent discrimination against people with disabilities and to ensure their integration into mainstream American life. . . . Statistics show that we face an increased qualified labor shortage. People with disabilities represent a large untapped resource of qualified labor. The ADA will help provide businesses with access to qualified labor, and allow qualified labor needed access to business."[22]

While the U.S. Chamber of Commerce did not support the legislation during its passage, the AFL-CIO has firmly supported the rights of people with disabilities. Reflecting the interests of the labor movement, Lane Kirkland, president of the AFL-CIO, said, "Organized labor is proud to have supported the ADA. This landmark legislation will give us the means to open up employment opportunities for millions of qualified Americans with disabilities."[23]

Dozens of people with disabilities testified during House and Senate committee hearings, providing Congress with personal insights into the nature of discrimination and the need for practical solutions. James Brady, the former White House press secretary who through extensive rehabilitation regained his abilities to walk, speak, and read after being shot in an assassination attempt on President Ronald Reagan, called the ADA the "most landmark federal civil rights legislation in over twenty-five years."[24] In testimony before Congress, Brady, who is vice chairman of the National Organization on Disability, said:

May I say at the start that I never thought I would be in the disability community. . . . The conservative columnist George Will has written that "we are barely at the

President Franklin D. Roosevelt in Hyde Park, New York, with Ruthie Bie and "Fala," February 1941. One of two known photographs of the president in a wheelchair. Courtesy of the Franklin D. Roosevelt Library/Margaret Suckley.

beginning of the last great inclusion in American life—the inclusion of people with disabilities." I believe that passage of the ADA will bring about the fundamental and necessary changes in the paternalistic way our country has traditionally looked at disability.[25]

Paul G. Hearne, as former executive director of the National Council on Disability, assisted in authoring the Americans with Disabilities Act. Hearne is president of the Dole Foundation for Employment of People with Disabilities and as a person with a mobility impairment, osteogenesis imperfecta, worked with Congress to advance and enact the ADA. Looking back at his work on the new law, Hearne said, "The Americans with Disabilities Act of 1990 was the culmination of work of many disabled advocates across the country. As a disabled person, this law initiates a new era for my quality of life in our society. As a professional, I was proud to participate in its construction and passage. It is a landmark for all disabled Americans."[26]

WHO ARE PEOPLE WITH DISABILITIES?

One in Seven Americans Has a Disability

As many as 43 million Americans have either a physical or mental disability, a total roughly equivalent to the combined populations of California and Florida, two of the nation's most populous states, according to the National Institutes of Health's *Report of the Task Force on Medical Rehabilitation Research*, published in 1990. Developed by one hundred of the nation's leading medical rehabilitation research scientists, the report estimates that the cost of disability to the United States economy is 6.5 percent of the gross national product. The report found that one in seven Americans has a disability—over 13 percent of the American population.[27]

Another report, *Disability in America: Toward an Agenda for Prevention*, co-sponsored by the National Council on Disability and published by the Institute of Medicine in 1991, found that disability affects "every individual, every community, neighborhood, and family."[28] The Institute of Medicine report states, "The Americans with Disabilities Act will have several beneficial effects. For example, the expected increase in the employment of people with disabling conditions should result in their enjoying higher standards of living and fuller integration into society."[29] The report was developed by a number of notable medical researchers including Henry B. Betts, M.D., medical director and CEO of the Rehabilitation Institute of Chicago and Julius B. Richmond, M.D., former surgeon general of the Public Health Service.

The problem of disability and unemployment has a disproportionate effect on women and minorities. Research reports based on the 1980 Census found that 16.7 percent of persons with disabilities (ages 16–64) are non-

Table 1.1
People with Disabilities in the United States

- 22 million who are hearing impaired, including 2 million who are deaf
- 18.4 million with orthopedic impairments
- 16.4 million with heart disease
- 13 to 14 million people with diabetes
- 6 million survivors of cancer
- 5.7 million with mental retardation, but nine out of ten mentally retarded persons are mildly retarded
- 3 million disabled veterans of working age, who represent almost one-half of all disabled men in the United States
    1,281,000 World War II disabled veterans
    767,000 disabled veterans of Vietnam Era
    581,000 disabled Korean Conflict veterans
    385,000 disabled veterans of other conflicts
- 2.5 million are severely visually impaired, unable to read a newspaper
    120,000 who are totally blind, and
    600,000 who are legally blind
- 2.4 million with epilepsy—80 percent are seizure-free on prescription medication
- 2.1 million with speech impairments
- 2 million with head injuries
- Between 1.7 and 2.4 million with a chronic mental illness
- 1 million estimated to be HIV-positive, including over 202,000 cases of Acquired Immunodeficiency Syndrome (AIDS)
- 1.6 million who are missing either a leg or arm
- 1.2 million who are partially or completely paralyzed
- 1 million people who use wheelchairs
- 950,000 with cerebral palsy
- 250,000 to 500,000 with multiple sclerosis
- 250,000 to 350,000 people with a spinal cord injury and there are 10,000 to 20,000 new cases each year
- 398,000 who wear a leg or foot brace
- 205,000 with an artificial leg or foot
- 500,000 who survived polio and 125,000 with post-polio syndrome, a progressive muscle weakness which develops 25 to 30 years after the initial disease
- 95,000 with autism
- 66,000 with an artificial arm or hand

SOURCE: National Center for Medical Rehabilitation Research, National Institutes of Health, 1991.

Table 1.2
People with Disabilities Who Are Women and Who Are Members of Minority Groups

- 59.1 percent of all working-age women had jobs but only 19.9 percent of working-age disabled women were employed.
- Disabled women represent 8.5 percent of all working-age women—one working age woman in twelve has a disability.
- 58.2 percent of disabled men and a significantly higher 76.5 percent of all disabled women in America are out of the work force.
- Hispanics have a 8.4 percent rate of disability and the majority of Hispanics with disabilties (53 percent) are women.
- One working-age black adult in every seven (14.1 percent) has a disability.
- Most black adults with disabilities (53.9) are women.
- 14.1 percent of all blacks of working age have one or more disabilities.
- 8.4 percent of whites of working age have disabilities.

SOURCE: President's Committee on Employment of People with Disabilities, *Disabled Women in America* and *Black Adults with Disabilities*, 1986.

white.[30] Proportionately, minority persons with disabilities out number white persons with disabilities by a factor of two to one. Disability is markedly more common among blacks than among whites, due to occupation and poverty status, according to a President's Committee on Employment of People with Disabilities report.[31]

THE DEFINITION OF DISABILITY

In the Americans with Disabilities Act, the term "disability" is defined as "a person with a physical or mental impairment that substantially limits one or more of the major life activities." The definition used in the ADA legislation is based on the Rehabilitation Act of 1973 but uses the much more widely accepted term "disability" rather than "handicap." Under the ADA legislation, a person with a disability is an individual who meets one or more of the following descriptions:

1. Has a physical or mental impairment that substantially limits one or more of the major life activities
2. Has a record of such an impairment
3. Is regarded as having such an impairment[32]

A major life activity includes walking, speaking, seeing, hearing, breathing, learning, working, and caring for oneself, for instance.

The ADA legislation does not provide a list of all the specific disabilities covered by the new law. The reason for the exclusion of a list is provided in a 1989 Senate report:

It is not possible to include in the [ADA] legislation a list of all the specific conditions, diseases, or infections that would constitute physical or mental impairments because of the difficulty of ensuring the comprehensiveness of such a list, particularly in light of the fact that new disorders may develop in the future. The term includes, however, such conditions, diseases, and infections as orthopedic, visual, speech, and hearing impairments, cerebral palsy, epilepsy, muscular dystrophy, multiple sclerosis, infection with the human immunodeficiency virus (HIV), cancer, heart disease, diabetes, mental retardation, emotional illness, and specific learning disabilities.[33]

The definition of disability also includes individuals who have recovered from a physical or mental impairment, which previously substantially limited their major life activities. The definition also covers an individual regarded by others to be a person with a disability and those who associate with people with disabilities. Three of the most common reasons people have a disability are a chronic health condition, an injury from an accident, or from wartime military service.[34] (For more information on individuals defined as having a disability, see chapter 4.)

A number of disorders and conditions covered by the Americans with Disabilities Act and the Rehabilitation Act of 1973 are frequently associated with prejudice, fear, and mistrust by society. In developing the ADA, Congress was careful not to exclude persons with disabilities, who due to stereotype or myth, are frequently discriminated against in the workplace. The ADA specifies that persons who pose "a direct threat," not a stereotyped fear, can be excluded from the law's coverage. The ADA states that "an individual shall not pose a direct threat to the health or safety of other individuals in the workplace." However, the Equal Employment Opportunity Commission (EEOC) issued final regulations that expand this exclusion to include "a direct threat to oneself or others."[35]

An applicant for employment or an employee who has a disability and is qualified for the position and who is not a direct threat to himself or others in the workplace is covered under the ADA legislation. For example, an employer cannot reject a qualified applicant who has a mental illness based on the employer's generalized fears that stress from the position may exacerbate the mental illness of the applicant in the future. As a publication by the National Mental Health Association states, "If a person is rejected from a job because of the myths, fears, and stereotypes associated with mental illness, and no job-related reason can be articulated by the employer, that individual would be covered by the test [definition of disability]."[36] (For more information on direct threat, see chapters 4 and 11.)

Conditions that are not by themselves considered disabilities are homosexuality, current illegal drug use, economic or cultural disadvantage, and obesity except in rare cases.[37] A person who is currently dependent on alcohol or has a history of alcohol dependency is covered under the ADA. An individual who was addicted to illegal drugs and is no longer using illegal drugs is covered under the ADA. (For more information on alcoholism and illegal drug use, see chapter 11.)

America's Largest Minority Is Largely Unemployed but Surveys Show They Are Productive Workers

President Bush said that people with disabilities "are the largest minority in America."[38] What makes the ADA so important is that it affects such a large segment of the population. America's largest minority is largely unemployed. As noted, a 1986 Louis Harris and Associates, Inc. survey of one thousand persons with a disability found that 66 percent were unemployed and not in the labor force. The survey also found that 82 percent would give up their government benefits in favor of full-time employment. Only one in four work full time, and another 10 percent work part time.[39]

Over 15 million people with disabilities are either unemployed or out of the work force. As a result of nonparticipation in the labor force, people with disabilities lose over $170 billion in potential earnings every year, according to the Bureau of the Census.[40] But study after study indicates that when people with disabilities have an opportunity to work, employers rate disabled employees as good or better than nondisabled workers in such critically important categories as job performance, productivity, attendance, punctuality, and the ability to work hard.[41]

A 1987 Louis Harris and Associates, Inc. survey of 921 companies found that managers overwhelmingly rated the job performance of employees with disabilities as good to excellent. The survey also found that these employees were working as well or better than other employees in the same job position. Only one in twenty managers said that job performance was only fair. The great majority of managers said that disabled employees work as hard or harder than nondisabled employees and are as reliable and punctual or more so. In rating attendance, productivity, desire for promotion, and leadership ability, people with disabilities were evaluated as the same or better than other employees.[42]

Most of the managers in the survey said that making accommodations for employees with disabilities is not expensive. The cost of accommodations rarely drives the cost of employment above the average range of costs for all employees. The survey concludes, however, "Strong performance evaluations and an absence of cost barriers have not translated into widespread hiring of disabled people."[43] A large percentage of the managers recognized that people with disabilities often encounter discrimination from employers.

Despite these favorable evaluations by managers of employees with disabilities, attitude barriers exist for both employers and people with disabilities. Both employers and people with disabilities say there is a lack of urgency in hiring people with disabilities, job discrimination, lack of training and education, and health and transportation problems. There is the fear of rejection on the part of job seekers and a fear of high costs by employers. The 1987 Louis Harris survey also found, "Large majorities of top managers, EEO officers, department heads/line managers, and small business managers feel that disabled people often encounter job discrimination from employers. . . . Until job discrimination and other employment barriers are eliminated, large numbers of disabled people may not enter the working mainstream of American life."[44]

LAST IN LINE FOR EQUAL EMPLOYMENT OPPORTUNITY

Federal equal employment opportunity (EEO) laws prohibit employment discrimination in seven major categories: race, color, religion, sex, national origin, age, and with the implementation of the Rehabilitation Act of 1973 and the ADA—disability became the seventh protected category. The first five categories were mandated by Title VII of the Civil Rights Act of 1964, which made it unlawful for employers of fifteen or more people to discriminate against prospective or current employees on the basis of race, sex, color, religion, or national origin.

The Civil Rights Act of 1964 affected not just those who were provided with new rights and protections but almost every American. Few other laws have had its impact, and "its most important thrust was with jobs and workers."[45] Title VII of the Civil Rights Act was called the Fair Employment Practice Law, and its significance is reflected in the 83 days of bitter debate before its adoption in the Senate. The Civil Rights Act of 1964, legislation that began in the House of Representatives in 1943, imposed upon employers, labor unions, and employment agencies a new set of responsibilities and obligations. It gave employees, job applicants, and members of minority groups and women new rights, and set up a new federal agency, the Equal Employment Opportunity Commission (EEOC), with the job of safeguarding and enforcing those new rights.[46]

The Civil Rights Act of 1964 represented the first significant federal civil rights law since the Reconstruction era following the Civil War with the adoption of the Thirteenth, Fourteenth, and Fifteenth Amendments to the Constitution and the short-lived Civil Rights Act of 1875. As Congressman George Meader said in 1964, "This was the first major civil rights measure enacted in 85 years."[47] After the Civil Rights Act of 1964 came other pieces of EEO legislation, which are also enforced by the EEOC. These two laws included the Equal Pay Act of 1963, which prohibits sex-based wage discrimination, and the Age Discrimination in Employment Act (ADEA) of 1967, which prohibits discrimination against persons forty years of age or older, based on age, in hiring and in other terms of employment. With the enactment of the ADEA legislation, age became the sixth protected equal employment opportunity category under the jurisdiction of the EEOC.

With the advent of the Rehabilitation Act of 1973, people with disabilities were added, *partially*, to the EEO list of protected minorities and women. People with disabilities were provided with EEO rights specifically in the federal government and in public and private programs funded and contracted by the federal government. It is estimated by the Small Business Administration that there are 50 thousand federal contractors, not including recipients of federal financial assistance.[48] The Rehabilitation Act under Section 503 and 504 for the first time created EEO rights for people with disabilities in the private sector, but only among those businesses or organizations receiving federal contracts or funding. It did not apply, however, to state and local governments that did not receive federal funds or to the vast majority of American businesses, estimated by the Small Business Administration to total over five million business establishments in 1991.[49]

With the implementation of the employment provisions of the ADA in July 1992, people with disabilities joined as the seventh and last group of people fully covered by EEO legislation. The ADA provided people with disabilities with full EEO coverage in all state and local governments and in a large segment of American nonprofit associations and business establishments.

ADA COVERS 87 PERCENT OF AMERICA'S PRIVATE SECTOR JOBS

The Americans with Disabilities Act affects the employment practices of all businesses and nonprofit associations, with some exceptions, who have fifteen or more employees beginning on 26 July 1994, and in the two-year preceding period, businesses and nonprofit associations with 25 or more employees. The ADA employment provisions will have their largest effect on business. While the ADA covers all state and local government employment, experts do not view this to be as significant as the business sector because at least 46 states have already adopted EEO laws protecting people with disabilities.[50] It is in the business sector where the ADA will cover over 38 million jobs by July 1994, according to the Small Business Administration.[51]

Estimates made by the Small Business Administration indicate there are 1,933,000 business establishments with 25 or more employees, consisting of a sizable 36 percent of all American business establishments in 1992. In 1994 there will be an estimated 2,682,000 business establishments with fifteen or more employees, which amounts to a significant 49 percent of all business establishments in the United States.[52]

But these businesses account for a disproportionately *greater* share of the labor market—87 percent of all of America's jobs in the private sector, according to the Equal Employment Opportunity Commission.[53] The ADA has expanded the EEO rights of people with disabilities to all state and local governments, to a large segment of nonprofit associations, and to the vast majority of jobs in American business. As a result of the ADA, there has been a very sizeable increase in private sector jobs covered by this new employment legislation. It is an expansion from about 1 percent of the business establishments in the private sector (jobs funded by federal contracts and grants) before the implementation of the ADA in July 1992 to 49 percent of America's private sector business establishments as a result of the ADA.

REASONABLE ACCOMMODATION

What makes the ADA unique in comparison to the preceding EEO legislation that covers race, religion, color, sex, national origin, and age is the ADA's fundamental principle of reasonable accommodation. Developed in the Rehabilitation Act of 1973, reasonable accommodation includes a number of possible modifications in the worksite itself, the use of readers and interpreters for blind and hearing-impaired individuals, and the use of adaptive devices, such as a headset for a telephone for an individual with limited arm or hand mobility. All reasonable accommodations are made, if necessary, when they are not an undue hardship on an employer, and on a case-by-case basis.

Examples of reasonable accommodation also include job restructuring, such as the elimination of non-essential tasks, flexible or modified work schedules, accessible facilities, and the purchase of adaptive equipment, also known as assistive devices. Reasonable accommodation ranges from installing a ramp for a person using a wheelchair to installing a telephone amplifier for an individual who is hearing impaired.

An applicant or employee is considered a "qualified individual with a disability" if that individual can perform the essential functions of the position *with* or *without* reasonable accommodation. According to the ADA, employers are obligated to make a reasonable accommodation to a qualified individual with a disability only when the employer is aware of the impairment, making it essentially the responsibility of the applicant or employee to request reasonable accommodation.

The majority of people with disabilities require no reasonable accommodation, and many forms of reasonable accommodation cost less than fifty dollars, such as a headset for a telephone. This reasonable accommodation, for instance, allowed an insurance salesperson with cerebral palsy to write while talking on the phone. (For more information on reasonable accommodation, see chapters 4, 7, 9, and 11.)

WHAT THE ADA IS AND WHAT IT IS NOT

In discussing the employment provisions of the ADA, it is important to understand what the new law *is not*. The ADA *is not* a mandate for quotas that specifies that certain numbers or ratios of persons with disabilities obtain employment. The ADA *is not* an affirmative action law. The ADA *does not* provide for preferential treatment in the hiring of people with disabilities. The ADA *does not* guarantee a person with a disability a job.

The ADA *is* an equal employment opportunity law for equal ability. The ADA *is* a nondiscrimination law. The employment provisions of the ADA are enforced under the same legal mechanisms that protect other minorities and women under Title VII of the Civil Rights Act of 1964. The ADA provides that employers must make work-related adjustments, when necessary, so that employees who use wheelchairs, for example, have access to all areas of the work environment, such as the break room, lunch room, and rest rooms.

THE ADA'S POTENTIAL

Prior to the ADA's implementation, millions of people with disabilities, when applying for a job, had to fill out pre-employment questionnaires regarding their disability and take medical tests before being considered for a job. This employment application process, which in addition to providing important information on an individual's skills, experience, and education, also revealed medical conditions or disabilities that were not always pertinent to the job, and it tended to screen out many otherwise qualified individuals with disabilities.

The ADA, in creating a level playing field for an applicant or employee with a disability, mandates that employers must comply with the following requirements: no pre-employment applications, medical examinations, including genetic testing, questions, or employment procedures, benefits, and promotions that tend to discriminate against qualified persons with a disability. Employers, who are covered under the law, are required to ask pre-employment questions that relate to the ability of an applicant to perform job-related functions. An employer cannot discuss an applicant's disability or ask whether a potential employee has a disability unless it is job related and consistent with business necessity.

This new federal civil rights law assists people with disabilities in obtaining employment in the private sector—in American business and industry and most nonprofit associations, and in state and local governments. The ADA's predecessor, the Rehabilitation Act of 1973, was limited to the federal sector: the federal government, federal contractors, and institutions awarded federal funds. The ADA, unlike the Rehabilitation Act of 1973, provides antidiscrimination protection in millions of places of business. The few organizations that have either qualified requirements or

Table 1.3
Public Support for the Americans with Disabilities Act

This 1991 Louis Harris and Associates survey found widespread support for the major components of the Americans with Disabilities Act.

- 83 percent support requiring employers of fifteen or more to make "reasonable accommodations" for disabled employees.
- 93 percent support making new public transportation accessible.
- 95 percent agree with banning job discrimination based on disability.
- 96 percent support prohibiting discrimination in public places, such as restaurants, hotels, theaters, stores, and museums.
- The goal of greater participation by disabled people is something the public is committed to and willing to spend money on.

SOURCE: Louis Harris and Associates, Inc. *Public Attitudes Toward People with Disabilities*, New York, 1991.

are exempt from the ADA are religious associations, Native American tribes, and private membership clubs.

The ADA provides people with disabilities with new opportunities for employment. These new employment opportunities are not affirmative action jobs, or government-sponsored work programs, nor do they provide for job quota systems. The implementation of the ADA is a shared responsibility of business and government. Employers, human resource managers, supervisors, office managers, and employees need to know how to comply with the new law in 1.9 million business establishments by July 1992 and 2.6 million business establishments by July 1994.[54]

The Americans with Disabilities Act signals the full inclusion of Americans with disabilities in the work force, and in access and utilization of public ground and rail transportation to get to and from work. The ADA also provides for the everyday physical access and full utilization of restaurants, hotels, pharmacies, physician offices, movie theaters, supermarkets—the "Main Streets" of America. The Americans with Disabilities Act is the first national effort, the first national mandate, that assists people with disabilities to become self-sufficient.

The Americans with Disabilities Act has a significant impact on 43 million people with disabilities, providing them with the full access and utilization, on a daily basis, to places of public accommodation, public ground transportation, telecommunications, and state and local government services. For over 22 million working-age people with disabilities, the law's broad sweeping changes will affect their ability to apply for work, take application tests that fairly measure their skills, obtain employment, and earn promotions. Most importantly for people with disabilities, the ADA provides protection against discrimination, as applicants and employees, based on disability.

For employers, human resource managers, supervisors, and employees of America's businesses, there are new responsibilities in understanding how to comply voluntarily with the new law. As a result of the employment provisions of the Americans with Disabilities Act, millions of places of business need to consider three major requirements:

1. Employers may not discriminate against a qualified applicant or employee on the basis of a disability.
2. Employers must have nondiscriminatory application procedures, qualification standards, and selection criteria.
3. Employers must reasonably accommodate the disabilities of qualified applicants or employees, unless there is undue hardship for the employer.

A PROVEN TRACK RECORD WITH BUSINESS

Prior to the ADA legislation, thousands of American businesses found that "hire the handicapped" was more than a slogan. Business owners and managers have found that in many instances disability does not make a difference. For example, numerous Department of Labor reports have shown that many people with disabilities are so eager to work that they have a lower absenteeism record than other employees.

Diversity in American business has become commonplace. The employment of women and minorities has been the fastest growing sector in the work force in the United States over the past 20 years.[55] Trends in the American work force by the year 2000, according to a Department of Labor study, are that workers will more likely be older, female, disadvantaged, or a member of a minority group. The Census Bureau predicts that by the year 2010, 47 percent of the work force will be women. People with disabilities have the potential of becoming a part of this trend as productive members of the American work force. Many corporations and small businesses have, since the 1970s and 1980s, initiated programs to employ workers with disabilities. Businesses, which had just begun to tap into the disabled labor force, did so for three major reasons: scarcity of labor, high productivity and job performance among disabled workers, and the importance of maintaining and creating diversity in the workplace.

E.I. du Pont de Nemours and Company, which has 2,745 employees with disabilities, found that its employees with disabilities help the company maintain diversity in its work force. Diversity helped to create a competitive edge for the company, according to a 1990 study.[56] The same study also found that Du Pont employees with disabilities were equivalent to other employees in job performance, attendance, and safety. A study by International Telephone and Telegraph of a 2,000 member plant with 125 disabled workers found that disabled workers had fewer absences than their co-workers.[57]

DISABILITY DOES NOT MAKE A DIFFERENCE

One of the first federal studies indicating that disability does not make a difference in the workplace was issued by the Department of Labor's Bureau of Labor Statistics in 1948. The study found that on the average, workers with disabilities had fewer accidents, were absent no more than other workers, and were as productive as their co-workers who did not have disabilities.[58]

Thousands of American businesses, both large and small, who have hired people with disabilities over the years, are aware of the productivity of these employees. For these businesses the goals and objectives of the Americans with Disabilities Act are not new. The managers of these companies will need to make little or no transition in meeting the legislative requirements of the ADA. They have been hiring workers with disabilities for years for one essential reason—good results.

Examples of large companies that have developed programs to attract and hire more employees with disabilities include the Marriott Corporation, Quaker Oats, American Express, Sears, Procter & Gamble, Coca-Cola, United Airlines, Burger King Corporation, Raytheon Company, American Can, General Motors Corporation, and Canon—to name a few. Large businesses have developed a number of programs to promote the employment of people with disabilities including management awareness and interview training. Many businesses have also been working with community disability organizations to locate applicants through job match programs.

Small businesses have been successfully utilizing disabled workers since the early part of the twentieth century. These small businesses include sneaker insole producers, computer companies, picture framing businesses, bakeries, fast food enterprises, printers, and bed and breakfast inns. Gopal Pati, a professor of business management at Indiana University, said, "Many small businesses have been utilizing workers with disabilities, especially young people, because they have a good track record as productive and hard working. Small businesses around the country have been increasingly hiring disabled workers in order to continue to be competitive. But disabled workers are still a large untapped labor source."[59]

These businesses have found an advantage in hiring qualified disabled people. For example, at Marriott, initially there were unfounded fears and concerns among some of the managers. These managers began to discover that many of the employees with disabilities took their jobs more seriously than many of the nondisabled workers and that they were positive additions to the work force. Managers and staff at Marriott found that morale had become higher because working with disabled co-workers had a broadening and enriching effect. Not only does Marriott view the employment of people with disabilities as advantageous, Marriott describes these workers as "an investment."[60]

The results at Marriott parallel those at many other companies: managers were at first cautious in working with disabled people until they discovered that people with disabilities, who were eager to prove themselves, earned the respect of managers, co-workers, clients, and consumers. The lesson for Marriott and for many other companies has been that workers with disabilities were found to be just as productive as anyone else. Mark Donovan, manager of community employment and training programs for the Marriott Corporation, testifying during the congressional hearings on the ADA, said:

> Marriott is recognized as a leader in the area of employment of people with disabilities. The reason is simple: it makes good, bottom line business sense. As a corporation operating in the hospitality industry, our employees are our life blood. It is only to the degree which we can find, attract, train, and retain able and motivated people that we can be successful. . . . From our perspective, not to draw on the resources represented by people with disabilities would be absurd.[61]

People with disabilities have a proven track record with business as successful and productive employees.

"A difference, to be a difference, must make a difference," said Wendell Johnson, a pioneering American educator of children with speech impairments.[62] The same can be said about a disability. As the Louis Harris, Du Pont, and International Telephone and Telegraph surveys and other studies strongly indicate, disability does not make a difference. People with disabilities are the equal of other workers in productivity, job performance, and attendance.

FAMOUS PEOPLE WITH DISABILITIES

Another example of a proven track record and the work capabilities and accomplishments of people with disabilities can be seen by looking at the achievements of famous people—where their ability, not disability, made a difference. The fact that these people have made so many important contributions and achievements certainly diminishes the importance of a label or description, such as "disabled" or "handicapped." Many of these famous individuals have a "hidden disability" such as epilepsy or a learning disability. These men and women, with many talents and from many backgrounds, include musicians, novelists, professional athletes, pilots, presidents and first ladies, generals, explorers, movie stars, cartoonists, engineers, and physicists.

A number of presidents—some not generally identified as having a disability—have successfully worked and achieved with a disability and have frequently overcome them. President Theodore Roosevelt lost vision in one eye from boxing during his younger years. President Woodrow Wilson had dyslexia, a learning disability. President Franklin D. Roosevelt would

Ivy Gunter is an international fashion model and she has a disability. She is an above-the-knee amputee who uses an artificial limb. Courtesy of Sabolich Prosthetic and Research Center, Oklahoma City, Oklahoma.

not allow photographers to take pictures of him in his leg braces or using a wheelchair; yet he founded the March of Dimes Birth Defects Foundation. President Dwight D. Eisenhower had a massive heart attack during his first term in office; his cardiologist, Paul Dudley White, M.D., was responsible for establishing what is today the National Heart, Lung and Blood Institute. President John F. Kennedy, as a result of an injury during his youth, used an orthotic back brace while in office. President Ronald Reagan began using a cochlear implant while in the White House due to a hearing impairment.[63]

A statement by President Franklin D. Roosevelt illustrates why presidents and a number of well-known people with disabilities have persevered, excelled, and achieved. "If you have spent two years in bed trying to wiggle your big toe, then anything else seems easy," said Roosevelt.[64] For many people with disabilities, it is not the disability itself that is a handicap but the attitudes of some members of society, which all too often translates into limited economic and employment opportunity.

OLD MYTHS AND MISCONCEPTIONS

The Americans with Disabilities Act is a comprehensive federal mandate that addresses the limited economic opportunities of people with disabilities. The ADA covers equal opportunity in employment, the access and utilization of public ground transportation, and telecommunications. The ADA also provides for public accommodation—the access and full use of America's "Main Streets" for shopping, working, and obtaining services in retail stores, restaurants, and the professional offices of physicians, dentists, and lawyers. In order to make these collective goals possible, the full inclusion of people with disabilities into American society, it was necessary for the congressional hearings and the law itself to refute the many old myths, misconceptions, fears, and stereotypes that have been linked to disability.

Why a new law for people with disabilities? The new law focuses the responsibility of people with disabilities to rely on themselves and not government in seeking and gaining employment. By becoming independent, the term "handicapped" is no longer a meaningful term. The term "handicapped" stems from a game of chance in England dating to the 1600s in which the players forfeited small articles that were picked without looking by "hand-in-cap." Extra articles were contributed to the cap as a bonus.[65] The term "handicap" came into use to describe a lack of an advantage, but like the old English game from which the word is derived, "handicap" is outdated and outmoded. The term has become stereotyped with negative connotations and is not used by people with disabilities.

The Senate Committee on Labor and Human Resources in a 1989 report on the Americans with Disabilities Act, stated, "As was made so strikingly clear at the hearings on the ADA, stereotypes and misconceptions about the abilities, or more correctly the inabilities, of persons with disabilities are still pervasive today. Every government and private study on the issue has shown that employers disfavor hiring people with disabilities because of stereotypes, discomfort, misconceptions, and unfounded fears about increased costs and decreased productivity."[66] The ADA, by emphasizing self-reliance and the importance of economic independence, is removing the antiquated image and stereotype.

The ADA has provided people with disabilities with the means to seek and gain employment without discrimination—and the stereotypes that often accompany prejudice and discrimination. The ADA is in essence a law that at its core refutes the "handicap" stereotype by recognizing the aspirations of millions of individuals with disabilities to be independent and to pursue employment and careers.

The new law, which makes discrimination against qualified applicants and employees illegal, enables people with disabilities to fulfill these aspirations by creating a level playing field. Far from the nonworking "handicapped" image, people with disabilities are contributing their energies and skills to the national economy as workers, producers, and consumers.

Do employers have to employ a person with a disability? Employers are free to select the most qualified applicant available and to make decisions based on reasons unrelated to the existence or consequence of a disability.

Won't people with disabilities increase business costs due to high turnover, absenteeism, and accident rates? Studies with many different types of disabled workers show an absenteeism rate equal to or *lower* than rates for co-workers. Pizza Hut has reported that after hiring 1,000 disabled employes, it *reduced* the restaurant chain's labor turnover costs by $2.2 million in a single year.[67]

People with disabilities do not have a higher accident rate than other workers. For example, the President's Committee on Mental Retardation reports that with workers with mental retardation the frequency of accidents *decreased*, and insurance rates did not increase.[68] When signing the ADA legislation, President Bush touched on the low turnover rate and loyalty of people with disabilities. "And remember this is a tremendous pool of people who will bring to jobs diversity, loyalty, proven low turnover rate, and only one request, the chance to prove themselves."[69]

Isn't the ADA going to place a burden on business for the costs of reasonable accommodations? One of the biggest myths is that the ADA is necessarily going to be more costly for American business. An article in *Businessweek* demonstrated how hiring people with disabilities actually *saved* money for businesses. For example, hiring workers with disabilities significantly decreased the turnover rate, *saving* money for the Boeing Company and Du Pont.[70]

More than 75 percent of people with disabilities do not need a reasonable accommodation in order to work. The costs of reasonable accommodation to an employer, according to a Job Accommodation Network survey, is fifty dollars or less for one-half of all accommodations. Senator Tom Harkin said, "Every study has found that fear of costs has proven to be unfounded."[71]

President Bush, during the ADA legislation signing ceremony, stated:

I want to say a special word to our friends in the business community. . . . I know there have been concerns that the ADA may be vague or costly, or may lead endlessly to litigation. But I want to reassure you right now that my administration and the United States Congress have carefully crafted this Act. We've all been determined to ensure that it gives flexibility, particularly in terms of the timetable of implementation; and we've been committed to containing the costs that may be incurred.[72]

Will compliance with the ADA hurt or help the economy? Ending discrimination in the workplace can have a direct impact on the federal government's expenditure of $57 billion annually on disability benefits and programs that tend to keep disabled people dependent on tax revenues rather than independent as employed taxpayers. The Bush administration reminded Congress that similar concerns were raised when the Rehabilitation Act was implemented in the 1970s:

The fears being raised now about the impact of the ADA are similar to the misgivings that were raised in the first few years following the implementation of Section 503 and 504 [of the Rehabilitation Act of 1973]. There were predictions that those covered by the regulations would be bankrupted or forced to severely curtail or alter their services. These doomsday predictions were based on ignorance and myth and proved false. Similar misgivings in the area of race discrimination surfaced in 1963 [after the Civil Rights Act of 1964] and proved to be equally unfounded. The administration believes that a similar fate awaits the misapprehensions that have been raised about the ADA.[73]

Federal studies of the major legislation preceding the ADA, the Rehabilitation Act of 1973, found that nondiscrimination in the employment of people with disabilities would have a substantial beneficial effect: reduced need for veterans benefits, rehabilitation, and disability, medical, and food stamp payments. A Department of Labor report in 1980 found, "When individuals [with disabilities] move from being recipients of various types of welfare payments to skilled taxpaying workers, there are obviously many benefits not only for the individuals but for the whole society."[74]

This finding is strikingly similar to the words of President Harry S. Truman that people with disabilities can "become taxpayers, not tax consumers." It is the view of the vast majority of experts that in the long run, the ADA will provide the economy with dividends in the form of *increased* national productivity, instead of costing the nation $300 billion a year in welfare payments, lost tax revenues, and lost productivity.

Why don't people with disabilities use restaurants and other public places like movie theaters, parks, or museums like everyone else? The congressional hearings provide answers to this question by illustrating the reasons for the development of Title III of the ADA—the right to the access and utilization of public accommodations. The Senate Committee on Labor and Human Resources 1989 report states:

Three major reasons were given by witnesses [for not using public accommodations]. The first reason is that people with disabilities do not feel that they are welcome and can participate safely in such places. The second reason is fear and self-consciousness about their disability stemming from degrading experiences they or their friends with disabilities have experienced. The third reason is architectural, communication, and transportation barriers.[75]

During the congressional hearings, former Senator Lowell Weicker, Jr. testified that people with disabilities spend a lifetime "overcoming not what God wrought but what man has imposed by custom and law."[76] The mandate of the ADA is to bring people with disabilities into full participation in American life. Congress recognized that full participation means full access and full use of America's "Main Streets"—restaurants, movie theaters, parks, museums, shops, stores, pharmacies, and doctor's offices. The ADA does not require, however, modifications that would fundamentally alter the nature of the services provided by a public facility or business establishment.

But don't we need workers to meet increasingly physically demanding jobs? Through the year 2000, according to the Bureau of Labor Statistics, more than 90 percent of the net new job openings will be in information-intensive and service-intensive occupations. As a result, employers will be "choosing brains over brawn and physical dexterity."[77] According to *Businessweek*, 90 percent of people with disabilities possess the skills for these new information and service jobs. It is fair to say that people with disabilities, provided with reasonable accommodations, when necessary, have the education and skills to fill the vast majority of America's future jobs.[78]

But the ADA goes much further than dispelling old myths and misconceptions about people with disabilities. Millions of Americans with disabilities now have new equal employment opportunity rights, enabling them to obtain employment on the basis of ability and protecting them from discrimination on the basis of a disability. People with disabilities are becoming enabled as part of the American social, business, and economic mainstream. The Americans with Disabilities Act of 1990 is providing the necessary opportunities for people with disabilities to become permanent and productive equal partners in American society and the American work force. People with disabilities, in the words of President Harry S. Truman, can now become "taxpayers, not tax consumers."

CHAPTER 2

The Purpose and Provisions of the Americans with Disabilities Act

When Congress passed the Americans with Disabilities Act, it created a mandate for America—a federal mandate to mainstream people with disabilities into the entire social and economic fabric of the nation. The ADA goes beyond equal employment opportunity rights and includes access to a full range of transportation and telecommunications services, and the full use of public and commercial services—from restaurants and movie theaters to sports stadiums and parks. The ADA mandates access for people with disabilities as consumers in obtaining goods and services in retail stores, hotels, barber shops, supermarkets, and grocery stores on the "Main Streets" of America. The ADA also mandates equal access for people with disabilities in transportation on buses and commuter trains, in access to telecommunications, and in obtaining services from state and local governments.[1] The ADA requires that affordable, round-the-clock telecommunications services be available to people who are hearing and speech impaired, allowing full utilization of the nation's telephone and telecommunications systems.

TITLE I   NONDISCRIMINATION IN EMPLOYMENT

Title I of the ADA provides for nondiscriminatory practices in the selection, testing, hiring, and promotion of new and current employees. Title I provides equal employment opportunity (EEO) protection for people with disabilities in almost two million places of business beginning in July 1992.[1] Unlike other EEO laws, the ADA also provides that a qualified person with a disability be provided reasonable accommodation, if necessary. These accommodations include a modified schedule, workplace, or assistive device, such as an amplified telephone. A reasonable accommodation is not required if it creates an undue hardship on the employer.[3]

TITLE II   ACCESS TO BUSES AND TRAINS, AND NONDISCRIMINATION BY STATE AND LOCAL GOVERNMENTS

Portions of Title II went into effect on 26 January 1991 and have two purposes. The first purpose is to prohibit discrimination against a qualified person with a disability by a department or agency of any state or local government. This part also requires that programs and services of all state and local governments be readily accessible to and usable by individuals with disabilities.

The second purpose of Title II is to prohibit discrimination based on disability in all public carriers that provide public rail or ground transportation.[4] Title II affects national, inter-city, and commuter railroads as well as public and privately operated buses, including school buses. Air carriers are subject to the Air Carriers Access Act and are not specifically addressed in the ADA.[5]

Public entities that operate fixed route transit systems and purchase or lease new buses, new rapid or light rail cars, or other new vehicles must assure they are accessible to individuals with a disability, including those who use wheelchairs. New vehicles must be equipped with lifts, ramps, and wheelchair spaces or seats. No retrofitting of existing buses, however, is required.[6]

Previously owned or used buses and rail cars that are purchased or leased for use on fixed route transit systems must also be accessible to people with disabilities, including those using wheelchairs. An exception exists if this equipment is unavailable despite the carrier's "demonstrated good faith efforts." Public ground transportation entities are also required to provide paratransit and other special transportation services at a level of service comparable to transit service afforded to individuals without disabilities. Key stations in commuter rail transportation systems and all stations used by Amtrak must be made accessible as soon as practicable. Amtrak must provide one accessible car per train by 1995.[7]

TITLE III   ACCESS TO PUBLIC ACCOMMODATIONS AND SERVICES: STORES, RESTAURANTS, MOVIE THEATERS, AND PHYSICIANS' OFFICES

What Title I does for economic independence, Title II accomplishes for transportation and mobility of people with disabilities. Title III provides for the physical access and use of the "Main Streets" of America—retail stores, restaurants, parks, grocery stores, banks, pharmacies, and the professional offices of physicians, lawyers, dentists, and accountants. Title III, which took effect on 26 January 1992, addresses places of public accommodation, commercial facilities and public transportation provided by

Table 2.1
The ADA's Twelve Categories of Public Accommodation

1. Places of lodging
2. Establishments serving food or drink
3. Places of exhibition or entertainment
4. Places of public gathering
5. Sales or rental establishments
6. Service establishments
7. Stations used for specified public transportation
8. Places of public display or collection
9. Places of recreation
10. Places of education
11. Social service center establishments
12. Places of exercise or recreation

SOURCE: Americans with Disabilities Act of 1990

private companies. These private companies and all businesses that provide public accommodations are prohibited from discriminating on the basis of disability and must provide customers who have disabilities with full and equal enjoyment of goods and services. These goods and services must be offered "in the most integrated setting appropriate to the needs of the individuals," except when the individual with a disability poses a direct threat to the health or safety of others.[8]

These places, which include millions of commercial facilities, must make reasonable modifications in order to afford people with disabilities access to their establishments, such as widening aisles or enlarging doors and signs. Places of public accommodation must make accessible any new buildings constructed after 26 January 1993. In existing structures, architectural and communication barriers must be removed if "readily achievable," which is defined as "easily accomplishable and able to be carried out without difficulty or expense."[9] If modifications that allow access to persons with disabilities are not readily achievable, places of public accommodation must make alternative arrangements to provide their goods and services to everyone by using, for example, curbside or home delivery service.

The breadth of ADA coverage on places of public accommodation is extensive. All privately operated establishments that affect interstate commerce fall within the law's domain. A non-exhaustive list includes hotels, motels, bars, theaters, convention centers, museums, libraries, zoos, amusement parks, shopping centers, clothing stores, all types of schools from nursery to post-graduate, dry cleaners, health spas, bowling alleys, and golf courses.[10]

Except for new construction that commenced after 26 January 1992, the law provides a grace period of six months during which time no civil action can be brought against a business that employs 25 or fewer employees with gross annual receipts of $1 million or less. In order to encourage businesses to comply with the accessibility provisions of the ADA, the Internal Revenue Code allows certain businesses to deduct up to $15,000 annually for removal of architectural barriers.[11]

TITLE IV   ACCESS TO TELECOMMUNICATIONS

Title IV of the ADA seeks to more fully integrate into society the nation's 24 million hearing-impaired and 2.8 million speech-impaired Americans by making the telephone system fully accessible. This title of the new law goes into effect on 26 July 1993, and amends Title II of the Communications Act of 1934 by requiring common carriers to provide interstate and intrastate telecommunications relay services to hearing- and speech-impaired individuals, enabling communication between nonhearing and hearing individuals. These telecommunication relay services must be continuously available and be no more expensive than functionally equivalent services. This is the first national telephone service of its kind for the hearing impaired in the United States. Provisions for confidentiality of communications are also included in Title IV.[12]

TITLE V   MISCELLANEOUS PROVISIONS INCLUDING THE GRANTING OF ATTORNEY'S FEES

A variety of miscellaneous regulatory and administrative matters are addressed in Title V of the ADA, such as the relationship between the ADA and the Rehabilitation Act of 1973. Essentially, the ADA is not to be interpreted to apply a lesser standard than that applied by the Rehabilitation Act or its regulations. Of course, the ADA does not invalidate or limit any other law that provides greater protection for the rights of individuals with disabilities. Title V provides special rules governing the alteration of historical buildings and the provision of attorneys' fees for successful litigants who bring suit for violations of the ADA.[13] Title V clearly makes states subject to suit for violations of the ADA and makes the ADA applicable to Congress and its related organizations, such as the Congressional Budget Office, the Library of Congress, and the General Accounting Office. The ADA, however, does not apply to federal employees or the federal government.

THE PURPOSE OF THE NEW LAW

The purpose and language of the Americans with Disabilities Act is to a very large degree built on previous federal civil rights law and legislation for people with disabilities. The employment provisions of the new law will affect the estimated 22.7 million working-age people with disabilities and a large segment of American business—in offices, department stores, hotels, insurance companies, telephone companies, accounting firms, factories, supermarkets, and restaurants, to name a few.

The employment rights of the ADA have an enormous potential for people with disabilities to become fully independent and full contributors and participants in the American economy. Even J. Kemp, Jr., chairman of the Equal Employment Opportunity Commission, emphasized the importance of these new rights when he said, "But the crux of the ADA is its employment provisions, for joblessness is the truly disabling condition."[14]

Chairman Kemp also said, "A staggering 58 percent of all men with disabilities and 80 percent of all women with disabilities are unemployed. So long as two-thirds of disabled Americans are unemployed, we will be unable to break the terrible cycle of dependency and segregation. And, if people with disabilities cannot break the grip of economic dependence, our society is doomed to spend more than $160 billion a year on benefits that most recipients would willingly trade for a good job."[15]

For people with disabilities, the ADA provides an opportunity to compete on an equal basis, and the new law addresses current and historic issues of isolation, inferior status, social, economic, and vocational disadvantages, and discrimination. The purpose of the ADA legislation, as stated in the law, is as follows:

1. To provide a clear and comprehensive national mandate for the elimination of discrimination against individuals with disabilities;
2. To provide clear, strong, consistent, enforceable standards addressing discrimination against individuals with disabilities;
3. To ensure that the federal government plays a central role in enforcing the standards established in this act on behalf of individuals with disabilities; and
4. To invoke the sweep of congressional authority, including the power to enforce the Fourteenth Amendment and to regulate commerce, in order to address the major areas of discrimination faced day-to-day by people with disabilities.[16]

CONGRESSIONAL FINDINGS ON THE SCOPE OF ISSUES

At the very beginning of the Americans with Disabilities Act of 1990, PL 101–336, there is a list of findings by Congress in committee hearings over a two-year period. It is interesting to note that almost all of the ADA findings relate to the very central issue of employment. These findings include the following:

1. Some 43 million Americans have one or more physical or mental disabilities, and this number is increasing as the population as a whole is growing older.

2. Historically, society has tended to isolate and segregate individuals with disabilities, and, despite some improvements, such forms of discrimination against individuals with disabilities continue to be a serious and pervasive social problem.

3. Discrimination against individuals with disabilities persists in such crucial areas as employment, education, transportation, communication, recreation, institutionalization, health services, voting, and access to public services.

4. Unlike individuals who have experienced discrimination on the basis of race, color, sex, national origin, religion, or age, individuals who have experienced discrimination on the basis of disability have often had no legal recourse to redress such discrimination.

5. Individuals with disabilities continually encounter various forms of discrimination, including outright intentional exclusion, the discriminatory effects of architectural, transportation, and communication barriers, overprotective rules and policies, failure to make modifications to existing facilities and practices, exclusionary qualification standards and criteria, segregation, and relegation to lesser services, programs, activities, benefits, jobs, or other opportunities.

6. Census data, national polls, and other studies have documented that people with disabilities, as a group, occupy an inferior status in our society and are severely disadvantaged socially, vocationally, economically, and educationally.

7. Individuals with disabilities are a discrete and insular minority who have been faced with restrictions and limitations, subjected to a history of purposeful unequal treatment, and relegated to a position of political powerlessness in our society, based on characteristics that are beyond the control of such individuals and resulting from stereotypic assumptions not truly indicative of the ability of such individuals to participate in and contribute to society.

8. The nation's proper goals regarding individuals with disabilities are to assure equality of opportunity, full participation, independent living, and economic self-sufficiency for such individuals.

9. The continuing existence of unfair and unnecessary discrimination and prejudice denies people with disabilities the opportunity to compete on an equal basis and to pursue those opportunities for which our free society is justifiably famous, and costs the United States billions of dollars in unnecessary expenses resulting from dependency and nonproductivity.[17]

WHAT IS DISCRIMINATION: CONGRESSIONAL FINDINGS

The House of Representatives Committee on Education and Labor in a 15 May 1990 report states:

People with disabilities have been subjected to unequal and discriminatory treatment in a range of areas ... resulting from stereotypical assumptions, fears and myths not truly indicative of the ability of such individuals to participate and contribute to society. ... The simple fact that this Act has taken this long to pass Congress, 25 years after other civil rights legislation had been passed, is a testament to that fact. This Act will finally set in place the necessary civil rights protections for people with disabilities.[18]

A House of Representatives report on the ADA from the Committee on Labor and Human Resources, 30 August 1989, presented additional examples of discrimination against people with disabilities:

1. Discrimination also includes exclusion, or denial of benefits, services or other opportunities that are as effective and meaningful as those provided to others.
2. Discrimination results from actions or inactions that discriminate by effect as well as by intent or design.
3. Discrimination also includes harms resulting from the construction of transportation, architectural, and communications barriers and the adoption or application of standards and criteria and practices and procedures based on thoughtlessness or indifference—benign neglect.
4. Discrimination also includes harms affecting individuals with a history of disability, and those regarded by others as having a disability as well as persons associated with such individuals that are based on false presumptions, generalizations, misconceptions, patronizing attitudes, ignorance, irrational fears, and pernicious mythologies.
5. Discriminating also includes the effects a person's disability or perceived disability may have on others. For example, a burn victim may have a stigmatizing condition but not a physical disability, but [that person] may be viewed by others including employers as having a physical disability.[19]

The congressional findings, the testimony of dozens of business managers and people with disabilities, and the overwhelming vote to enact the Americans with Disabilities Act are not the only barometers of public opinion. Louis Harris, chairman and CEO of Louis Harris and Associates, Inc., measured the number of voters with disabilities in 1988 and found "that fully 10 percent of the entire electorate were people with disabilities."[20] At a press conference, after completing a cross-section survey of American opinion about the ADA, in September 1991, Harris said, "The reaction to the ADA is overwhelming. Between 83 percent and 96 percent support key provisions [in which] employers will be prohibited from discriminating against a qualified person for a job because he or she is disabled [and] that employers must provide accommodations for employees with disabilities."[21]

THE ADA LANGUAGE

Like other important federal legislation, the Americans with Disabilities Act has spawned a new language and vocabulary. Many of these terms are relatively new, having been developed since 1964. The term "public ac-

Table 2.2
Public Attitudes toward People with Disabilities in the Workplace

- The public has very positive opinions about disabled workers.

- More than four out of five Americans believe that disabled workers are equally or more productive than average workers. However, only just over half of those with a regular job rate their employers' policies for employment of the disabled positively.

- Economics, compassion, and civil rights are all accepted as rationales for working to increase participation by disabled people. More than 90 percent support each of these reasons for increasing participation.

- When members of the public who work regularly with a disabled person were asked to assess their productivity, 82 percent said disabled workers are equally or more productive than the average worker.

- Two-thirds of the public is ready to have more people with disabilities join them and their co-workers in the workplace, although only one-half said their employers are doing a good job at developing policies that attract more people with disabilities.

- 81 percent of the public believes disabled people under 65 want to get jobs rather than stay at home and live on disability payments.

- The public is largely aware of the kind of life that people with disabilities lead in this country. They understand that two-thirds of working-age disabled persons who are not working would like to find a job.

- 66 percent of the public feel disabled people are discriminated against in equal access to employment.

- 78 percent of the public views disabled people as having under used potential to contribute to the economy rather than as a burden supported through government payments.

- Both in general terms and specifically in reference to the work force, the public overwhelmingly accepts the characterization of disabled people as a great untapped resource.

SOURCE: Louis Harris and Associates, Inc. *Public Attitudes Toward People with Disabilities,* September 1991, New York.

commodation," however, goes back to the Civil Rights Act of 1875. Passed by Congress during the Reconstruction era, the short-lived law provided blacks with the "full and equal enjoyment of accommodations"—inns, theaters, and places of public amusement.[22] Understanding the ADA's language is crucial to obtaining a clear grasp of the purpose, provisions, and objectives of this landmark federal civil rights legislation.

Covered entities. In the ADA legislation, this term refers to small businesses, companies, nonprofit associations (religious organizations are a qualified exception), state and local governments, employment agencies, labor organizations, and joint labor management committees.

Covered employers. The antidiscrimination coverage of the ADA is comprehensive and affects all public and private employers with fifteen or more employees. Between 26 July 1992 and 26 July 1994, however, businesses with 25 or more employees must comply with the law.

Covered applicants or employees. The employment provisions of the ADA cover all applicants or employees who are qualified to perform the essential functions of an employment position.

Definition of disability. A person satisfies the ADA definition of disability if the individual meets the requirements of one of the following three categories:

1. The individual has a mental or physical impairment that substantially limits one or more major life activities such as walking, seeing, or hearing.

2. The individual has a record of an impairment that is used by the employer to discriminate against the individual, whether or not the individual still has the impairment. (This category encompasses people with mental impairments or past impairments that are usually no longer active.)

3. The individual is regarded by others as having a disability, whether or not the individual is impaired at all. (This category encompasses individuals with acquired immunodeficiency syndrome [AIDS] or who are HIV positive, for instance, and addresses discrimination against people based on fears, myths, and stereotypes.)[23]

Exclusions to the disability definition. Several categories of individuals are excluded from coverage under the ADA, including those who currently use illegal drugs, those who are homosexuals, and those who have specific sexual-related disorders. (For a more extensive definition of disability under the ADA, see chapter 4.)

Employment. Title I of the ADA is a federal nondiscrimination law designed to remove barriers that prevent all qualified individuals with disabilities from enjoying the same employment opportunities that are available to all people without disabilities, regardless of any ties to federal funding. In its most practical form, the ADA has three basic requirements:

1. Employers must make employment determinations based on ability and not on disability.

2. Employers must treat people with disabilities just like other applicants or employees except where accommodation is necessary to enable them to perform the job.

3. Employers must accommodate people with disabilities unless to do so would impose an undue hardship on the employer.

It is estimated that Title I, the employment provisions of the ADA, will extend nondiscrimination coverage to 20 million employees not already covered by the Rehabilitation Act of 1973 or state statutes comparable to the ADA.[24] If state statutes similar to the ADA are included, 15 million employees will be newly covered, according to the Equal Employment Opportunity Commission.[25] The employment discrimination provisions of the ADA are based on the protections and enforcement mechanisms established in the Civil Rights Act of 1964 and the Rehabilitation Act of 1973.

Discrimination against people with disabilities. The employment provisions of the ADA affect all aspects of employment, including hiring, firing, promotion, compensation, job training, and benefits of employment. An employer who discriminates against a qualified individual with a disability because of the disability in any aspect of employment, including the application process, is in violation of the ADA.

Reasonable accommodation. Once the applicant or employee raises the need for reasonable accommodation, the employer must enter into a discussion with the individual to attempt to provide a reasonable accommodation that will eliminate barriers to the workplace. Reasonable accommodation is an action taken by an employer, mutually determined with a qualified applicant or employee with a disability, that assists that individual in performing the essential functions of a specific job. Job restructuring, part-time or modified work schedules, reassignment to a vacant position, and the use of assistive devices are examples of reasonable accommodation.

Job restructuring. A type of reasonable accommodation, job restructuring means modifying a job, by eliminating some of the non-essential elements or reassigning tasks, so that a person with a disability can perform the essential functions of the position.

Qualified individual with a disability. Not all persons who have disabilities are necessarily qualified. An employer is not required to hire or retain an individual who is not qualified. As defined in the ADA, a qualified person with a disability is a person who "with or without reasonable accommodation, can perform the essential functions of the employment position that such individual holds or desires." The ADA regulations define a qualified person with a disability as an individual with a disability who "satisfies the requisite skill, experience, education and other job-related requirements of the employment position such individual holds or desires."[26]

Undue hardship. An employer does not have to provide an applicant or employee with a reasonable accommodation if no form of accommodation can be agreed upon that does not impose an undue hardship on the employer. Undue hardship includes undue financial burdens or a fundamental alteration of the operation of the business.

Public accommodation. In addition to nondiscrimination rights in employment, the ADA also provides antidiscrimination rights to all persons with disabilities in their access and full utilization of places of public accommodation, such as retail businesses, hotels, restaurants, zoos, movie theaters, parks, recreational areas, and the offices of physicians, lawyers, and accountants.

Readily accessible. This term refers to the degree by which a person with a disability can enter or fully utilize a facility.

Readily achievable. This term refers to the degree of ease or difficulty that confronts a business operator in removing a barrier or in making a change that is "easily accomplishable and able to be carried out without much difficulty or expense."[27] Under the ADA, places of public accommodation are required to remove structural barriers in existing facilities only if the removal is readily achievable. Examples include changing the arrangement of tables in a restaurant or the addition of raised letters and braille markings on elevator control buttons and the addition of braille to restaurant menus.

CHAPTER 3

A Blueprint for Change

Congress has enacted nearly thirty laws containing broad prohibitions against discrimination against people with mental and physical disabilities.[1] The history of federal legislation for people with disabilities can be traced to the Smith-Sears Veterans Rehabilitation Act of 1918, which provided vocational rehabilitation to World War I veterans. The first civilian vocational rehabilitation legislation, the Smith-Fess Act of 1920, ushered in the federal and state partnership of funding and administering civilian vocational rehabilitation programs.

The Rehabilitation Services Administration of the Department of Education has reported that during the last seventy-five years, the federal-state vocational rehabilitation program's annual budget has grown from $750,000 to $1.5 billion.[2] These programs have provided millions of people with disabilities with training and higher education. But due to discrimination in employment practices, and without even partial EEO legislation until 1973, a high proportion of people with disabilities who had successfully *completed* training and education programs, including college education, had trouble finding employment.

THE BEGINNING OF A FEDERAL MANDATE
THE 1960s TO 1970s

The history of the disability rights movement can be traced to a sunny, spring day in Washington, D.C. in 1964 when Hugh Gregory Gallagher, a Senate legislative aide who uses a wheelchair as a result of polio, wanted to conduct research at the Library of Congress. The unwillingness of the librarian of congress to provide Gallagher, who worked on the staff of Senator E. L. "Bob" Bartlett (D-Alaska), with a ramp signaled the beginning of a series of new federal legislation and a federal mandate for people with disabilities.

According to Gallagher, "I literally needed an act of Congress to have the ramp installed." Gallagher no longer wanted to be carried up the two steps by two guards in order to gain access to the Library of Congress. Senator Bartlett placed a line item for $5,000 for the ramp in an appropriation measure, and when it passed, a cast iron ramp was installed, a ramp that still stands today. Gallagher, who wanted to be able to visit the Smithsonian Institution and the Kennedy Center, was soon responsible for initiating their efforts to become accessible. Senator Bartlett, at Gallagher's suggestion, requested that the new federal building in Juneau, Alaska, be made accessible. This was the beginning of the first in a series of federal laws leading to the ADA.

From the one federal building in Juneau, Gallagher had a model for new federal legislation and authored the Architectural Barriers Act of 1968, covering "any facility constructed wholly or in part with federal funds." Like the ADA, the Architectural Barriers Act enjoyed a virtual unanimous vote in Congress and was signed into law by President Lyndon Johnson. Gallagher, who is the author of *F.D.R.'s Splendid Deception*, said:

When I drafted the Architectural Barriers Act twenty-five years ago, my idea was a simple one: equality in the civil rights sense. Disabled people paid their taxes just like other people. Surely, I argued, any building or facility built with tax revenues should be accessible to all taxpayers—including the disabled. The argument was unassailable back then, and it still is. My concept has been extended to public education, to federal employment, and now, with the bipartisan Americans with Disabilities Act, across the land. It sparked a revolution. Who would have guessed, twenty-five years ago?[3]

Due to the efforts of Gallagher and many others, the federal government began to demonstrate an increased interest and awareness of the need for legislation for people with disabilities. It was the beginning of a long road to what would become the ADA. During the late 1960s, there was a shift away from entitlement programs, such as Social Security Supplemental Income (SSI), to a new focus on civil rights. The following were among the most important civil rights laws for people with disabilities during this period: the Architectural Barriers Act of 1968, which provided access to federally funded public buildings by an estimated 20 million people with physical disabilities; the Rehabilitation Act of 1973 (especially Section 504); and the Education for All Handicapped Children Act of 1975, now known as the Individuals with Disabilities Education Act (IDEA).

For employment of people with disabilities, certainly, the most significant legislation prior to the ADA was the Rehabilitation Act of 1973, and the "linchpin" of the Rehabilitation Act was Section 504.[4]

Table 3.1
Federal Legislation Affecting People with Disabilities

The Civil Rights Act of 1991
The Americans with Disabilities Act of 1990
The Technology-Related Assistance for Individuals with Disabilities Act
  of 1988
Handicapped Children's Protection Act of 1986
Protection and Advocacy for Mentally Ill Individuals Act of 1986
The Orphan Drug Act of 1983
Developmental Disabilities Assistance and Bill of Rights Act of 1975
  (amended in 1984)
Education for All Handicapped Children Act of 1975 (IDEA)
  (amended in 1984)
The Rehabilitation Act of 1973 (amended in 1986)
Architectural Barriers Act of 1968
Civil Rights Act of 1964
The Social Security Act of 1935 (and amendments in 1956)
The Smith-Fess Act of 1920
The Smith-Sears Veterans Rehabilitation Act of 1918

SOURCE: U.S. Department of Education, *Summary of Existing Legislation Affecting Persons with Disabilities*, August 1988.

The language used in the Civil Rights Act of 1964 was utilized in framing Section 504, which created protections for people with disabilities against discrimination in programs funded in part or whole by the federal government. Section 504 of the act states: "No otherwise qualified handicapped individual in the United States . . . shall, solely by reason of his handicap, be excluded from the participation in, be denied the benefits of, or be subjected to discrimination under any program or activity receiving federal financial assistance or under any program or activity conducted by any executive agency or by the United States Postal Service."[5]

The key problem with the Rehabilitation Act of 1973 was a gap in coverage in that it only covered federal employees, parties with federal contracts, and those organizations or businesses receiving over $2,500 per year from the federal government. Because of this gap, the Rehabilitation Act did not have a substantial impact on private sector employers or employees.[6] In addition, the only way to enforce Section 504 was to bring a private cause of action or a complaint with the Office of Civil Rights under the particular federal funding agency where the alleged discriminatory institution was funded. While this led to some enforcement by private parties, it was fairly unusual for the government to sue or participate in suits.[7] By contrast, under the ADA, the government may investigate charges and file lawsuits directly through the commissioner of the Equal Employment Opportunity Commission and the attorney general.

Optimism over the Americans with Disabilities Act is not shared by everyone. There has been criticism despite the overwhelming bipartisan support in Congress and the advantages of enabling people with disabilities to become independent workers rather than welfare consumers. The ADA also has the potential for increasing economic growth instead of sustaining continued annual lost productivity and tax revenues estimated at $300 billion per year. Some critics have forecast a flurry of litigation with the implementation of the ADA and a corresponding burden on American businesses.[8] The same fears were raised in the first few years following the implementation of the Civil Rights Act of 1964 and Section 504 of the Rehabilitation Act of 1973.[9]

The Civil Rights Act of 1964 prohibits discrimination against people on the basis of race, color, religion, national origin, and sex. The Rehabilitation Act of 1973 incorporated many of the enforcement and administrative principles of the Civil Rights Act of 1964. Section 501 of the Rehabilitation Act prohibited the federal government from discriminating against its employees with disabilities. Section 503 of the Rehabilitation Act extended the prohibition against discrimination on the basis of disability to all employers with federal contracts for goods and services. Section 504 prohibits discrimination based on disability under any program or activity receiving federal financial assistance. This includes state and local government agencies, colleges, universities or school systems, corporations, or private organizations that receive federal financial assistance. The Rehabilitation Act of 1973, specifically Section 504, has been the principal law relied upon by litigants in disability discrimination cases over the past sixteen years.[10] As a result of a series of court decisions in the mid–1980s that significantly limited the application of Section 504, Congress passed the Civil Rights Restoration Act of 1987 (PL 100–259), which reasserted the broad coverage of the law.

THE SEARCH FOR MORE COMPREHENSIVE LEGISLATION
THE 1980s

Advocates for people with disabilities in the 1980s began to look at the Civil Rights Act of 1964 as the basis of a potential blueprint for a civil rights law for people with disabilities that would go further than the Rehabilitation Act of 1973. A common thread that can be seen between the Civil Rights Act of 1964 and the Americans with Disabilities Act of 1990 is that they are both based on the commerce clause of the Constitution. Speaking on the floor of the Senate on behalf of the Civil Rights Act of 1964, Senator Hubert H. Humphrey said, "The constitutional basis for Title VII is, of course, the commerce clause. The courts have held time and again that the commerce clause authorizes Congress to enact legislation to regulate employment which affects interstate and foreign commerce."[11]

Twenty years later in 1984, two attorneys, Robert L. Burgdorf, Jr. and Christopher G. Bell, argued persuasively for a blueprint for federal legislation that would prohibit discrimination against people with mental and physical disabilities in an article in the *Mental and Physical Disability Law Reporter* published by the American Bar Association.[12] These two nationally recognized experts in the field of disability law compared the Civil Rights Act of 1964 with the then current federal civil rights provisions and protections for people with disabilities and found them to be inadequate. They questioned why Congress could not invoke the commerce clause and create federal legislation for people with disabilities comparable to the Civil Rights Act of 1964:

In some civil rights measures, particularly the Civil Rights Act of 1964, Congress has made use of its authority to regulate interstate commerce to prohibit discrimination in all agencies and businesses that affect interstate commerce. To date, laws prohibiting discrimination against handicapped people have applied only to federal agencies and recipients of federal grants, contracts, and other forms of federal assistance. Discrimination against handicapped persons should be prohibited in all the contexts where Congress has seen fit to outlaw other forms of discrimination. Congress should invoke its interstate commerce authority to expand the coverage of handicap discrimination laws to all entities that affect interstate commerce.[13]

Six years later, in 1990, Congressman Steny H. Hoyer (D-Maryland), the chief supporter of the Americans with Disabilities Act in the House of Representatives, said that with the ADA, Congress "is invoking the sweep" of its authority, "including the power to regulate commerce."[14] Congressman Hoyer told his colleagues in the House of Representatives, "The Fourteenth Amendment gives Congress the power to enforce that amendment through appropriate legislation. Congress has authority under this section to prohibit discrimination in state and local governments."[15]

The blueprint for constructing a *comprehensive* federal civil rights law for people with disabilities had been drawn. The next step was to see what resources were available. There was an array of necessary materials for building the foundation: the overwhelming support by members of Congress; hearings, reports, and testimony provided by congressional committees in Washington, D.C., Boston, and Houston; the active support of the White House; the National Council on Disability's publication of its recommendations in *Toward Independence*; the concerns voiced by national organizations and advocates with disabilities; and supportive public opinion as measured in national surveys. In addition to the commerce clause, Congress had the Civil Rights Act of 1964 and the Rehabilitation Act of 1973 as precedents and models for the Americans with Disabilities Act of 1990.

The Civil Rights Act of 1964 serves as a foundation for the Americans with Disabilities Act and there are a number of similarities between the two pieces of legislation. Title I of the ADA seeks to reward employees based on merit in the hiring and promotion arenas. In this regard, the ADA is similar to the 1964 Civil Rights Act because disability is placed on the same level as race, color, religion, national origin, and sex when determining the merits of a prospective employee. The Americans with Disabilities Act, like the Civil Rights Act and Section 504 of the Rehabilitation Act, does not establish quotas or require preferences favoring individuals with disabilities over those without disabilities. In fact, the ADA incorporates the remedial enforcement provisions of the Civil Rights Act of 1964. The remedies for discrimination based on disability include reinstatement of the employee, back pay, attorney's fees to the prevailing party, and other compensation that the court decides is proper.[16]

The Civil Rights Act of 1964 prohibits any consideration of personal characteristics such as race, religion, or sex when determining issues of employment. The ADA adopts this same principle but goes one step further. The ADA prohibits employers from treating people differently on the basis of personal characteristics, namely disability. As Christopher Bell, the attorney advisor to the chairman of the Equal Employment Opportunity Commission, stated, "The ADA requires the employer to treat people differently, when they need to be treated differently. But only to the extent they need to be treated differently, and only to the extent it doesn't affect [the] business operation unduly."[17]

During the mid–1980s the National Council on Disability, an independent federal agency, was also studying the problem of inadequate federal protections for people with disabilities. The effectiveness of the Rehabilitation Act of 1973 was beginning to be questioned. There was a lack of definitive employment statistics regarding the implementation of Section 504 of the Rehabilitation Act, preventing an accurate analysis of the effectiveness of the law.[18] Despite some advances in the employment of people with disabilities at the federal level, and congressional intervention to re-establish the breadth of Section 504, the Rehabilitation Act of 1973 was largely viewed as ineffective in the private sector area of employment and not comprehensive enough to fully assimilate America's working-age disabled population into the national economic mainstream. After the National Council on Disability produced the report, *Toward Independence*, on the effectiveness of federal legislation for people with disabilities in 1986, the stage was set for the expansion of the rights of people with disabilities through what came to be known as the Americans with Disabilities Act.[19]

THE ADA FINAL REGULATIONS

As stated in the legislative history of the Americans with Disabilities Act, it was the intention of Congress to pattern the regulations of the

ADA after the regulations of Section 504 of the Rehabilitation Act of 1973, as amended. In this way, the ADA benefits from an established regulatory framework and a proven track record of case law. In furthering the congressional intention to make the ADA regulations comprehensive and easily understood, the ADA final regulations specify terms not previously defined in the regulations implementing Section 504 of the Rehabilitation Act.

As Senator Harkin stated, "Every key term used in the ADA has an extensive history or is specifically defined in the legislation and further clarified in the reports accompanying the bill."[20] These new terms include "substantially limits," "essential functions," and "reasonable accommodation." In addition, the ADA is highly detailed in contrast to other legislation in its class. As a result, the agencies responsible for formulating the ADA regulations had little discretion when elaborating upon the language of the law. Most of the final ADA regulations, which were published in the *Federal Register*, 26 July 1991, provide guidance on the law's provisions and rely on existing case law.

This reliance on established civil rights law is seen as one of the major strengths of the ADA. The uniformity of terms was designed to eliminate or severely diminish the need to have courts interpret the language of the statute in ADA lawsuits. People with disabilities and the businesses that employ them will be able to look to the cases that have been decided for over two decades for guidance. The goal of this approach is to focus attention on compliance with the ADA and away from after-the-fact lawsuits. According to the *Labor Lawyer*, published by the American Bar Association, the majority of ADA litigation will center on Title I, the employment provisions of the law, where claimants will stand to gain the most economically by court-enforced compliance with the ADA.[21]

Because of the economic stakes, several critics raised serious opposition to the Bush administration's forecast of smooth ADA implementation.[22] These authors predict a great deal of Title I litigation despite the uniform language of the law. The ADA cannot possibly detail every situation where a legal or factual issue may exist. These conflicts may have to be decided in the courtroom. For example, an employer who denies employment to a qualified person with a disability because the employee is said to have "a high probability of substantial harm to oneself or others" could end up before the Equal Employment Opportunity Commission or in court explaining the reason for the decision. In addition to the ADA's inability to fully address every potential disagreement, lawsuits based on discrimination of people with disabilities will inevitably increase due to the vast number of businesses and individuals with disabilities affected by the law.

THE ADA: LEARNING LESSONS FROM PAST
LEGISLATION
THE 1990s

The drafters of the ADA learned lessons from the implementation of Section 504 and refined the statutory and regulatory language of the ADA to make for smoother implementation and to eliminate loopholes. In general, the EEOC's regulations and interpretive appendix to the ADA provide more detailed guidance than existed under the Rehabilitation Act on important terms such as "substantially limits," "working," "disability," and "essential functions."

A notable expansion of ADA coverage concerns the prohibition of Section 504 against discrimination of any "handicapped person *solely* on the basis of handicap." This language often allowed employers to escape liability if they had mixed motives or had more than one reason for discriminating against applicants or employees who happened to have a disability. The language of the ADA is not as limited because it does not use the word "solely" and as a result closes a potential loophole caused when an important term is qualified or limited.

The ADA specifically includes job reassignment as an example of a reasonable accommodation, an issue of substantial controversy throughout the implementation of Section 504. The language of Section 504 and its regulations do not define the key concept of "undue hardship" to an employer, but merely states three factors to consider when making determinations of undue hardship. The ADA not only defines undue hardship as "significant difficulty or expense" but expands and refines the factors to consider when determining whether an accommodation creates an undue hardship on the employer. While litigation is still probable on this issue and courts may still disagree in result, the ADA removes some of the ambiguity that existed under Section 504 of the Rehabilitation Act.

The ADA provides important limitations on the employer's ability to deny employment opportunities to people with disabilities because the qualified applicant or employee poses a threat to the health or safety of "oneself or others." The courts had read an "elevated risk" standard into Section 504 cases in this area. In other words, employers could claim that the risks associated with hiring or promoting a person with a disability doubled if the risk of injury increased from one in one thousand to two in one thousand by hiring the disabled person over the nondisabled person. The ADA regulations heightened this standard primarily to protect individuals with a mental illness or a history of mental illness from the myths and stereotypes of being prone to violence.

The ADA regulations specify that an employer may deem a person unqualified for a particular job only if the individual poses *a high probability of substantial harm* to oneself or others that cannot be eliminated or reduced by reasonable accommodation.[23] Although this heightened standard provides more protection to people with disabilities than existed under Section 504, many disability advocates have expressed concern that employers may discriminate against disabled applicants and employees by utilizing the "threat to oneself" language in the ADA regulations.

People with disabilities have responsibilities and obligations to the employer under the ADA. While the new law provides new and expanded rights for people with disabilities, it does not relieve a disabled individual from performing the essential functions of the job. On the contrary, the ADA's goal is to enable people with disabilities to compete in the workplace based on the same performance standards and requirements that employers expect of people without physical or mental disabilities. The ADA provides for equal employment opportunity for an applicant or employee based not on disability, but on qualification—competence, educational background, skill, and ability to perform a specific job.

DIFFERENCES WITH PREVIOUS LEGISLATION

The ADA regulations improve upon Section 504 by clearly addressing the practical reality of pre-employment inquiries. While the employer may not ask the disabled applicant or employee about certain issues, such as worker's compensation claims, the employer can ask the visibly disabled applicants or employees to explain or demonstrate how they can perform a particular job with a reasonable accommodation. This approach is consistent with Section 504 but takes it one step further. It allows the doubting employer to be shown, not simply told, that an applicant or employee with a disability is qualified to perform the job.

While both the Rehabilitation Act and the ADA generally restrict pre-employment inquiries of people with disabilities, the Rehabilitation Act regulations specifically permit self-identification of one's disability for affirmative action purposes or to remedy past discrimination. The ADA did not adopt this provision, and the ADA does not utilize affirmative action. In another development, the ADA refined the central concept of reasonable accommodation created by the Rehabilitation Act. The ADA provides a generic definition of reasonable accommodation, detailing the interactive process between employer and applicant or employee. The new law guides an employer in deciding to provide reasonable accommodation to an applicant or employee, when necessary, on an individual, case-by-case basis. This determination involving both employer and employee is based on a number of factors, including the employer's resources. The objective of reasonable accommodation is to create a level playing field for a *qualified* applicant or employee to ensure that an individual can perform the essential functions of the job.

Not all disabled workers require accommodation. Louis Harris and Associates, Inc. reported that only 35 percent of one thousand disabled workers who participated in a survey required accommodation in the workplace.[24] The EEOC has reported in its proposed regulations an average figure of $261 per disabled employee who needs a reasonable accommodation.[25] However, when a potential employee's disability impedes job performance and requires the employer to attempt to reasonably accommodate the disabled individual, the employer will not be required to accommodate the disabled person if it would impose an undue hardship on the employer.

Another major difference between the Rehabilitation Act of 1973 and the Americans with Disabilities Act was the time-consuming struggle between Capitol Hill and the White House before the Rehabilitation Act became enacted and implemented. President Richard Nixon vetoed the Rehabilitation Act twice, stating that it would "cruelly raise the hopes" of people with disabilities.[26] Nixon was in no hurry to implement the law when he finally signed a veto-proof revision of the legislation on 26 September 1973. It was not until three-and-a-half years later in May 1977 that Section 504 was implemented. One of the key reasons that Section 504 finally became a reality was due to demonstrations by people with disabilities in nine different cities on 5 April 1977, making front-page news in metropolitan newspapers around the country.[27]

The major political differences between the Rehabilitation Act and the ADA are striking. First, unlike Nixon, President Bush supported the ADA and invited three thousand guests, a majority of whom had disabilities, to the South Lawn of the White House for the signing ceremony on 26 July 1990. Second, Congress requested the testimony and direct involvement of dozens of people with disabilities in committee hearings as it studied and then created the landmark legislation. Third, all of the federal agencies responsible for developing regulations for the ADA met the congressional deadline for publication in the *Federal Register* within one year after the ADA was signed into law. The fourth difference is that the ADA symbolizes how people with disabilities have increasingly become part of the political system, at the ballot box, in peaceful demonstrations, and with the support of influential senators and congressmen—a number of whom either have disabilities or have close relatives with disabilities.

One of the most important differences is that with the enactment of the Americans with Disabilities Act, people with disabilities have as citizens been specifically recognized. As Burgdorf and Bell state in their blueprint for a new civil rights law for people with disabilities:

The experiences of women and racial and ethnic minorities in battling for civil rights in our society have provided an invaluable model for handicapped people's civil rights efforts. But the remedies for the discrimination faced by handicapped people cannot be achieved by merely copying the remedial legislation secured by previous civil rights groups. Improvements to existing legislation providing civil rights protections for handicapped people can be framed only by focusing on the great diversity of disabled people, the common experience of discrimination they share, the nature, sources, and dynamics of that discrimination, and the ways in which existing legislation has failed to adequately address and eliminate such discrimination.[28]

The Americans with Disabilities Act was enacted because existing legislation was incomplete and not comprehensive in its scope. The common experience of discrimination that people with disabilities shared was all too common. Congress chose to address and remedy discrimination against people with disabilities with a comprehensive mandate. As stated at the beginning of the ADA, Congress enacted the legislation by invoking "the sweep of congressional authority, including the power to enforce the Fourteenth Amendment and to regulate commerce, in order to address the major areas of discrimination faced day-to-day by people with disabilities in creating equal opportunity for the advancement of people with disabilities in American society."[29]

A blueprint for change was enacted. The responsibility for working to build a more equal nation was no longer just in the hands of Congress or the federal government. As a new federal civil rights law, it is the law of the land. As Congressman Steve Bartlett (D-Texas) said during a congressional hearing, "The world is changing and it is going to change even faster with the ADA."[30]

IMPLEMENTING THE ADA

The federal government is responsible for implementing and enforcing the ADA. The four federal agencies that have the primary responsibility for implementation are the Department of Justice, the Equal Employment Opportunity Commission, the Department of Transportation, and the Federal Communications Commission. The two agencies with primary responsibility for implementing the employment provisions of the ADA are the EEOC and the Department of Justice. The EEOC is primarily responsible for the enforcement of the ADA's nondiscrimination provisions in employment. As in the case of Title VII, which is also primarily enforced by the EEOC, the Department of Justice also has litigation authority under the ADA with respect to nondiscrimination in employment by state and local governments. The EEOC issued final regulations for the enforcement of the ADA's employment provisions on 26 July 1991. (For an analysis of the ADA final employment regulations, see chapters 4, 5, and 11.)

Evan J. Kemp, Jr., former EEOC chairman, summarized the agency's experience and perspective for the future when he stated, "EEOC has a critical role to play in implementing the ADA. In its capacity as an administrative appellate body, EEOC has grappled with many difficult issues under the Rehabilitation Act that will arise under the ADA as well. These include questions concerning the definition of disability as well as the scope of an agency's duty to provide reasonable accommodation."[31]

The EEOC has three thousand employees in fifty district and local offices throughout the United States. During fiscal year 1989, the EEOC received 55,926 new charges of employment discrimination in private sector employment, and it closed a total of 66,209 charges. According to Chairman Kemp, "The enactment of the ADA will result in perhaps an additional ten thousand to twelve thousand charges being filed with the commission alleging discrimination on the basis of disability, an increase of approximately fifteen to twenty percent in the commission's workload."[32] Congress recognized the necessity of informing the public about the Americans with Disabilities Act and its extensive provisions affecting employment, commerce, public accommodations, transportation, and telecommunications.

To implement this landmark legislation, the Department of Justice, the Equal Employment Opportunity Commission, the Department of Transportation, the Architectural and Transportation Barriers Compliance Board, and the Federal Communications Commission are coordinating the dissemination of technical assistance manuals and information on the ADA to the public. The ADA authorizes each of these agencies to render technical assistance to individuals, businesses, and organizations that have rights or duties under the new legislation. In addition, the President's Committee on Employment of People with Disabilities, created in 1947, operates the Job Accommodation Network (JAN), which provides a free consulting service, on a case-by-case basis, with information on available aids, devices, and methods for accommodating workers with disabilities. (For federal agency information on the ADA, see the appendix.)

Congress has authorized 36 technical assistance programs to aid in implementing the Americans with Disabilities Act through the Equal Employment Opportunity Commission, the Department of Justice, and the Department of Education. Ten of the Department of Education National Institute on Disability and Rehabilitation Research programs are business accommodation centers located in each of ten regions around the country. Information on the ADA for the business community and people with disabilities is available through these federal agencies and federally funded technical assistance programs. (For information on the ADA Regional Disability and Business Accommodation Centers, see the appendix.)

CHAPTER 4

The Principal Employment Concepts of the ADA

As with many large pieces of legislation, Congress relied on particular federal agencies to issue the final regulations that specify the legal requirements of the Americans with Disabilities Act. By reviewing these regulations, one may obtain an in-depth understanding of how the employment provisions of the ADA are applied and work in everyday practice. Most of these regulations were to be issued within one year of the enactment date, as directed by the language of the law. Final federal regulations for Title I, which consist of the employment provisions of the ADA, were issued by the Equal Employment Opportunity Commission on 26 July 1991, one year after the enactment of the ADA.

This chapter and the next provide an analysis of the final federal regulations covering the principal employment areas of the Americans with Disabilities Act:

- The definition of disability
- Who is a qualified individual with a disability
- Reasonable accommodation and undue hardship
- Nondiscriminatory employment practices

In addition, an attempt is made to clarify the regulatory language with examples and with an "implications section" following each major regulatory area. This detailed analysis of the final federal regulations regarding the employment provisions of the ADA can assist both employers and people with disabilities better understand their responsibilities and obligations under the new law. A good example of why it is important to understand the regulations is that an important definition of "direct threat" was substantially changed and expanded in the final regulations, differing from the definition in the ADA legislation.[1]

The language of Title I of the ADA is relatively detailed in comparison to other laws. According to the EEOC's Notice of Proposed Rulemaking, "Title I of the ADA is an unusual statute in that it contains a level of detail more commonly found in regulations, leaving very little room for regulatory discretion."[2] The final regulations covering Title I, issued by the EEOC, explain the language of the law and provide guidance on the legislation's requirements by relying primarily on existing case law derived from lawsuits brought under existing nondiscrimination disability law. It was the intent of Congress that the ADA employment regulations be easily understood, comprehensive, and reflect the format of the regulations implementing Section 504 of the Rehabilitation Act of 1973, as amended.[3]

It is important to note that these regulations have the full force and effect of law and carry as much weight as the actual language in the legislation, according to the legislative history of the ADA.[4] The appendix to the EEOC regulations, the "interpretive guidance," provides analysis and technical assistance to consider when interpreting the ADA law and regulations. The interpretive guidance provided by the EEOC does not carry the force and effect of administrative law and in this discussion is distinguished from the EEOC regulations.

The congressional intent, as reflected in the legislative history, to give Title I regulations the full force and effect of law, is a significant departure from the relationship between the law and the regulations of other protected groups covered by Title VII of the Civil Rights Act of 1964. The regulations issued under Title VII to protect people from discrimination on the basis of race, color, sex, religion or national origin, merely serve as guidance and do not retain as much legal significance as the regulations detailing discrimination based on age, and now based on disability, under the ADA.[5]

This is not to say, however, that the validity of particular ADA regulations will be protected from legal attacks by employers or employees who feel that the regulations go unreasonably beyond the intent of Congress. ADA lawsuits based on the validity of EEOC regulations, however, will not likely be successful, in light of the congressional authority to issue binding regulations, as expressed in the legislative history.[6] A good example of a potential legal challenge to a particular EEOC regulation concerns the validity of the "direct threat" defense for employers. Title I states that an employer can reject a person with a disability from a particular position if the person poses a direct threat to the health or safety of other individuals in the workplace.[7] The ADA legislation defines a "direct threat" as a "significant risk to the health or safety of others that cannot be eliminated by reasonable accommodation."[8] The EEOC regulations, however, expand this definition to include an individual with a disability who poses a direct threat to his or her own health or safety, in addition to the health or safety of others.[9] This regulation, issued by the EEOC, seems to exceed the language of the law, and at least one commentator believes this particular regulation should be held invalid.[10] (For more information on direct threat, see chapter 11.)

WHICH EMPLOYERS ARE COVERED BY THE LAW?

Nearly every American business will be affected by some aspect of the ADA, whether it be in the areas of transportation, accessibility, or communication. The employment provisions, however, exclude businesses that employ fewer than 15 people from ADA coverage and does not cover employees of the federal government. The new law states that all public and private employers, employment agencies, labor organizations and joint labor-management committees are covered by the ADA if their industry affects commerce—and all industries do—and have fifteen or more employees. These employees must be employed for twenty or more calendar weeks in the current or preceding calendar year. Between 26 July 1992 and 26 July 1994, however, only employers who have 25 or more employees are affected by the law.[11]

Virtually every employer in the United States who has fifteen or more employees must eventually adhere to the employment provisions of the ADA or face the consequences of noncompliance. This includes for-profit and nonprofit associations and other organizations. Entities not covered by the ADA include the United States government and its wholly owned corporations, Native American tribes, and private membership clubs other than labor organizations. In addition, the ADA provides a qualified exception to religious organizations, such as religious corporations, associations, educational institutions, and societies when giving preference to its members or followers when hiring and promoting employees. (For more information on hiring in religious organizations, see chapter 11.)

WHO IS PROTECTED BY THE LAW?

Individuals protected by the ADA are persons with disabilities and those who associate with people with disabilities. Employers may not discriminate against individuals who are known to have a family, business, or social relationship with a person with a disability. The first determination that employers should make when considering an applicant or employee with a disability is whether the person is considered "disabled" under the definition provided by the new law. There will undoubtedly be instances where potential employees consider themselves disabled but do not qualify under the ADA's definition. An individual who is classified as a disabled veteran, for instance, is not automatically considered to have a disability under the ADA.

Conversely, there will also be situations where potential employees will clearly be considered disabled under the ADA definition but will not choose to avail themselves of the benefits of the legislation for a variety of reasons. As stated in the appendix to the EEOC regulations, "The determination of whether an individual has a disability is not necessarily based on the name or diagnosis of the impairment the person has, but rather on the effect of that impairment on the life of the individual."[12]

THE THREE-PRONGED DEFINITION OF DISABILITY

Primarily for the purpose of uniformity, the ADA adopts a similar definition of disability to that which appears in the Rehabilitation Act of 1973 describing an individual with a "handicap." The change in terminology from "handicap" to "disability" largely reflects the preference of people with disabilities and advocates of people with disabilities. The term "disability" has a three-pronged definition in the ADA:

A physical or mental impairment that substantially limits one or more of the major life activities of such individual; a record of such an impairment; or being regarded as having such an impairment.[13]

Implications: Meeting any one of the three prongs in the definition will qualify a person as an individual with a disability. This is a functional definition and not an enumerated list of disabilities that qualify under the ADA. A person may be considered, under this definition, to be disabled in one of three specific ways. According to the appendix of the 1977 regulations that helped implement Section 504 of the Rehabilitation Act, this flexible approach was deliberately taken to avoid the difficulty of developing a comprehensive list of disabling conditions and to account for medical conditions that have not yet been identified as disabling. Because this definition of disability has been in effect since the Rehabilitation Act of 1973, those interpreting the requirements of the ADA can look for guidance to the regulations and case law that have interpreted the meaning of the components of this definition over the past two decades.

Physical or Mental Impairment

Most applicants and employees who qualify as persons with disabilities under the ADA will satisfy the first prong of the disability definition. People who qualify under this prong have physiological or mental impairments that create significant limitations on the performance of the activities of daily life, such as walking, seeing, speaking, and hearing. "Physical or mental impairment" is defined as:

1. Any physiological disorder, or condition, cosmetic disfigurement, or anatomical loss affecting one or more of the following body systems: neurological, mus-

culoskeletal, special sense organs, respiratory (including speech organs), cardiovascular, reproductive, digestive, genito-urinary, hemic and lymphatic, skin, and endocrine.

2. Any mental or psychological disorder, such as mental retardation, organic brain syndrome, emotional or mental illness, and specific learning disabilities.[14]

Implications: As one can observe from the broad regulatory definition, the ADA does not confine itself to "traditional" disabilities but covers a wide spectrum of individuals with physical and mental impairments. Although the ADA purposely did not provide a "laundry list" of qualifying disabilities, the following impairments will likely qualify under the new law: orthopedic, visual, speech, and hearing impairments, amputation, paralysis, serious back conditions or respiratory illnesses, epilepsy, cerebral palsy, muscular dystrophy, multiple sclerosis, cancer, heart disease, diabetes, deviated septum, human immunodeficiency virus (HIV), mental retardation, emotional illness, and recovered (or recovering) alcoholics, as well as recovered drug addicts.

The ADA definition of disability specifically excludes a number of conditions that do not qualify under the new law. One significant change from the disability regulations of Section 504 of the Rehabilitation Act of 1973 is the exclusion of coverage under the ADA of current users of illegal drugs and people with disorders that arise from illegal drug use. However, the ADA does cover people who have successfully completed or are participating in supervised drug rehabilitation programs and who are no longer using illegal drugs. The ADA also covers those individuals who have been erroneously regarded as illegal drug users but who are not engaging in drug use. According to the EEOC, the ADA does not encourage, authorize, or prohibit drug tests.

The ADA regulations state that conditions such as pregnancy, homosexuality, and bisexuality are not impairments and are not considered disabilities under the new law. The ADA also excludes from coverage transvestism, transsexualism, pedophilia, exhibitionism, voyeurism, gender identity disorders not resulting from physical impairments, and other sexual behavior disorders. Compulsive gambling, kleptomania, and pyromania are also not covered by the new law. In addition, advanced age, or cultural, educational, environmental, and economic disadvantages are not impairments under the ADA. Only impairments that substantially limit major life activities qualify as disabilities under the ADA definition of disability.[15]

Major Life Activities

What the ADA means by "major life activities" is clearly spelled out in both the 1977 regulations for the Rehabilitation Act and the ADA regulations. "Major life activities" are defined as:

Functions such as caring for oneself, performing manual tasks, talking, seeing, hearing, speaking, breathing, learning, and working.[16]

Implications: Major life activities are those basic activities that the average person in the general population can perform with little or no difficulty. When comparing a potentially disabled person's ability to that of the "average person in the general population," the ADA regulations note that this is not intended to imply a mathematical "average." According to the interpretive guidance of the ADA regulations, the list of major life activities is not exhaustive. Other activities include sitting, standing, lifting, or reaching, to name a few. Other activities may be included in this list, such as "procreation" and "intimate personal relations" as major life activities, according to a legal opinion on Section 504 published in 1989 by the Department of Justice.[17]

Disability—Substantially Limits Major Life Activity

Determining whether an applicant or employee has a physical or mental impairment is the first step in determining whether the individual has a disability. An impairment is covered by the ADA definition of disability only if it "substantially limits" one or more of the individual's major life activities. The regulations go into great detail to explain the process of determining what is considered to be a substantial limitation. The term "substantially limits" means:

1. Unable to perform a major life activity that the average person in the general population can perform.
2. Significantly restricted as to the condition, manner, or duration under which an individual can perform a particular major life activity as compared to the condition, manner, or duration under which the average person in the general population can perform that same major life activity.[18]

The following factors should be considered in determining whether an individual is substantially limited in a major life activity:

1. The nature and severity of the impairment.
2. The duration or expected duration of the impairment.
3. The permanent or long-term impact, or the expected permanent or long-term impact resulting from the impairment.[19]

Implications: The appendix to the EEOC regulations clearly explains that the determination of whether an individual's impairment substantially limits one or more major life activities should be made on a case-by-case basis and without taking into account the "availability of medicines, assistive devices, or other mitigating measures."[20] In other words, a lower limb amputee would be substantially limited in the major life activity of walking and would be considered disabled under the ADA definition, even though that person had learned to function well with an artificial leg.

Similarly, people with diabetes, who effectively regulate their blood sugar levels with insulin, are considered substantially limited in major life activities because without medication they could eventually lapse into a coma. The ADA does not exclude from coverage those disabled individuals who have successfully rehabilitated themselves through medical and technological means.

The regulations note several factors to consider when determining whether an individual is substantially limited in a major life activity. These include the nature and severity, the duration, and the long-term impact of the impairment. According to the appendix to the ADA regulations, "the term 'duration,' as used in this context, refers to the length of time an impact persists, while the term 'impact,' refers to the residual effects of an impairment."[21]

For example, a broken leg is an impairment of short duration and is not considered a disability under the ADA. If the broken leg does not heal properly, however, the resulting permanent limp is the impact of the impairment and may be considered a disability under the ADA if the major life activity of walking is substantially limited as a result.

According to Chai R. Feldblum, a visiting professor at Georgetown University Law Center and an attorney who participated in the drafting of the ADA legislation, "Most serious medical conditions do have a substantial impact on basic life activities."[22] For example, an individual who is paralyzed will be substantially limited in walking; a legally blind person has a substantial limitation in the major life activity of seeing. These types of impairments are inherently limiting. Other less severe impairments can be measured by their effect on the life of the individual. The stage of the disease or disorder and the existence of other impairments will be factors in determining whether the individual is substantially limited in major life activities.

The ADA regulations make clear that if an individual's multiple impairments combine to substantially limit one or more major life activities, that person can be considered disabled under the ADA, even though the particular impairments would not substantially limit major life activities if considered separately. However, as the appendix to the EEOC regulations explains, "Temporary, non-chronic impairments of short duration, with little or no long-term or permanent impact, are usually not disabilities."[23] This type of impairment includes injuries such as broken limbs, sprained joints, concussions, appendicitis, and influenza. Except in rare cases, obesity is not considered a disabling impairment.

Substantially Limits the Ability to Work

According to the appendix to the ADA regulations, if an applicant or employee is not substantially limited in any other major life activity, the individual's ability to perform the major life activity of working should be considered. Conversely, if an individual is found to have a substantial limitation in any other major life activity, no determination should be made as to the individual's limitation to work. For example, a deaf job applicant is substantially limited in the major life activity of hearing. There is no need to determine whether that person is also substantially limited in the activity of working. Because this determination is also made on a case-by-case basis, the ADA regulations outline specific factors to consider when determining an individual's limitations on the ability to work. With respect to the major life activity of working, the term "substantially limits" means:

Significantly restricted in the ability to perform either a class of jobs or a broad range of jobs in various classes as compared to the average person having comparable training, skills, and abilities. The inability to perform a single, particular job does not constitute a substantial limitation in the major life activity of working.[24]

Implications: An individual need not be completely unable to work in order to be substantially limited in the major life activity of working. The individual, however, must be significantly restricted in the ability to perform a class of jobs or a broad range of jobs in different classes when compared with the average person with comparable skills. For example, individuals who have back conditions that prevent them from lifting heavy objects are substantially limited in the major life activity of working because they cannot perform a class of jobs due to their impairment.

In addition to the nature and severity of the impairment and the duration and impact of the impairment, the ADA regulations list additional factors that may be considered when determining whether an applicant or employee is substantially limited in the major life activity of working. These factors are relevant to this question but not required to be shown. The additional factors that may be considered include the following:

1. The geographical area to which the individual has reasonable access.
2. The job from which the individual has been disqualified because of an impairment, and the number and types of jobs utilizing similar training, knowledge, skills, or abilities within that geographical area, from which the individual is also disqualified because of the impairment (class of jobs).
3. The job from which the individual has been disqualified because of an impairment, and the number and types of other jobs not utilizing similar training, knowledge, skills, or abilities within that geographical area, from which the individual is also disqualified because of the impairment (broad range of jobs in various classes).[25]

Implications: The appendix to the ADA regulations provides an example for the individual whose impairment substantially limits his or her ability to perform a broad range of jobs in various classes. Suppose an individual has an allergy to a substance found in most high-rise office buildings, but seldom found elsewhere, which makes it difficult for that individual to breathe. This allergy would substantially limit the individual's ability to perform a broad range of jobs in various classes that are conducted in high-rise office buildings within a geographical area that is reasonably accessible. In this case, the applicant or employee would be substantially limited in the major life activity of working.

The factors to consider when deciding whether an individual is substantially limited in working include these two terms: the "number and types of jobs" and the "number and types of other jobs" in relation to which jobs the individual with a disability is disqualified from performing. These terms do not require precise numbers or a great deal of evidence to prove the existence of these employment demographics.

It is important to note that an individual's inability to perform a particular specialized job or a narrow range of jobs does not qualify that individual as substantially limited in the major life activity of working. Additionally, an inability to perform jobs that require extraordinary skill, prowess, or talent do not qualify the person as substantially limited. For instance, a professional baseball player whose ability to pitch is substantially limited due to an elbow impairment is not substantially limited in working under the ADA definition of disability.

Having a Record of an Impairment

The second and less common definition of disability is designed to protect individuals who have a history of disability from discrimination. Individuals who qualify as disabled under the first prong of the disability definition, by having a physical or mental impairment, need not qualify under the second or third prong as well. As long as one prong of the definition is satisfied, the individual is considered disabled for purposes of the ADA. To have "a record of such an impairment" means:

The individual has a history of, or has been misclassified as having, a mental or physical impairment that substantially limits one or more major life activities.[26]

Implications: Individuals who satisfy this prong of the disability definition may not currently have an impairment but either had one in the past or were misclassified as having an impairment. According to the regulations of Section 504 concerning this section, individuals who frequently satisfy this prong are people with cancer, heart disease, and mental or emotional disorders. People who are commonly misclassified include individuals with learning disabilities or mental retardation.

Many types of educational, medical, and employment records may contain information or references to an individual's past or potential impairments. This prong of the disability definition is satisfied if an employer rejects an applicant or employee by relying on a record that indicates the existence of a physical or mental impairment that substantially limits a major life activity.

Regarded as Having an Impairment

Assuming an applicant or employee cannot satisfy the first or second prong of the ADA's disability definition, the individual may be considered disabled under the third prong of the definition in one of three ways. The "regarded as" prong of the definition prohibits discrimination against people who have impairments that are not substantially limiting or who have no impairment at all but are treated by their employers as though they are disabled. To be "regarded as having such an impairment" means that the individual

1. Has a physical or mental impairment that does not substantially limit major life activities but is treated by the employer as constituting such a limitation;
2. Has a physical or mental impairment that substantially limits major life activities only as a result of the attitudes of others toward such an impairment; or
3. Has none of the [physical or mental] impairments defined in the first prong of the disability definition but is treated by the employer as having a substantially limiting impairment.[27]

Implications: The "regarded as disabled" definition is designed to address the discrimination that flows from fears, myths, and stereotypes associated with people with disabilities. A rejected applicant or employee whose employer regards that individual as disabled, whether or not the employer's perception is shared by others or whether the individual is actually mentally or physically impaired, is covered under the ADA. This prong of the disability definition addresses misconceptions and attitudinal barriers that frequently result in the exclusion of people with disabilities. According to the appendix to the ADA regulations, these attitudinal barriers include concerns regarding safety, productivity, attendance, accommodation and accessibility expenses, insurance, liability, worker's compensation costs, and acceptance by co-workers and customers.

In summary, there are three ways an individual can be regarded as disabled under the third prong of the ADA disability definition. Under the first part, the individual has a physical or mental impairment that is not substantially limiting, but the employer perceives the impairment as being substantially limiting. Take, for example, an employee who has high blood pressure that is not substantially limiting. If the employer reassigns the employee to less strenuous work because of unsubstantiated fears that the individual might suffer a heart attack in performance of the more strenuous job, the employee would satisfy this definition by being regarded as disabled.

The second part of the "regarded as" definition of disability addresses the situation where an individual's impairment is substantially limiting only because of the attitudes of others. A person who is not substantially limited in any major life activity but is facially disfigured due to scarring or burns, or has a condition that periodically causes a jerk of the head, will be regarded as disabled under this category. If these individuals are rejected by the employer on the basis that their conditions are regarded as disabilities, then these individuals will be protected under the ADA provisions.

The third way that an individual may be regarded as disabled under the ADA occurs when the employer believes that an individual has a substantially limiting impairment that the person actually does not have. This part of the disability definition would be satisfied if an employer discharged an employee based on unfounded information that the employee was infected with the human immunodeficiency virus (HIV). In this situation, the individual is regarded as disabled and is being discriminated against on the basis of disability, even though the person has no impairment at all. People who test positive for HIV or who have AIDS or AIDS-related complex (ARC) would also be considered disabled because they have a physical impairment that substantially limits major life activities.

PRACTICAL APPLICATION OF BEING REGARDED AS DISABLED

The United States Supreme Court has interpreted the "regarded as being disabled" language of the disability definition in a lawsuit brought under Section 504. In *School Board of Nassau County v. Arline*, 480 U.S. 273 (1987), the court considered whether Gene Arline, a public school teacher who had a record of having tuberculosis in 1957, was discriminated against on the basis of a disability when she was fired in 1978. Arline was terminated after several relapses of the disease allegedly because of fear of current contagiousness, not because of the existence of an underlying disease. The court discussed the "regarded as" disabled language and decided that employers could not separate the underlying disease from its contagious effects and discriminate against individuals on the basis of the contagious effects of a disease.[28] Although an individual with acquired immunodeficiency syndrome (AIDS), or who is HIV positive, is covered under the first prong of the disability definition, the *Arline* case is widely regarded as being applicable to individuals who are HIV positive or have AIDS.

According to the *Labor Lawyer*, "the regarded as being disabled" prong of the disability definition was "as concerned about the effect of an impairment on others as it was about its effect on the individual."[29] This prong was designed to cover the child with cerebral palsy who was able to attend school, but because he produced "a nauseating effect" on his classmates, he was excluded from class. It was also designed to address the case of the woman who was "crippled by arthritis" and denied a job because college personnel thought "normal students shouldn't see her."[30] In short, as stated in the *Arline* opinion, "Congress acknowledged that society's accumulated myths and fears about disability and diseases are as handicapping as are the physical limitations that flow from actual impairment" (*Arline*, 480 U.S. at 284).[31]

As explained in the appendix to the ADA regulations, if an individual can show that an employer made an employment decision based on a "myth, fear, or stereotype" of disability, the "regarded as" part of the definition will likely be satisfied. In this case, an inference can be drawn that the employer was acting on the basis of myth, fear, or stereotype unless the employer can articulate a nondiscriminatory reason for the employment action.

A Qualified Individual with a Disability

In addition to satisfying the ADA definition of disability, applicants or employees must be qualified to do the job for which they are applying or the one they currently hold. A "qualified individual with a disability" is defined in the ADA as follows:

An individual with a disability who, with or without reasonable accommodation, can perform the essential functions of the employment position that such individual holds or desires.[32]

Implications: There is a two-step process in determining whether the applicant or employee is a qualified individual with a disability. The employer must first decide whether the individual with a disability has the skill, experience, education, and other job-related requirements of the employment position that the person holds or desires. For instance, the employer must first decide whether a paralyzed individual who applies for an attorney position holds a license to practice law, or whether a blind individual who applies for a public teaching position is certified to teach.

It is important to note that "other job-related requirements" may be considered in addition to one's skill, experience, and education. Section 504 of the Rehabilitation Act established this same inquiry, but the process is referred to as determining whether a disabled individual is "otherwise qualified" for the position the person is seeking. Once the determination has been made that the individual possesses the requirements for the position, the employer must then determine whether the individual can or cannot perform the essential functions of the position that is held or is desired by the individual, with or without reasonable accommodation.

The purpose of this second step of identifying the essential functions of the job is to ensure that individuals with disabilities who cannot perform marginal or incidental aspects or tasks of a particular job are not rejected if they can perform the essential functions of that position. The terms "essential functions" and "reasonable accommodation" are key concepts of the ADA and are discussed at length later in this chapter. Reasonable accommodation is "any modification or adjustment to a job or the work environment that will enable a qualified applicant or employee with a disability to perform essential job functions."[33] Essential job functions refer to the fundamental duties of a particular position of employment.

The appendix to the EEOC regulations clearly explains that this two-step process to determine whether an individual with a disability is qualified must take place at the time of the employment decision. The determination should be based on the capabilities of the individual at that time and should not be based on speculation that the employee may become unable to perform functions in the future. The possibility that health insurance premiums or workers compensation costs will increase due to the employment of an individual with a disability cannot be a consideration.

The Three-Pronged Disability Definition in Practice

As noted, a qualified applicant or employee with a disability is an individual who either currently has, has a record of, or is regarded as having a mental or physical impairment that substantially limits one or more major life activities. In addition, the individual must be qualified to perform the essential functions of the particular job, with or without reasonable accommodation.

The following examples illustrate the practical application of the ADA to particular physical or mental conditions. The following examples are from an article written by Chai R. Feldblum, "The Americans with Disabilities Act: Definition of Disability."[34]

A person who is an alcoholic. Under Section 504 of the Rehabilitation Act and the ADA, a person who is dependent on alcohol is considered to have an "impairment" and, therefore, satisfies the first prong of the disability definition. Under the ADA, a person who is an alcoholic is considered a person with a disability whether the individual is currently drinking alcohol or not. In order to qualify under the ADA, or Section 504, a person with an alcohol dependency must be able to perform the essential functions of the job, with reasonable accommodation, if necessary. The ADA specifically addresses this issue and allows employers to make rules that prohibit employees from using alcohol during work hours and rules that ensure an alcohol-free workplace. Employers may also hold individuals who are alcoholics to the same performance standards as other employees, even if poor job performance is directly related to the employee's alcoholism. (For more information on alcoholism, see chapter 11.)

A person with a bad back. Even minor back conditions are considered physiological impairments. A person will only qualify under the first prong of the ADA if the impairment substantially limits the ability to lift objects or walk, for instance. If the back condition is not substantially limiting, but the employer rejects the applicant or employee for fear that employees with back conditions might cause problems, the employer is discriminating on the basis of disability under the "regarded as" prong of the ADA definition.

A person who uses a hearing aid. A hearing aid is an example of an assistive device that corrects an impairment that substantially limits the major life activity of hearing. Because the determination of disability under the ADA is made without respect to assistive devices, a person with a hearing aid qualifies under the first prong of the ADA.

A person with a manic-depressive disorder. Many people with mental health disabilities successfully control their impairment with prescription medication. If a person is controlling manic depression with the prescription medication lithium, for instance, and is qualified for a particular job, an employer cannot discriminate against the individual on the basis of the disability. However, the ADA legislation contains specific conditions under which an employer can reject an applicant or terminate an employee with a mental illness. Employers are not under an EEO responsibility to employ people with mental health disabilities who pose a direct threat to other employees or who are simply not qualified to perform the job.

It is important to note that the EEOC regulations expand the definition of "direct threat" to *also* include "a direct threat to oneself." The regulations specify that a direct threat is "a significant risk of substantial harm to the health or safety of the individual [with a disability] or others, which cannot be eliminated or reduced by reasonable accommodation."[35] If an individual is successfully controlling a manic-depressive disorder, however, and is otherwise qualified for the position, that person cannot be disqualified for a position on the basis of a disability.

A person who uses illegal drugs. Applicants or employees who currently use illegal drugs are not considered qualified individuals with disabilities under the ADA, regardless of the impact of the drug use on the employee's performance or the frequency of the drug use. Even if an employee has a legitimate disability, the employer may fire or refuse to hire any person who uses illegal drugs. However, individuals with a history of addiction to illegal drugs who can prove they are no longer using illegal drugs and are either receiving treatment or have been successfully rehabilitated *are* covered by the ADA. Drugs taken under the supervision of licensed health care professionals, including experimental drugs, are not considered illegal drugs under the ADA. (For more information on ADA coverage of people addicted to illegal drugs, see chapter 11.)

Individuals who abuse prescribed drugs, however, such as valium or sleeping pills, are not considered to be taking these drugs under the care of licensed health care professionals and are excluded from the protections of the ADA. As stated previously, individuals who have successfully been rehabilitated and are no longer using illegal drugs are covered by the new law. In addition, people who are not drug users but are regarded as users of illegal drugs due to their dress, behavior, or a faulty drug test are covered under the ADA.

Essential Functions of the Job

The term "essential functions" is defined in the regulations as "the fundamental job duties of the employment position the individual with a disability holds or desires." Marginal or incidental functions of the position are not considered to be essential, and an applicant's or employee's inability to perform these functions should not be used as a basis to deny employment to the individual. The regulations list a number of factors to consider when determining whether a particular job function is essential. A function may be considered essential for any of several reasons, including but not limited to the following:

1. The function may be essential because the reason the position exists is to perform that function.
2. The function may be essential because of the limited number of employees available among whom the performance of that job function can be distributed.
3. The function may be highly specialized so that the incumbent in the position is hired for his or her expertise or ability to perform the particular function.[36]

The regulations elaborate upon this issue by detailing specific evidence that will tend to show whether a particular job function is essential. Again, this evidence includes but is not limited to:

1. The employer's judgment as to which functions are essential
2. Written job descriptions prepared before advertising or interviewing applicants for the job
3. The amount of time spent on the job performing the function
4. The consequences of not requiring the incumbent to perform the function
5. The terms of a collective bargaining agreement

6. The work experience of past incumbents in the job

7. The current work experience of incumbents in similar jobs[37]

Implications: The question of which functions of a particular job are essential is crucial to whether an individual with a disability is qualified. While the regulations list specific evidence to consider when resolving this question, other types of relevant evidence may be included to show whether a particular function is essential. The individual with a disability must be able to perform the essential functions of a particular job, whether unaided or with the assistance of reasonable accommodation, in order to be qualified for the position.

The appendix to the regulations cautions that the inquiry of whether a function is essential to a job is not intended to second guess the employer's business judgment on the issue of quality and quantity standards required by the employer's workers. The ADA is not an affirmative action law and does not require employers to lower their standards in order to hire or promote people with disabilities.

As the appendix to the EEOC regulations explains, "If an employer requires its typists to be able to accurately type 75 words per minute, it will not be called upon to explain why an inaccurate work product, or a typing speed of 65 words per minute, would not be adequate."[38] The employer may be required to show, however, that in practice, it actually holds its employees to such a standard and that the standard was not intentionally adopted to discriminate against people with disabilities.

Are the job functions actually essential? The determination of this question begins with a focus on whether the functions that the employer identifies are actually essential to the particular job. For example, if typing is stated by the employer to be a fundamental job duty, but the person holding the position in the past has not been required to type in daily practice, this would not be an essential function of the job. If, however, the position actually does require the performance of a particular job duty, such as typing, the focus then turns to whether removing the function from the list of job duties would fundamentally alter that position.

Judgment of the employer. A number of other factors are listed in the ADA regulations that are intended to guide the case-by-case determination of whether a particular function is essential. While the judgment of the employer carries weight, it cannot be presumed that the job function is essential merely because the employer makes that assertion. The ADA legislative history indicates that Congress rejected the notion of establishing a "rebuttable presumption" in favor of the employer. A "rebuttable presumption" means that the employer's judgment is presumed to be valid unless it is challenged by evidence presented by the employee. Instead, under the ADA both an individual with a disability and an employer are on a level playing field if an employer's judgment on essential job functions is questioned.

Written job descriptions. Although written job descriptions, prepared prior to advertising and interviewing for a position, are specifically not required to be developed and maintained by employers in order to comply with the ADA, written job descriptions are important indicators of the essential functions of a job. It is highly recommended that employers, in their efforts to comply with the ADA, develop or review written job descriptions that detail essential functions of specific positions. This step toward ADA compliance will serve the employer well in all phases of employment of people with disabilities and provides the employer with a written record as evidence of compliance with the law.

Time spent performing the job function. The time that an employee actually spends performing the job function at issue is important to a determination of whether it is essential. For instance, if an employee spends the vast majority of the workday operating a cash register, that would be an important factor in determining whether the ability to operate a cash register is an essential function.

Other factors. The appendix to the regulations makes it clear that the terms of a collective bargaining agreement and the work experience of past employees in that job or current employees in similar jobs are important factors when determining whether a particular function is essential to the performance of an employment position. Again, this list is not exhaustive and other evidence that is not listed may be equally important to the determination.

TYPES OF REASONABLE ACCOMMODATION

Modifying the Work Environment

If one were pressed to describe the Americans with Disabilities Act in two words, it would come down to the concept of reasonable accommodation. Implementation of this term under Section 504 of the Rehabilitation Act in the employment of federal grantees has established a significant and useful history. Reasonable accommodation, and assistive devices and technologies that often embody reasonable accommodation, has been a key principle of nondiscrimination law for people with disabilities. In addition to the case law under Section 504 that defines the parameters of this important principal, the ADA provides a generic definition of reasonable accommodation in the regulations. Still, several critics have expressed concern that the relatively loosely defined concept of reasonable accommodation will create extensive litigation before its dimensions are fully understood.[39] The term "reasonable accommodation" means:

1. Modifications or adjustments to a job application process that enable a qualified applicant with a disability to be considered for the position such qualified applicant desires.
2. Modifications or adjustments to the work environment, or to the manner or circumstances under which the position held or desired is customarily performed, that enables a qualified individual with a disability to perform the essential functions of that position.
3. Modifications or adjustments that enable [an employee] with a disability to enjoy equal benefits and privileges of employment as are enjoyed by [an employer's] other similarly situated employees without disabilities.[40]

Implications: In essence, an accommodation is any change in the work environment that enables an individual with a disability to enjoy equal employment opportunities. The ADA requires the employer to take steps to reasonably accommodate individuals with disabilities in three primary areas: the application and promotion process, the work environment, and in the area of benefits and privileges of employment. This requirement, of course, does not prohibit the employer from taking further steps to accommodate its employees in other areas related to employment. The language of the ADA itself lists some of the typical employment-related accommodations that are generally considered to be reasonable. This list in no way limits the employer and employee from negotiating other forms of accommodation on an individual basis. Reasonable accommodation may include but is not limited to the following:

- Making existing facilities used by employees readily accessible to and usable by individuals with disabilities
- Job restructuring
- Part-time or modified work schedules
- Reassignment to a vacant position
- Acquisition or modification of equipment or devices
- Appropriate adjustment or modification of examinations, training materials, or policies
- The provision of qualified readers or interpreters
- Other similar accommodations for individuals with disabilities[41]

Implications: It is the responsibility of the individual with a disability to make the employer aware of the disability and to request accommodation. The list of common reasonable accommodations is designed to provide guidance when an employer initiates an informal, interactive discussion with the applicant or employee with a disability to determine the appropriate reasonable accommodation. The provision of a reasonable accommodation may enable the individual with a disability to actually become

Cyndee Pearson, who has post-polio syndrome, works as a pharmacist's assistant in a modified workspace. Courtesy of the National Easter Seal Society.

qualified for a particular position or may simply allow the individual to more easily perform the job. This individualized process should identify the precise limitations resulting from the disability and the potential reasonable accommodations that could overcome those limitations, according to the appendix of the EEOC regulations.

An example of an appropriate reasonable accommodation would be the provision of reserved parking spaces for employees who have difficulty walking. An example of a reasonable accommodation in the workplace is when an employer agrees to obtain a portable handset telephone amplifier for an employee who is hearing impaired. Other examples of reasonable accommodation would be when an employer agrees to permit the use of accrued paid leave for necessary medical treatment or when an employer makes transportation, which is available to other employees, accessible to employees with disabilities.

A reasonable accommodation that is not required by the EEOC regulations but is discussed in the interpretive guidance is the provision of personal assistants. The use of personal assistants can be defined as the human support needed by an individual with a disability to be able to benefit from or participate in a program, activity, or, in terms of employment, to perform safely the essential functions of a job at a satisfactory level. Because this form of reasonable accommodation appears in the interpretive guidance and not in the regulations themselves, their provision by employers is suggested but not required. Personal assistants take the form of aides and attendants, such as a page turner for an employee with no arms or a travel guide for a blind employee who occasionally travels on business. These attendants may assist a disabled employee with office tasks, business travel, and grooming and eating, when necessary. The EEOC, however, does not require this form of reasonable accommodation but recommends that employers provide personal assistants when an undue hardship would not exist.[42]

The appendix to the EEOC regulations states that reasonable accommodation includes a situation where an employer permits a worker to use assistive aids, equipment, or services even though this assistance is not provided by the employer. For instance, as a reasonable accommodation, an employer may allow a blind employee to use a guide dog at work, even though the employer would not be required to provide a guide dog to the employee.

One of the reasonable accommodations listed in the ADA that may result in some degree of expense to the employer is the accommodation of making existing facilities used by employees readily accessible to and usable by workers with disabilities. This includes all work-related and non-work-related structures such as rest rooms, cafeterias, break rooms, lunch rooms, and training rooms.[43]

Modifying the Job

Job restructuring. In order to be considered a qualified individual with a disability, the individual must be able to perform the essential functions of the position of employment. Any restructuring of job duties to accommodate the individual with a disability should not, under the law, include the reallocation of essential functions. It is permissible, however, to alter when and how the essential function is performed in order to accommodate the person with a disability. For instance, a job duty traditionally performed in the early morning may be rescheduled to later in the day to accommodate the disabled employee if this is necessary for the employee and not unduly burdensome on the employer. Similarly, an employee with a disability who has difficulty writing may be permitted to perform the essential duty of record keeping by the use of a computer instead of manually.

Marginal, non-essential job functions, however, may be reallocated and redistributed to accommodate individuals with disabilities who cannot perform all of the marginal functions of a particular position. The employer may extract a combination of marginal functions from two positions and allocate these functions to one employee with a disability who can perform them. The remaining marginal functions would be allocated to the remaining employment position.[44]

Reassignment to a vacant position. The accommodation of reassignment is only available to qualified employees with disabilities, not qualified applicants. Generally, the accommodation of reassignment should only be considered when accommodation to the employee in his or her current position would create an undue hardship on the employer. For example, a salesman who, as a result of an accident becomes unable to walk, should be considered for reassignment to the company's accessible headquarters if structural alterations in the employee's field office would create an undue hardship on the employer.

Much care must be taken by the employer when reassigning employees with disabilities. Reassignment must not be used to segregate or discriminate against individuals with disabilities by placing disabled employees in undesirable positions or isolated offices. Reassignment should be to equivalent positions, with equal pay and status. If a qualified employee seeking reassignment waits a reasonable amount of time for a vacant position to become available, the employer may reassign the worker with a disability to a lower graded position if no vacancy in the higher grade arises. The employer is not required to maintain that employee's salary if the salary of a nondisabled employee would not be maintained in the same situation. It is important to note that the employer is not required to promote an individual with a disability as an accommodation.[45] (For more information on reasonable accommodation, see chapter 9.)

UNDUE HARDSHIP

As stated in the ADA, an employer is required to reasonably accommodate a qualified individual with a disability unless that accommodation would impose an undue hardship on the employer. In the event the accommodation does pose an undue hardship, an employer is not required to provide that applicant or employee with a disability with that form of accommodation. Instead, the employer must provide another form of accommodation if one is found to be reasonable and would enable the applicant or employee to become qualified to perform the job. If the cost of the accommodation is the reason for the undue hardship on the employer, the employee can offer to pay for that portion of the particular accommodation that is claimed to be unduly burdensome on the employer.

If no form of reasonable accommodation can be found, the applicant or employee can be rejected by the employer without fear of a potentially successful lawsuit being brought against the business. The defense of "undue hardship" is the key defense of employers when a claim is made that they have violated the mandate of the ADA in the employment arena. Not surprisingly, critics assert that this issue will be frequently argued in the court system. The language of the ADA and the regulations define undue hardship as follows:

With respect to the provision of an accommodation, significant difficulty or expense incurred by [an employer], when considered in light of several factors.[46]

Implications: The fact that an undue hardship on an employer must involve significant difficulty or expense limits the employer to assert this defense only when the provision of reasonable accommodation will have a substantial impact on the operation of the employer's business, not merely an incidental effect. Although cases interpreting Section 504 of the Rehabilitation Act have centered on the issue of financial burden as a way of proving undue hardship, the impact is not strictly financial.

For example, assume an applicant with a disabling vision impairment applies for a job as a waiter in a nightclub. If the applicant asks the employer of the nightclub to brightly light the establishment as a form of reasonable accommodation, the employer could claim that satisfying this request would impose an undue hardship on the operation of the business by detracting from the club's ambience. If another form of reasonable accommodation were possible that would not create an undue hardship, however, the employer would be required to provide the alternative accommodation.

The language of the ADA and the regulations list several factors to consider when determining whether a particular accommodation would impose an undue hardship on the employer. These factors primarily address the issue of financial burden but also guide the inquiry based on other reasons. This is not intended to be an exclusive list. Other factors may be used in the individualized process of negotiating reasonable accommodation. In determining whether an accommodation would impose an undue hardship on an employer, factors to be considered include the following:

1. The nature and net cost of the accommodation needed under this part, taking into consideration the availability of tax credits and deductions, and/or outside funding.

2. The overall financial resources of the facility or facilities involved in the provision of the reasonable accommodation, the number of persons employed at such a facility, and the effect on expenses and resources.

3. The overall financial resources of the employer, the overall size of the business of the employer with respect to the number of its employees, and the number, type, and location of its facilities.

4. The type of operation or operations of the employer, including the composition, structure, and functions of the work force of the employer, and the geographic separateness and administrative or fiscal relationship of the facility or facilities in question to the employer.

5. The impact of the accommodation upon the operation of the facility, including the impact on the ability of other employees to perform their duties and the impact on the facility's ability to conduct business.[47]

Implications: In determining whether the cost of an accommodation creates an undue hardship on the employer, the factors focus on the relative financial resources of the business and its ability to absorb the cost of accommodation. One important issue centers around whose financial resources should be considered when making this determination. The relationship of a particular business to a parent company or a franchise should be considered.

In a case where an individual business will bear the actual costs of the accommodation, and not a parent company for instance, the focus should be on the particular business to determine whether the employer can absorb the cost of the accommodation without causing an undue hardship. If a close relationship exists between a particular business and a parent company or franchise, financial or otherwise, the ability to absorb the cost of the accommodation should be determined by focusing on the larger business entity.

If an employer can show that the accommodation would impose an undue hardship, it would still be required to provide accommodation if an alternative funding source can be located to pay for the accommodation. According to the appendix to the EEOC regulations, state vocational rehabilitation agency assistance, and federal, state, and local tax deductions and tax credits are often available to offset the cost of particular accommodations.[48] In the event that the accommodation would impose an undue financial burden on an employer and an alternative funding source cannot be found, the individual with a disability requiring the accommodation should be given the option of paying for that portion of the particular accommodation that is claimed by the employer to impose the undue hardship. (For more information on tax credits for worksite modifications, see chapter 7, and for more information on reasonable accommodation, see chapter 9.)

CHAPTER 5

The ADA Mandate for Nondiscrimination

NONDISCRIMINATION IN ALL ASPECTS OF EMPLOYMENT

The Americans with Disabilities Act mandate for nondiscrimination based on disability in the workplace comprehensively addresses all aspects of employment. The ADA states the general rule of nondiscrimination as follows:

No [employer] shall discriminate against a qualified individual with a disability because of the disability of such individual in regard to job application procedures, the hiring, advancement, or discharge of employees, employee compensation, job training, and other terms, conditions, and privileges of employment.[1]

Implications: By virtue of this language in the new law, every aspect of state and local government employment and private employment in the United States is affected by the requirements and protections of the Americans with Disabilities Act. The scope of the ADA is to be interpreted in the same way that Section 504 of the Rehabilitation Act has been applied. The ADA, as noted, does not require employers to lower the quality standards of their work force. Employers may continue to use job-related criteria to select qualified employees who can perform the fundamental aspects of the job. The regulations elaborate upon the ADA definition of discrimination and provide a comprehensive list of every employment issue that must meet the ADA nondiscrimination mandate. Employers must not discriminate against people with disabilities, on the basis of disability, in the following areas of employment:

• Recruitment, advertising, and job application procedures

- Hiring, upgrading, promotion, award of tenure, demotion, transfer, layoff, termination, right of return from layoffs, and rehiring
- Rates of pay or any other form of compensation and changes in compensation
- Job assignments, job classifications, organizational structures, position descriptions, lines of progression, and seniority lists
- Leaves of absence, sick leave, or any other leave
- Fringe benefits available by virtue of employment, whether or not administered by the employer
- Selection and financial support for training, including: apprenticeships, professional meetings, conferences, and other related activities, and selection for leaves of absence to pursue training
- Activities sponsored by an employer, including social and recreational programs
- Any other term, condition, or privilege of employment[2]

Implications: As the regulations suggest, ADA coverage of the workplace is extremely comprehensive. To illustrate a few of the more important employment issues listed in the regulations, employers can no longer overlook people with disabilities when advertising available positions or recruiting qualified people to the work force. Simply hiring qualified people with disabilities is not enough. Promotions, awards of tenure, and transfers must also comply with the nondiscrimination mandate. Once a person with a disability is ready to return to work after sick leave, whether or not the leave was caused by the employee's disability, the employer must afford that person the same treatment as employees without disabilities. The right to return to work after a layoff and the entire rehiring process must comply with the ADA. (For more information on the employment process, see chapters 7 and 8.)

Equal Pay and Other Benefits of Employment

People with disabilities must not be paid less than people with comparable jobs who are not disabled and must not receive differing fringe benefits from their employer and others. An employer's decision to send employees to conventions, conferences, and training programs must not be based on an employee's disability. Finally, invitations to the firm's Christmas party or company picnic must be made with accessibility in mind so as not to exclude employees with disabilities from social and recreational events.

The text of the ADA itself specifically lists several actions throughout the employment process that are included in the definition of discrimination as it applies to people with disabilities. The term "discriminate" includes the following:

1. Limiting, segregating, or classifying a job applicant or employee based on disability in a way that diminishes the opportunities or status of that person.
2. Participating in a contract or other arrangement that has the effect of discriminating against people with disabilities.
3. Using standards, criteria, or methods that have the effect of or perpetuate discrimination on the basis of disability.
4. Denying equal jobs, benefits, or generally discriminating against a qualified person who is known to associate with a person who has a disability.
5. Not making reasonable accommodations for a qualified applicant or employee with a disability and, therefore, denying employment opportunities to that individual, unless undue hardship on the employer would result.
6. Using qualification standards, employment tests, or other selection criteria that tend to screen out people with disabilities or classes of people with disabilities unless these tests are job related and consistent with business necessity.
7. Failing to give applicants and employees the kinds of employment tests that accurately rate their abilities and do not merely reflect their physical or mental impairments in taking the particular tests.[3]

Implications: The ADA further refines its nondiscrimination mandate by including in the law and explaining in the regulations these specific aspects of the employment process.

Limiting, Segregating, and Classifying

This section was designed to prevent employers from limiting people with disabilities to certain job duties, job opportunities, or lines of promotion based on stereotypes and myths that people with disabilities either cannot or will not want to participate in job categories comprised of people without disabilities. Of course, segregating people with disabilities into a particular building, office, or eating facility is strictly prohibited by the ADA. It would be a violation of this section to deny a person with a disability a job based on generalized fears of safety or potential absenteeism. These issues must be resolved on an individual basis.

Health insurance. Congress intended the ADA to ensure that people with disabilities have equal access to the same health insurance provided to all employees. Pre-existing condition clauses are permissible under the ADA, as long as these clauses are not used to evade the purposes of the new law. For instance, under the ADA, an employer is allowed to offer a health insurance policy that limits certain health care procedures to a number of times per year, for example, x-rays, even though a particular employee with a disability may need more than the allotted number. It would not be permissible to deny that employee medical care in the setting of a broken leg, for instance, even though the plan would not be responsible for the cost of the x-rays over and above the number provided by the policy.

If the employer is going to restrict medical coverage in its health insurance policy, it will be permissible under the ADA only if the restrictions apply to all employees, and even if it has a negative impact on people with disabilities. Reductions in benefits, however, that are adopted for discriminatory purposes are in violation of the ADA. (For more information on health insurance, see chapters 7 and 10.)

Contractual and Other Arrangements

According to the appendix of the EEOC regulations on this section of the ADA, an employer may not do through a contractual or other relationship what it is prohibited from doing directly. To illustrate, suppose an employer seeks to establish a contract with another company to train its employees in certain job duties. The responsibility remains with the employer to provide reasonable accommodation to its employees with disabilities even though a separate company has been contracted to provide the training. If the training facility were inaccessible, the employer would have to ensure that persons with disabilities were reasonably accommodated unless it would create an undue hardship. This provision applies whether or not the employer intended the contractual relationship to have a discriminatory effect.

This provision applies to both contracting parties. Employers whose workers both provide and receive services must ensure that those workers are not discriminated against on the basis of disability. For instance, a copier company may be required to provide a step stool as a reasonable accommodation to one of its service representatives who is small in stature, in order for the service representative to perform repairs on copying machines. This does not mean, however, that an employer would have to make structural changes to a customer's inaccessible premises where copiers may be located as a form of reasonable accommodation.

Relationship or Association with a Person with a Disability

As already noted, the ADA extends nondiscrimination coverage to people who associate with individuals with disabilities. This section is designed to deter discrimination based on disability against those who are known to have a family, business, social, or other relationship with a person with a disability. This provision prohibits an employer from rejecting an applicant or employee because the applicant does volunteer work with people with acquired immunodeficiency syndrome (AIDS). It also protects the employee who is discriminated against because the employee's spouse is disabled and the employer fears excessive absenteeism on behalf of the employee in order to care for the individual with the disability.

It is important to realize that employers are not required to provide reasonable accommodation to people who are associated with people with disabilities. In other words, an employee without a disability would not be entitled to a modified work schedule in order to enable the employee to care for a disabled spouse.

Not Making Reasonable Accommodation

If an employer fails to reasonably accommodate a qualified person with a disability, the employer violates the ADA unless undue hardship can be shown. In addition, it is illegal for an employer to base an employment decision on an individual's need for an accommodation. The fact that the employer did not receive technical assistance in complying with the law is not an excuse for the employer's failure to adhere to the ADA provisions. An individual with a disability is not required to accept a reasonable accommodation where it is neither requested nor needed. If, however, the individual was not able to perform an essential function of the job without accommodation and still refused to accept an assistive device or modification to the work environment, the employer could reject the individual as not qualified for the job.

As the appendix to the EEOC regulations states, "The reasonable accommodation requirement is best understood as a means by which barriers to the equal employment opportunity of an individual with a disability are removed or alleviated."[4] The obligation to reasonably accommodate qualified employees with disabilities covers all services and programs provided by the employer and all nonwork facilities maintained by the employer. Cafeterias, lounges, gymnasiums, auditoriums, means of transportation, and counseling services that are provided by the employer must be accessible to people with disabilities. Other forms of reasonable accommodation for qualified individuals with disabilities include modified work schedules and job procedures. (For specific examples of how reasonable accommodation is used in the workplace, see chapter 9.)

The obligation to provide reasonable accommodation itself is a form of nondiscrimination. While it applies to the hiring and promotion processes, the employer has no obligation to provide modifications or assistive devices that are primarily for the personal benefit of the individual with a disability. The obligation covers accommodations that will assist the employee in the performance of job functions, not in daily activities unrelated to the fundamental duties of the job. For example, the employer is not required to purchase a personal item such as an artificial limb, a wheelchair, or eyeglasses for an employee with a disability. However, that employer may be required to purchase for a vision-impaired employee eyeglasses that are specifically designed to enhance the employee's vision of office computer monitors.

Finally, it is the employee's responsibility to make the employer aware of the need for reasonable accommodation. The employer is not obligated to provide reasonable accommodation for a disability of which the employer is unaware. In the case of a hidden disability, the employer may require documentation before providing reasonable accommodation. Even with individuals who clearly have disabilities, such as wheelchair users, the employer has no obligation to provide the best accommodation possible for the applicant or employee. As long as the accommodation is sufficient to meet the job-related needs of the applicant or employee, the ADA is satisfied.

TESTING, HIRING, AND PROMOTING PEOPLE WITH DISABILITIES: THE PRE-OFFER STAGE

Prohibited Pre-Employment Inquiries

In the past, disclosure of an applicant's or employee's disability had been a common and acceptable topic on job application forms and in employment interviews. The presence of a disability such as diabetes or heart disease often meant the exclusion of a disabled applicant, even before the abilities of the person to perform the job could be measured and evaluated.[5] The ADA seeks to eliminate this discriminatory bias by regulating the job interviewing process in the pre-offer and post-offer stages of employment.

During the employment interview process, the employer may or may not know of the existence of an applicant's or employee's disability. Even if the applicant or employee clearly seems to have a disability, the employer may not ask the applicant or employee about the existence, nature, severity, or origin of a disability. The ADA regulations clearly spell out the parameters of pre-employment examinations and inquiries with respect to new applicants.

[Except for specific situations that are detailed later in this chapter,] it is unlawful for [an employer] to conduct a medical examination of an applicant or to make inquiries as to whether an applicant is an individual with a disability or as to the nature or severity of such disability.[6]

Similar language appears in the ADA regulations that prohibit these same inquiries of current employees who may or may not be in the process of promotion. Examination or inquiry of employees is defined as follows:

Except [for specific situations that are detailed later in this chapter], it is unlawful for [an employer] to require a medical examination of an employee or to make inquiries as to whether an employee is an individual with a disability or as to the nature or severity of such disability.[7]

Implications: Unless a job applicant clearly identifies the existence, nature, and severity of his or her disability, the ADA regulations clearly prohibit employers in a pre-offer stage of the job selection process from asking about an applicant's disability. The employer is prohibited from inquiring about a disability either directly or by requiring the applicant to take a medical examination. Employers are also prohibited from asking applicants about their worker's compensation history or other questions related to disability or illness and its treatment. Before making a conditional job offer, an employer may not request any information about a job applicant from a previous employer, family member, or other source that it may not itself request of the job applicant.

The ADA regulations specifically prohibit employers from requiring current employees to take medical tests or answer medical inquiries that do not serve a legitimate business purpose. For instance, employees who begin to look unhealthy, use increasing amounts of sick leave, or inquire about their health insurance coverage are protected from employers who might otherwise require the employee to undergo tests for HIV infection or cancer, for instance.[8] Employers can require tests of this nature if they can demonstrate that the medical tests or inquiries are job related and consistent with business necessity. (For more information on testing, see chapters 7 and 11.)

Acceptable Pre-Employment Inquiries

While direct inquiries and requirements to take pre-offer medical exams that could detect the presence of a disability are strictly prohibited by the ADA regulations, all questions related to the ability to perform functions of the job are allowed, as long as the questions are not phrased in terms of disability. Acceptable pre-employment inquiries are described as follows:

[An employer] may make pre-employment inquiries into the ability of an applicant to perform job-related functions, and/or may ask an applicant to describe or to demonstrate how, with reasonable accommodation, the applicant will be able to perform job-related functions.[9]

Implications: As long as an employer's pre-employment questions are not phrased in terms of a disability, an employer may ask questions about the applicant's ability to perform job functions. The appendix to the EEOC regulations provides examples to illustrate this often challenging proposition. For instance, if driving were a function of a particular job, an employer could ask if the applicant has a driver's license but could not ask whether the applicant has a visual impairment that prevents the applicant from driving. If the job position required the employee to assemble small parts, the employer could describe and even demonstrate the particular job function and inquire whether the applicant or employee with a disability could perform that function.

The employer can ask about the applicant's ability to perform both essential and marginal job functions. The employer, however, cannot deny the job to an applicant with a disability merely because the disability prevents the applicant from performing marginal or incidental functions of a job.[10] For instance, if an applicant with a disability could answer telephones well but was not able to type, and typing was an incidental function to the desired receptionist position, an employer could not refuse to hire the applicant if that individual was the most qualified at the essential functions of the job. A prospective employer may ask a job applicant's previous employer about the applicant's job performance, job functions, attendance record, and other job-related issues that do not relate to disability.

An employer may make certain pre-employment, pre-offer inquiries regarding the use of alcohol or the illegal use of drugs. An employer may ask whether an applicant drinks alcohol or whether the individual is currently using drugs illegally. However, an employer may not ask whether an applicant is a drug addict or an alcoholic, nor inquire whether the individual has ever been in a drug or alcohol rehabilitation program. Under the ADA, an employer may require an applicant to undergo a drug test prior to an offer of employment. After a conditional offer of employment has been made, an employer may also ask any questions concerning past or present drug or alcohol use. However, the employer may not use such information to exclude an individual with a disability, on the basis of a disability, unless it can show that the reason for exclusion is job related and consistent with business necessity, and that legitimate job criteria cannot be met with a reasonable accommodation.

Demonstration of Job Functions

The second half of this important regulation allows an employer to ask an applicant to describe or to demonstrate how, with reasonable accommodation, the applicant will be able to perform job-related functions. This is a significant change from the Rehabilitation Act of 1973, which did not provide for demonstrations from potential employees. This provision will go a long way toward alleviating the apprehensions and doubts of employers who may question the true ability of applicants with disabilities to perform job functions.[11] No longer must employers exclusively rely on applicants' statements but can be shown, with or without reasonable accommodation, how the person with a disability can perform the essential job functions of the employment position.

The appendix to the EEOC regulations clearly states that all applicants or employees in the same job category may be asked to demonstrate their ability to perform job-related functions, regardless of the existence of a disability. When the known disability of an applicant or employee interferes with or prevents the performance of a job-related function, the employer can ask the individual with a disability to demonstrate the ability to perform that function, even if other disabled or nondisabled applicants are not required to demonstrate the function. However, there must be a connection between the known disability and the performance of a job-related function.[12]

This EEOC regulation can be illustrated with the following example. Suppose a qualified applicant for an electrician position has one leg. His prospective employer is not allowed to ask about the reason for the amputation or the prognosis, the amount of leave anticipated for treatment or incapacitation, or the cost of an assistive device such as an artificial limb. The employer can, however, ask the applicant to explain or demonstrate his ability to get into a customer's basement with a heavy toolbox, in order to perform electrical repairs. However, an employer could not ask an applicant with one leg to demonstrate his ability to assemble small parts while seated at a table, unless the employer routinely asks all applicants to provide this demonstration.

Employers who require applicants with disabilities to demonstrate the performance of job-related functions must provide reasonable accommodations to applicants who request them. If a reasonable accommodation cannot be readily provided, applicants with disabilities may explain how they would demonstrate the function if the reasonable accommodation were provided. As already stated, an inability to perform marginal or incidental functions does not give an employer grounds to reject the applicant with a disability. The employer must provide a reasonable accommodation to enable the applicant to perform the function, restructure the job description to eliminate the marginal function, or exchange functions with another position that the applicant is capable of performing.[13]

As already noted, employers cannot ask applicants with disabilities about their anticipated leave requirements due to treatment or incapacitation. The employer may, however, state the attendance requirements of the job and ask whether the applicant with a disability can meet those requirements. Employers are completely prohibited from using job application forms that list potentially disabling impairments. To do so is patently against the letter and spirit of the ADA.

The ADA is not an affirmative action law. Employers who have federal contracts, however, must still comply with the affirmative action requirements of Section 503 of the Rehabilitation Act of 1973. For the purposes of these affirmative action reporting requirements imposed on federal contractors, employers may collect information and invite employees to identify themselves as individuals with disabilities without violating the ADA.

Standards, Criteria, or Methods of Administration

Despite good faith efforts by management to incorporate people with disabilities into the work force, employment standards, job criteria, or methods of administration may tend to implicitly or explicitly discriminate against people with disabilities. The text of the ADA law makes a strong statement on this issue, but the EEOC regulations provide an exception. The regulations on standards, criteria, or methods of administration are as follows:

It is unlawful for [an employer] to use standards, criteria, or methods of administration which are not job-related and consistent with business necessity, and:

1. That have the effect of discriminating on the basis of disability or

2. That perpetuate the discrimination of others who are subject to common administrative control.[14]

Implications: As the regulation reads, employers may not use standards, criteria, or methods of administration that tend to perpetuate or have the effect of discrimination against people with disabilities. This much of the regulation is completely consistent with the language of the ADA. The EEOC regulations provide an exception to this rule by allowing discriminatory employment standards, job criteria, and methods of administration if they are job related and consistent with business necessity, thereby allowing employers a defense that is not explicitly provided by the language of the ADA law.

Qualification Standards, Tests, and Other Selection Criteria

The ADA further regulates the selection criteria used by employers that may tend to discriminate against people with disabilities. The three principal obligations that employers must satisfy in this area include the following:

1. Employers must not reject applicants or employees with disabilities because of an inability to perform non-essential or marginal functions of the job.

2. Employment selection criteria that screen out or tend to screen out applicants or employees with disabilities must be job related and consistent with business necessity.

3. Reasonable accommodation must be provided to applicants or employees with disabilities in order to assist in meeting legitimate employment selection criteria.[15]

Qualification standards, tests, and other selection criteria are as follows:

It is lawful for [an employer] to use qualification standards, employment tests, or other selection criteria that screen out or tend to screen out an individual with a disability or a class of individuals with disabilities, on the basis of disability, unless the standard, test or other selection criteria, as used by the [employer], is shown to be job-related for the position in question and is consistent with business necessity.[16]

Implications: This provision is designed to enable an employer to determine whether an applicant or employee is qualified to perform the essential functions of a particular job in a way that does not screen out people with disabilities or classes of people with disabilities because of their physical or mental impairment. According to the appendix of the regulations, the goal of this section "is to ensure that individuals with disabilities are not excluded from job opportunities unless they are actually unable to do the job. It is to ensure that there is a fit between job criteria and an applicant's (or employee's) actual ability to do the job."[17] This section applies to all types of selection criteria, including safety, vision and hearing requirements, walking and lifting requirements, and employment tests in general. This regulation is not intended, however to second guess the business judgment of the employer with regard to production standards.

Qualification standards and selection criteria that tend to exclude people with disabilities, whether intentional or not, may not be used under the ADA unless the employer can show that the criteria are both related to the position in question and are consistent with business necessity. The term "business necessity" has the same meaning as it is used in Section 504 of the Rehabilitation Act. By definition, selection criteria that tend to exclude people with disabilities and do not test the ability to perform *essential* functions of the job are not consistent with business necessity and would likely be illegal under the ADA.

Conversely, job selection criteria that tend to exclude people with disabilities, but do test the ability to perform essential functions of a job, may be consistent with business necessity and, therefore, allowable under the ADA. In this case, an individual with a disability may not be rejected if the individual could satisfy the criteria with the provision of reasonable accommodation. Most challenges of discriminatory selection criteria under Section 504 of the Rehabilitation Act were resolved by providing the individual with a disability a reasonable accommodation. Challenges to selection criteria under this part of the ADA will likely be resolved in a similar manner. To illustrate the interrelationship between essential functions, job relatedness, and reasonable accommodation in the employment selection process, note the case of Mr. Sheller who has dyslexia and is applying for a heavy equipment operator position.[18]

Mr. Sheller meets all of the selection criteria for the job but, due to his dyslexia, cannot pass the written test required to enter the training program for that particular position. The written test tends to discriminate against people with dyslexia. The requirement to take a written test for acceptance into the training program and the program's reading requirements must be job related and essential to the performance of the heavy equipment operator position. If the ability to read and write are essential requirements of the job, the ADA is not violated and the employer may reject Mr. Sheller for employment. Because Mr. Sheller is qualified for the position under all of the other selection criteria, however, he is entitled to a reasonable accommodation in order to satisfy the reading and writing requirements, such as the provision of someone to act as a reader. If the ability to read and write are not job related and essential requirements of the job, Mr. Sheller cannot be rejected from the heavy equipment operator position because of his dyslexia.[19]

Administration of Tests

In addition to regulating the content of job selection criteria, the ADA regulates the manner in which employment tests are administered. The ADA mandates that employment tests be given in the most effective manner that will accurately reflect the true abilities of the applicant or employee.

It is unlawful for [an employer] to fail to select and administer tests concerning employment in the most effective manner to ensure that, when a test is administered to a job applicant or employee who has a disability that impairs sensory, manual, or speaking skills, the test results accurately reflect the skills, aptitude, or whatever other factor of the applicant or employee that the test purports to measure, rather than reflecting the impaired sensory, manual, or speaking skills of such employee or applicant (except where such skills are the factors that the test purports to measure).[20]

Implications: This section of the ADA is similarly designed to limit or reduce the negative effects that flow from an applicant's disability when the taking of a test is a prerequisite to the job. The protections of this section are extended to all eligible applicants or employees whose disabilities impair sensory, manual, or speaking skills. The employer is required to provide test formats that do not require the use of the applicant's impaired skill, unless those skills are the factors the test is designed to measure.[21]

The test must be given in the most effective manner that will not inaccurately reflect the effects of an applicant's impaired skill upon potential job performance. To illustrate, it would be a violation of this section for an employer to give a written employment test to an individual who is unable to read due to a vision impairment, if the ability to read were not the skill being tested and the employer knew of the disability before the administration of the test.

The employer has an obligation to test qualified people with disabilities in alternate formats (i.e., oral, written) only if the individual has given the employer prior notice of the necessity for reasonable accommodation. In the event the applicant or employee with a disability discovers the need for reasonable accommodation at the beginning of the test (i.e., the print is too small to read), the employer may be required to provide reasonable accommodation at that time. Other alternative formats for employment testing include large print or braille, the provision of a sign interpreter, and the allowing of more time to complete the exam, unless the purpose of the test is to measure speed. If testing through alternative formats is not possible due to undue hardship, the employer may, as a form of reasonable accommodation, evaluate the applicant or employee in a different manner, such as interviews, or review of educational licenses or work experience.

The appendix to the EEOC regulations cautions that these provisions do not give all applicants their choice of test formats. Only people whose disabilities impair sensory, manual, or speaking skills are eligible under this section. In addition, this regulation does not apply if the employment test itself is designed to measure sensory, manual, or speaking skills. For instance, in the previous example, the employer could require an applicant with dyslexia to take a written test if the employer were testing the ability to read. The test, however, could not be used to exclude the applicant unless the particular skill was necessary to perform the essential functions of the job and no reasonable accommodation was available that would allow the employer to accurately test the applicant's ability to perform the fundamental duties of the job.

HIRING AND PROMOTING PEOPLE WITH DISABILITIES: THE POST-OFFER STAGE

Medical Examinations of Job Applicants: Employment Entrance Exams

There are certain situations in the diverse context of employment that legitimately call for the testing of potential employees through the use of medical examinations. The ADA does not prohibit all medical exams and inquiries of applicants and employees, just those medical exams and inquiries that occur before an offer of employment has been made.[22] The ADA adopts this approach in an effort to eliminate or reduce bias against people with disabilities in the job selection process. The parameters of legitimate medical exams and inquiries, either requested after an offer of employment has been made or requested on a voluntary basis, are clearly identified in the ADA legislation itself and in the EEOC regulations.

[An employer] may require a medical examination (and/or inquiry) after making an offer of employment to a job applicant and before the applicant begins his or her employment duties, and may condition an offer of employment on the results of such examination (and/or inquiry), if all entering employees in the same job category are subjected to such an examination (and/or inquiry) regardless of disability.[23]

Implications: Inquiries of applicants or employees as to their medical history or condition are equivalent to requests for formal medical examinations under the ADA.[24] Both medical exams and inquiries are permitted after an applicant or employee has been offered a job but before the potential employee actually starts working. The offer of employment may be conditioned on the results of the medical exam or inquiry as long as the employer adheres to three rules:

1. All entering employees in the same job category must be subjected to the same medical exam or inquiry, regardless of whether an entering employee does or does not have a disability.
2. All information obtained regarding the medical history or condition of the potential employee must be kept confidential.
3. The results of these medical exams or inquiries must only be used in accordance and consistent with this part of the ADA.[25]

Medical exams must apply to all potential employees. Individual applicants who have been made an offer of employment cannot be singled out and subjected to a medical examination that is a condition to employment. Post-offer medical exams and inquiries can occur only if all of the entering employees in the same job category are subjected to the same test. Medical examinations under this part of the ADA do not have to be job related or consistent with business necessity as long as all incoming employees in the same job category are subjected to the same test. For example, a state may require all potential police officers to take a medical exam but not require other state workers to take a similar exam. This exception to the general rule against medical inquiries serves the employer's need to discover certain disabilities that may limit the employee's ability to perform a specific job.[26]

The results of a post-offer, pre-employment medical exam "cannot be used to discriminate against a person with a disability if the person is still qualified for the job."[27] If a particular medical examination, however, reveals that a potential employee does not satisfy certain employment criteria, and the offer of employment is therefore withdrawn, the specific criterion that resulted in the rescinded offer must meet three tests:

1. The specific criterion must not screen out or tend to screen out individuals with disabilities or classes of individuals with disabilities.
2. The specific criterion must be job related and consistent with business necessity.
3. In showing that specific criteria are job related, the employer must also show that there is no reasonable accommodation that would allow the rejected applicant with a disability to perform the essential functions of the job.[28]

For instance, suppose an essential function of a particular job is that the potential employee work every day for the next three months. After receiving a conditional offer, a medical examination uncovers a disabling impairment in the applicant that, according to reasonable medical judgment, will prohibit the applicant from satisfying the attendance requirement of the job. Under these circumstances, the employer would be able to withdraw the offer of employment without violating the ADA.[29]

The appendix to the EEOC regulations describes the allowance of post-offer medical examinations as a recognition that some industries, especially air transportation and construction, must have employees who meet certain physical and psychological requirements. Post-offer medical examinations given prior to employment help ensure that only individuals who meet the physical and psychological criteria of the job, with or without reasonable accommodation, will actually be hired and begin working.[30]

It should be noted that the ADA does not consider physical agility tests and drug tests to be medical examinations. Physical agility tests can be administered at any time throughout the application or employment process. These tests, however, must meet the same ADA guidelines as medical examinations in that they must be given to all similarly situated applicants or employees regardless of disability. If the physical agility test tends to screen out individuals with disabilities, the employer must show that the test is job related and consistent with business necessity and that performance cannot be achieved with reasonable accommodation.[31]

All medical information must be kept confidential. The language of the ADA itself and the EEOC regulations clearly establish the confidentiality of all information on the medical history and condition of applicants or employees obtained from post-offer, pre-employment medical examinations and inquiries. This information must be collected and maintained on separate forms and in separate medical files and must be treated as confidential medical records. There are three exceptions to the confidentiality of medical records that are spelled out in the language of the law. Exceptions to the confidentiality of medical records include the following:

1. Supervisors and managers may be informed regarding necessary restrictions on the work or duties of the employee and necessary accommodations.

2. First aid and safety personnel may be informed, when appropriate, if the disability might require emergency treatment.

3. Government officials investigating compliance with this part shall be provided relevant information on request.[32]

Implications: In addition to the supervisor, emergency, and government official exceptions of the confidentiality requirement, "medical information obtained in an examination pursuant to the post-offer, pre-employment stage may be used by the employer as baseline data to assist the employer in measuring physical changes attributable to on-the-job exposures."[33] In this way, employers will be able to measure, evaluate, and adjust existing work situations that may cause or increase the severity of work-related physical and mental impairments.

Use of information obtained from employment entrance exams. The language of the ADA states that results from post-offer, pre-employment medical examinations shall be "used only in accordance with this title."[34] The EEOC regulations restate this phrase as, "The results of such examination shall not be used for any purpose inconsistent with this part."[35] The regulatory language arguably allows for greater use of this medical information. The appendix to the EEOC regulations allows the disclosure of employee medical information in response to requests from state worker's compensation offices or second injury funds in accordance with state worker's compensation laws. "The ADA is not intended to override any legitimate medical standards or requirements established by federal, state or local law, or by employers or applicants for safety or security-sensitive positions, if the medical standards are [not consistent with the ADA]."[36]

Information obtained in the course of permitted employee entrance exams or inquiries may also be used during the underwriting and administration of health and life insurance, as well as other benefit plans, according to the EEOC regulations.[37] A question remains whether this medical information can be used in the defense of worker's compensation claims and other legal proceedings that may involve the medical condition of an employee.[38]

Medical Examinations of Current Employees

As mentioned earlier in this chapter, employers are generally prohibited from subjecting employees to medical examinations and inquiries. Once a person is hired, the employer cannot require the employee to take a medical exam, answer a medical inquiry, or inquire as to the existence, nature, or severity of an employee's disability. An exception to this general rule, however, allows employers to subject employees to medical exams and inquiries when they are job related and consistent with business necessity. By definition, a medical examination or inquiry that is not job related serves no legitimate business purpose and is therefore unlawful under the ADA. As is the case in the pre-employment context, employers may make inquiries about the employee's ability to perform functions of the job.[39]

[An employer] may require a medical examination (and/or inquiry) of an employee that is job-related and consistent with business necessity. [An employer] may make inquiries into the ability of an employee to perform job-related functions.[40]

Implications: This provision addresses the practical reality of employees whose job duties impact upon public health and safety. When an employer needs to conduct a "fitness for duty exam," for instance, in order to determine whether an employee is still able to perform the essential functions of the job, this section of the ADA permits the employer to do so. This section also allows employers to make inquiries and conduct medical examinations necessary to the reasonable accommodation process. Employers are permitted under this part to conduct periodic physicals and other medical monitoring required under federal, state, or local law. The ADA does not override medical standards established under these laws as long as the inquiries and exams are consistent with the ADA, or in other words, job related and consistent with business necessity.[41]

To illustrate the interaction between the ADA's medical exam requirements and federal safety standards, the transportation industry is a prime example. Under federal safety regulations, bus and truck drivers must undergo medical examinations at least once every two years.[42] Similarly, pilots and flight attendants must continually meet certain medical requirements in order to ensure public safety and health. The ADA is not an obstacle to the fulfillment of these legitimate standards.

The periodic testing for health reasons of employees under the Occupational Safety and Health Act of 1970 (OSHA), the Federal Coal Mine Health and Safety Act of 1969, and similar statutes are prime examples of the interaction between the ADA and other federal laws that prescribe medical examinations and inquiries. The periodic medical monitoring of employees exposed to toxic and hazardous substances under these and other laws is not limited by the ADA in any way.[43]

All information obtained as a result of medical exams and inquiries imposed upon current employees must meet the same confidentiality requirements and is subject to the same exceptions as acceptable medical exams and inquiries imposed upon applicants. This medical information must similarly be used only in a manner "not inconsistent with this part" of the ADA.

Voluntary Examinations and Inquiries

Because of past successes with preventive medical monitoring programs, such as "corporate wellness" programs, the ADA specifically allows employers to conduct medical examinations and inquiries of a voluntary nature.

[An employer] may conduct voluntary medical examinations and activities, including voluntary medical histories, which are part of an employee health program available to employees at the worksite.[44]

Implications: While employers may not require medical exams that are not job related and consistent with business necessity, voluntary medical examinations and medical histories, as part of employee health programs, are specifically allowed under this section of the ADA. Examples of voluntary medical exams include tests for high blood pressure, glaucoma, cancer detection, and weight control, to name a few. The appendix to the EEOC regulations also includes monitoring of blood pressure and the administration of prescription drugs, such as insulin, as permissible medical inquiries in a voluntary medical program.[45] Employees can use the results of voluntary exams to obtain treatment in the early stages of the disease or disorder.

Medical exams and inquiries under this part of the ADA are subject to the same confidentiality requirements and exceptions as medical examinations and inquiries given to applicants and employees. Information derived from voluntary medical exams and inquiries must not be used in a manner inconsistent with the ADA. For example, this information must not be used to limit or affect the employee's eligibility for health insurance.[46]

Record-Keeping and Reporting Requirements under the ADA

The Americans with Disabilities Act requires all employers who have one hundred or more employees to file with the EEOC copies of Standard Form 100, as revised (otherwise known as "Employer Information Report EEO-1") on or before 30 September of each year. Every employer that is subject to Title VII of the Civil Rights Act of 1964 is required to supply this form to the EEOC. While the EEOC will distribute this form to all known employers who fall within the requirements of the record-keeping and reporting section of the ADA, it is the employer's responsibility to obtain the necessary forms from the EEOC.

If an employer claims that the preparation or filing of the report would create an undue hardship, the employer may apply to the commission for an exemption. In addition, employers may seek and obtain from the EEOC alternative filing dates and periods for which data is reported. Also, special reporting procedures or systems may be granted upon specific written proposals to the EEOC by the employer. When the EEOC has received an allegation or has reason to believe that a person has not complied with the record-keeping and reporting requirements of the ADA, the commission may conduct an investigation of the alleged failure to comply.[47]

CHAPTER 6

Requirements of Places of Public Accommodation and State and Local Governments

ACCESSING PLACES OF PUBLIC ACCOMMODATION

A vast majority of the facilities that affect commerce are operated by *private* entities in the United States and must comply with Title III of the Americans with Disabilities Act. These places of public accommodation include the millions of businesses that operate on America's "Main Streets," from dry cleaners to supermarkets to hotels and movie theaters. Many of these businesses, business organizations, and nonprofit associations are concerned with the potential for excessive costs from implementation and potential litigation as a result of the ADA, particularly the public accommodation provisions. These fears are largely unfounded and will likely be proved untrue, just as apprehensions with regard to the Civil Rights Act of 1964 were for the most part baseless.

What many business owners may fail to realize is that the Americans with Disabilities Act will bring a large new segment of American consumers into the marketplace. Presumably, over the course of the next decade, an important new market segment will emerge, composed of workers with disabilities entering the work force. This new market segment will be patronizing facilities and businesses that comply with the ADA's accessibility and nondiscrimination mandates in order to purchase goods and services. In addition, untold billions of dollars may be saved by enabling people with disabilities to break the cycle of isolation and dependency on government benefits and entitlements. Resources will be devoted to enabling people with disabilities to become productive taxpayers instead of disenfranchised tax consumers. American business owners, in complying with the public accommodation provisions of the ADA, are making a long-term human investment in workers with disabilities and a long-term investment in a new market segment of over 22 million adult consumers.

Title III of the ADA is administered by the U.S. Department of Justice and went into effect on 26 January 1992. Title III prohibits discrimination on the basis of disability by *private* entities in places of public accommodation and requires publicly used commercial facilities to be designed, constructed, and altered in order to comply with established accessibility standards. Public entities, defined as state and local governments and their instrumentalities, are not considered places of public accommodation but are covered by the ADA nondiscrimination mandate under Title II, discussed later in this chapter. Private membership clubs and religious organizations are exempted from the requirements of Title III.

Access to commercial facilities and other establishments is only one of the requirements of Title III. A public accommodation may not subject an individual or a class of individuals on the basis of a disability or disabilities, directly or through contractual relationships, to a denial of the opportunity to participate in or benefit from the goods, services, facilities, privileges, advantages, or accommodations of a place of public accommodation.[1] For example, a public accommodation cannot refuse to serve a person with a disability because its insurance company sets its coverage or rates without taking disability into account.

The opportunity to benefit from the goods, services, and privileges of a place of public accommodation must be equal to that afforded to other individuals without disabilities. In other words, a business may not offer an accommodation to a person with a disability that is different or separate from goods, services, or privileges provided to other individuals. The exception is when an alternative means is necessary to facilitate the provision of goods, services, privileges, or opportunities to the individual; however, the alternative must be as effective as that provided to others. A business is only permitted to provide separate benefits "when necessary" and must do so in "the most integrated setting appropriate to the individual."[2] This language allows for the designation of parking spaces for persons with disabilities, for instance, without fear of violating the ADA prohibition of separate benefits.

Similar to the employment provisions of Title I, a place of public accommodation is prohibited from avoiding its obligations under the ADA by doing indirectly, through a contractual, licensing, or other arrangement what it may not do directly. However, Title III is not intended to encompass the clients or customers of other businesses. As a result, a place of public accommodation is not liable under the ADA for discrimination that may be practiced by those with whom it has a contractual relationship, when that discrimination is not directed against its own clients or customers. For example, if an amusement park contracts with a food service company to operate its food stands at the park, the amusement park is not responsible for other operations of the food service company that do not involve clients or customers of the amusement park.[3]

Table 6.1
Places of Public Accommodation under the Americans with Disabilities Act

1. An inn, hotel, motel or other place of lodging (except for an establishment located within a building that contains more than five rooms for rent)
2. A restaurant, bar, or other establishment serving food or drink
3. A motion picture house, theater, concert hall, stadium, or other place of exhibition or entertainment
4. An auditorium, convention center, lecture hall, or other place of public gathering
5. A bakery, grocery store, clothing store, hardware store, shopping center, or other sales or rental establishment
6. A laundromat, dry-cleaner, bank, barber shop, beauty shop, travel service, shoe repair service, funeral parlor, gas station, office of an accountant or lawyer, pharmacy, insurance office, professional office of a health care provider, hospital, or other service establishment
7. A terminal, depot, or other station used for specified public transportation
8. A museum, library, gallery, or other place of public display or collection
9. A park, zoo, amusement park, or other place of recreation
10. A nursery, elementary, secondary, undergraduate, or postgraduate private school, or other place of education
11. A day care center, senior citizen center, homeless shelter, food bank, adoption agency, or other social service center establishment
12. A gymnasium, health spa, bowling alley, golf course, or other place of exercise or recreation

SOURCE: *The Americans with Disabilities Act Handbook,* published by the Equal Employment Opportunity Commission and U.S. Department of Justice, 1991.

Places of public accommodation are prohibited, directly or through contractual or other arrangements, from utilizing standards, criteria, or methods of administration that have the effect of discriminating on the basis of disability or that perpetuate the discrimination of others who are subject to "common administrative control." This provision of Title III incorporates a disparate impact standard, or unintentional discrimination standard, to ensure the effectiveness of the legislative mandate to end discrimination. This rule, however, is subject to several limitations. A place of public accommodation is not required to adhere to this provision, if out of necessity or safety concerns, it is not practicable to do so.[4]

Places of public accommodation located in private residences are also covered by the ADA's accessibility and nondiscrimination mandate where a portion of the residence is used exclusively in the operation of a professional practice or a day care center, for instance. The portion of the residence that is used to enter the place of public accommodation, including the homeowner's front sidewalk, door or entryway, hallway, and rest rooms must be accessible to persons with disabilities. The Department of Justice, in formulating its regulations for Title III, recognized that many businesses operating out of public residences are quite small and employ only the homeowner. In this situation, the range of required actions in order to comply with the ADA would be quite modest. If it is not readily achievable to remove existing architectural barriers, a place of public accommodation located in a private residence may meet its obligations under the ADA by providing its goods or services to clients or customers with disabilities through the use of alternative measures, such as home delivery or house calls.[5]

Accessibility: New Construction

The ADA provides that newly constructed or altered places of public accommodation or commercial facilities must be readily accessible to and usable by individuals with disabilities.

No individual shall be discriminated against on the basis of disability in the full and equal enjoyment of goods, services, facilities, privileges, advantages, or accommodations of any place of public accommodation by any private entity who owns, leases (or leases to), or operates a place of public accommodation[6]

Implications: This general prohibition is patterned after the basic, general prohibitions that exist in other civil rights laws that prohibit discrimination on the basis of race, sex, color, religion, or national origin. This requirement contemplates a high degree of convenient access and ensures that patrons and employees of places of public accommodation are able to access, enter, and utilize facilities. Both the landlord who owns the building that houses a place of public accommodation and the tenant who owns or operates the place of public accommodation are subject to the requirements of Title III of the ADA. The landlord and the tenant can determine the allocation of responsibility for complying with the accessibility and nondiscrimination obligations of the ADA by lease or other contract.[7]

The ADA is realistic about the time needed to fully implement the mandate of accessibility. For instance, the ADA states that after 26 January 1993, design and construction of new facilities for first occupancy must be in compliance 30 months after the enactment of the ADA. It is clearly a law geared toward the future, its goal being that, over time, access will be the rule, rather than the exception. The ADA requires all new construction and alterations of existing buildings to be accessible.

Removing Barriers in Existing Facilities

For existing facilities, the new law requires modifications that remove accessibility barriers in a manner that the ADA language describes as "readily achievable"—without much difficulty or expense. Simply stated, the ADA requires existing places of public accommodation to alter their facilities by making modifications that are "cheap and easy."

Readily achievable modifications may take many forms. Examples include the repositioning of store shelves that are not readily accessible and the rearranging of tables, chairs, vending machines, display racks, and other furniture to enable easy access. The ADA requires that to the maximum extent possible facilities must be accessible to and usable by individuals with disabilities. It is not sufficient to provide such features as accessible routes, elevators, or ramps, if those features are not maintained in a manner that enables individuals with disabilities to use them. For example, inoperable elevators and locked accessible doors do not meet the standards established in the ADA. A place of public accommodation must maintain in operable working condition those features and equipment of its facilities that allow access and use to persons with disabilities. However, temporary interruptions in services or access due to maintenance or repairs are not considered violations of the ADA, unless the condition of disrepair persists beyond a reasonable period of time.[8]

An exception to full compliance with Title III of the ADA for construction facilities exists where the business can demonstrate that it is structurally impracticable to meet the requirements. "Structural impracticability" will only apply in rare circumstances when the unique characteristics of terrain prevent the incorporation of accessibility features. If full compliance with Title III's accessibility and nondiscrimination provisions would be structurally impracticable, compliance is required to the extent that it is possible. In other words, any portion of a facility that can be made accessible should be made accessible to the extent it is not structurally impracticable. This includes ensuring accessibility to persons other than individuals who use wheelchairs, if ramps and elevators are not structurally practicable. For instance, places of public accommodation are not relieved from the requirements to ensure accessibility to persons who use crutches or have sight or hearing impairments, even though they may not be able to accommodate persons in wheelchairs.[9]

The Elevator Exemption

The ADA also provides an elevator exemption for new construction in certain instances. Small buildings with less than three stories, or less than three thousand feet per story, are exempt from the requirement to install an elevator to provide access to people who use wheelchairs. Having *either* less than three thousand square feet per story or less than three stories qualifies a facility for the exemption; it need not qualify for the exemption on both counts. In creating this elevator exemption, however, Congress decided that the exemption would not apply to certain facilities such as shopping centers, shopping malls, or professional offices of health care providers. In addition, terminals, depots, or other stations used for public transportation, including loading and unloading zones, baggage claim areas, and dining facilities, must be accessible and, therefore, may not utilize the elevator exemption.[10]

Creating Accessibility in Existing Facilities

Title III of the ADA requires that alterations to existing facilities be made in a way that ensures that the altered portion is readily accessible to and usable by individuals with disabilities. The ADA does not require alterations. It simply provides that when alterations are undertaken, they must be made in a manner that provides access.

Any alteration of a place of public accommodation or a commercial facility, after January 26, 1992, shall be made so as to ensure that, to the maximum extent feasible, the altered portions of the facility are readily accessible to and usable by individuals with disabilities, including individuals who use wheelchairs. An alteration is deemed to be undertaken after January 26, 1992 if the physical alteration of the property begins after that date.[11]

Implications: Alterations to existing facilities include remodeling, renovation, rehabilitation, reconstruction, historic restoration, and changes or rearrangement in structural parts of the building or facility. Title III does not consider alterations to include normal maintenance such as re-roofing, painting or wallpapering, removing asbestos, or changes in mechanical or electrical systems that do not affect the usability of the building. If it is virtually impossible to comply fully with the accessibility standards of Title III when altering facilities, the accessibility and nondiscrimination provisions should be met to the maximum extent feasible.[12]

Any alteration to an existing facility that affects the accessibility of a facility that contains a primary function should be made to ensure that, to the maximum extent possible, the path of travel to the altered area and the rest rooms, telephones, and drinking fountains serving the altered area, are readily accessible to and usable by individuals with disabilities. Examples of "primary functions" include customer service departments, lobbies, dining areas, and meeting rooms. Storage and supply rooms, janitor closets, and rest rooms are not areas containing primary functions. These alterations should be carried out unless the cost and scope is disproportionate to the cost of the overall alteration of the facility. Alterations made to provide an accessible path of travel to the altered area will be deemed disproportionate to the overall alteration when the cost exceeds 20 percent of the cost of the accommodation to the primary function area.[13]

Historic Buildings

The ADA provides for significant limitations on the necessity to alter historic buildings in order to provide physical access. If a place of public accommodation exists within a historic property, eligible for listing in the National Register of Historic Places under the National Historic Preservation Act, the obligation to provide physical access is severely reduced if the alteration will threaten or destroy the historic significance of the building or facility. In this event, however, alternative methods of access must be provided.[14]

Nondiscrimination in Places of Public Accommodation

The ADA prohibits the imposition of "eligibility criteria" that screen out or tend to screen out individuals with disabilities from fully enjoying any goods, services, facilities, privileges, advantages, and accommodations unless the criteria are necessary for the provision of the goods and services being offered.[15] For example, a restaurant cannot use a "no pets" policy to deny service to a blind woman who uses a guide dog. Such a policy would discriminate against all blind persons with guide dogs, which is prohibited by the ADA.

A public accommodation, however, may impose legitimate safety requirements that are necessary for safe operation. Similar to Title I, these safety requirements must be based on actual risks and not on mere speculation, stereotypes, or generalizations about individuals with disabilities. Examples of safety qualifications that would be justifiable in appropriate circumstances would include height requirements for certain amusement park rides or a requirement that all participants in a recreational rafting expedition be able to meet a necessary level of swimming proficiency. In addition, a public accommodation may not impose a surcharge on a particular individual with a disability to cover the costs of providing auxiliary aids, removing barriers, and making reasonable modifications in policies and procedures in order to meet the ADA nondiscrimination mandate. A place of public accommodation that placed a sign in its window, for example, that implied that the establishment did not allow the patronage of persons with disabilities could be found in violation of Title III if the sign "screened out or tended to screen out" persons with disabilities.

Places of public accommodation must be flexible when considering the

ADA rights of persons with disabilities and the obligations imposed by the ADA to modify policies, practices, or procedures.

A [place of] public accommodation shall make reasonable modifications in policies, practices, or procedures when the modifications are necessary to afford goods, services, facilities, privileges, advantages, or accommodations to individuals with disabilities, unless the [place of] public accommodation can demonstrate that making the modifications would fundamentally alter the nature of the goods, services, facilities, privileges, advantages, or accommodations.[16]

Implications: The hallmark of Title III of the ADA on places of public accommodation is flexibility. A parking garage, for example, would be required to modify a rule barring all vans with raised roofs, if an individual who uses a wheelchair-accessible van wishes to park in that facility and if the garage's overhead fixtures are high enough to accommodate the height of the van. The garage would not, however, be required to fundamentally alter the structure of its facility if the height of the garage were too low to accommodate the van. Similarly, a department store may need to modify a policy of only permitting one person at a time in a dressing room, if an individual with mental retardation needs and requests assistance in dressing from a companion.

Making Referrals to Other Service Providers

In general, a public accommodation may refer an individual with a disability to another public accommodation, if that individual is seeking services outside of the area of specialization of the referring public accommodation. This, of course, assumes that the public accommodation would refer the person with a disability in the normal course of its operations and would make a similar referral to an individual without a disability who seeks or requires the same treatment or services.[17]

The regulations of Title III provide an illustration of the concept of appropriate referrals of persons with disabilities with respect to medical specialties. A health care provider may refer an individual with a disability to another provider, if that individual is seeking or requires treatment or services outside of the referring provider's area of specialization, and if the referring provider would make a similar referral for an individual without a disability who seeks or requires the same treatment or services. A physician who specializes in treating only a particular condition cannot refuse to treat an individual with a disability for that condition, but the physician is not required to treat the individual for a different condition.

For example, it would not be discriminatory for a physician who specializes only in burn treatment to refer an individual who is deaf to another physician for treatment of an injury other than a burn injury. To require physicians to accept patients outside the realm of their specialty would fundamentally alter the nature of their medical practice and, therefore, would not be required by the ADA. Additionally, a clinic specializing exclusively in drug rehabilitation could similarly refuse to treat a person who is not a drug addict, but it could not refuse to treat a person who is a drug addict simply because the patient tested positive for HIV.[18]

Providing Auxiliary Aids and Services

In general, a place of public accommodation must take those steps that may be necessary to ensure that no individual with a disability is excluded, denied services, segregated, or otherwise treated differently than any other individual because of the absence of auxiliary aids and services.

A [place of] public accommodation shall take those steps that may be necessary to ensure that no individual with a disability is excluded, denied services, segregated, or otherwise treated differently than other individuals because of the absence of auxiliary aids and services, unless the public accommodation can demonstrate that taking those steps would fundamentally alter the nature of the goods, services, facilities, privileges, advantages, or accommodations being offered or would result in an undue burden, i.e., significant difficulty or expense.[19]

Implications: In order for places of public accommodation to satisfy the responsibility to provide auxiliary aids and services, the public accommodation must communicate effectively with its customers, clients, patients, or participants who have disabilities that affect hearing, vision, or speech. Auxiliary aids and services include a wide range of services and devices for ensuring effective communication. Use of the most advanced technology is not required as long as effective communication exists. Auxiliary aids and services include qualified interpreters, note takers, computer telephone handset amplifiers, assistive listening devices, telecommunication devices for deaf persons, or other effective methods of making aurally delivered materials available to individuals with hearing impairments. Personal devices such as prescription eyeglasses and hearing aids are not considered auxiliary aids. A place of public accommodation may only challenge the request for auxiliary aids and services if the provision of these accommodations would fundamentally alter the nature of the goods or services, or result in an undue hardship on the operation of the business.[20]

Barrier Removal That Is Readily Achievable

A place of public accommodation is required under the ADA to remove architectural barriers in existing facilities, including communication barriers that are structural in nature, where removal is "readily achievable."

Again, "readily achievable" is defined as "easily accomplishable and able to be carried out without much difficulty or expense."[21] A list of barriers that may be removed without much difficulty or expense includes the installation of ramps, curb cuts, the repositioning of shelves, tables, vending machines, and other furniture, and the widening of doors to allow easy access. Additional examples include the installation of grab bars in toilet stalls, the rearrangement of toilet partitions to increase maneuvering space, the creation of designated accessible parking spaces, and the addition of elevator signage and restaurant menus in braille.

In the event that extensive and costly alterations are required in order to eliminate accessibility and communication barriers in particular places of public accommodation, alternative methods may be utilized if those methods are readily achievable. Examples of alternatives to extensive barrier removal include the provision of goods by curb service or home delivery, the retrieval by salespersons of merchandise from inaccessible shelves or racks, and/or the relocation of activities to accessible locations.[22]

Again, the ADA strikes a balance between the interests of business owners and managers of places of public accommodation and the interests of people with disabilities. It was not the intention of the drafters and supporters of the ADA to place great pressures, strains, and burdens on American business. The ADA strives to afford all members of American society with the opportunities and privileges that many individuals take for granted.

Enforcement of Title III

As noted, the Department of Justice has jurisdiction over violations of Title III of the Americans with Disabilities Act. Unlike the necessity to file a charge with the EEOC for violations under Title I of the ADA, Title III allows private lawsuits by individuals who have reasonable grounds to believe that they either have been or are about to be subjected to discrimination in violation of the new construction and alteration requirements that facilities be readily accessible to and usable by individuals with disabilities. Preventive relief is available in civil actions of this nature, including permanent or temporary injunctions and restraining orders to prevent construction of facilities with architectural barriers not in compliance with Title III of the ADA. The court may, in its discretion, permit the Attorney General to intervene in a civil action if the Attorney General believes the case is of general public importance.

In order to avoid unnecessary lawsuits, an individual bringing a private lawsuit for violation of Title III must have "reasonable grounds" for believing that a violation is about to occur but is not required to engage in a futile gesture, such as attempting to enter an inaccessible business, if the individual has notice that a person or organization covered by Title III of the ADA does not intend to comply with its provisions.[23]

Injunctive relief: In the case of violations of several parts of Title III, injunctive relief, known as a "shall include" order, directs a place of public accommodation to alter its facilities to make them readily accessible to and usable by individuals with disabilities to the extent required by the ADA. A report of the Energy and Commerce Committee of the House of Representatives notes that "an order to make a facility readily accessible to and usable by individuals with disabilities is mandatory under the shall include language."[24] Other appropriate injunctive relief includes requiring the provision of an auxiliary aid, service, a modification of a policy, or the provision of alternative methods in order to carry out the purposes and obligations of the ADA.[25]

Any individual who believes to have been subjected to discrimination prohibited by Title III may file a charge and request the Department of Justice to institute an investigation. Where the Attorney General has reason to believe that there may be a violation of Title III, a compliance review may be initiated, leading to a civil action. This civil action would be based on reasonable cause that a person or group engaged in a pattern or practice of discrimination in violation of Title III, or a person or group has been discriminated against in violation of Title III and the discrimination raises an issue of general public importance.[26]

The court has authority in a civil action brought under Title III of the ADA to grant equitable relief, such as temporary, preliminary, or permanent injunctions, providing auxiliary aids and services, modifications, or alternative methods to make facilities readily accessible to and usable by individuals with disabilities. The court may also award appropriate monetary damages to persons aggrieved if the Attorney General requests this relief and may, in order to vindicate the public interest, assess a civil penalty against the entity that violated Title III. The amount of the penalty may not exceed $50,000 for a first violation or $100,000 for any subsequent violation. Punitive damages are not available for violations of Title III of the ADA.[27]

Although Title III generally took effect on 26 January 1992, 18 months after the enactment of the Americans with Disabilities Act, several exceptions exist with respect to the filing of civil lawsuits. Except for violations of new construction and alterations requirements, no civil action may be brought for violation of Title III that occurs before 26 July 1992 against businesses with twenty-five or fewer employees and gross annual receipts of $1 million or less. In addition, no civil action may be brought under Title III, except with respect to violations of new construction and alterations requirements before 26 January 1993 against businesses with ten or fewer employees and gross annual receipts of $500,000 or less.[28]

DISCRIMINATION PROHIBITED BY STATE AND LOCAL GOVERNMENTS

As previously noted, Section 504 of the Rehabilitation Act of 1973 imposed a mandate of nondiscrimination on the basis of disability on all entities that receive federal financial assistance or federal contracts. For instance, several programs within every state and many local governments receive federal financial assistance for a variety of government programs. As a result, every state and many local governments have twenty years of experience in meeting the federal employment and government service needs of individuals with physical and mental disabilities.

Comparing Title I with Title II of the ADA

Title I, the employment provisions of the ADA, applies to all private employers who have more than 15 employees beginning on 26 July 1994. Private sector employers who have 25 or more employees were affected by Title I on 26 July 1992.

The provisions of Title II of the ADA concern nondiscrimination against people with disabilities with regard to employment, services, programs, and activities provided by "public entities," primarily state and local governments. Title II adopts requirements for making programs accessible to individuals with disabilities and for providing equally effective communications. This section took effect on 26 January 1992 and is directly patterned after the regulations issued for Section 504 of the 1973 Rehabilitation Act. Title II of the ADA, however, does not limit its nondiscrimination mandate to those state and local governments that receive federal financial assistance, as Section 504 does. Title II, which is essentially identical to the language of the law and regulations for Section 504 of the Rehabilitation Act, applies to all state and local governments, regardless of their ties to federal funds.

Put another way, since 26 January 1992, every state and local government, whether it receives federal funds or not, has been and will continue to be prohibited from discriminating against people with disabilities pursuant to Title II of the ADA. Since 26 July 1992, all state and local governments that employ more than 25 employees must comply with the employment provisions of Title I of the ADA. All state and local governments with less than 25 employees must still comply with Title II, the ADA equivalent of Section 504. After 26 July 1994, all state and local governments with fifteen or more employees must comply with Title I, while state and local governments with less than 15 employees must comply with Title II of the ADA.[29]

State and Local Government Obligation in Providing
Programs and Services

The ADA provisions of Title II apply to employment services, programs, and activities conducted by more than just state and local governments. Title II of the ADA applies to all public entities that are defined in the language of the ADA itself. The term "public entity" includes the following:

1. Any state or local government.
2. Any department, agency, special purpose district, or other instrumentality of a state or states or local government.
3. The National Railroad Passenger Corporation [commonly known as Amtrak], and any commuter authority (as defined in Section 103(8) of the Rail Passenger Service Act).[30]

Implications: Title II of the ADA applies to all public entities that can be identified with a state or local government, including any of its departments or branches. The ADA does not cover federal employees. In addition, all public transit authorities are included in the term "instrumentality of a state and local government."[31] For the sake of convenience, however, the term "state and local government" can be used to refer to all public entities under Title II.

Under Title II, a qualified individual with a disability is defined according to the established Section 504 definition. It combines the definition for employment ("a handicapped person who, with reasonable accommodation, can perform the essential functions of the job in question") with the definition for other services ("a handicapped person who meets the essential eligibility requirements for the receipt of such services.")[32] The ADA, however, uses the term "person with a disability" rather than a "handicapped person." Under Title II, the term "qualified individual with a disability" means:

An individual with a disability who, with or without reasonable modifications to rules, policies, or practices, the removal of architectural, communication, or transportation barriers, or the provision of auxiliary aids and services, meets the essential eligibility requirements for the receipt of services or the participation in programs or activities provided by a public entity.[33]

Implications: For the purposes of employment, the definition of a qualified individual with a disability under Title II of the ADA parallels the definition that appears in Section 504. The language of the Section 504 definition is very similar to the definition that appears in Title I of the ADA. Under Section 504 and Title I of the ADA, an individual with a disability must be substantially limited in a major life activity. A significant difference between the two laws is the ADA's inclusion of "working" as a major life activity.

In order to receive state and local government services, a person with a disability must meet essential eligibility requirements. This means that if the manifestations of a person's disability impose a substantial interference with or a direct threat to the operation of the state or local government program, the person with the disability can be denied the service or participation in the program.[34] It should be noted that prejudices against people with disabilities are not considered "substantial interference" with the operation of the government program.

State and Local Government Programs and Services Must Be Accessible

The regulations under Title II provide a general definition for discrimination in state and local government programs, services, and activities against individuals with disabilities, and a specific definition related to discrimination in employment against people with disabilities. Discrimination is prohibited generally as follows:

[Except with regard to construction on new and existing facilities], no qualified individual with a disability shall, because a public entity's facilities are inaccessible to or unusable by individuals with disabilities, be excluded from participation in, or be denied the benefits of the services, programs, or activities of a public entity, or be subjected to discrimination by any public entity.[35]

Implications: This is the general nondiscrimination principle underlying the program accessibility requirements of state and local governments. Title II again parallels Section 504 and describes several exceptions to this rule for existing facilities and for new construction and alteration of facilities. This section of the ADA provides that all facilities and parts of facilities in which construction or alteration commenced after 26 January 1992 must be readily accessible to and usable by individuals with disabilities.

Design, construction, or alteration of state and local government facilities must conform to the Federal Accessibility Standards or with the ADA Accessibility Guidelines for Buildings and Facilities, or must provide equivalent access.[36] This section includes construction on roads, highways, and intersections, including curb cuts.[37]

The regulations make clear that state and local governments should adhere to the general rule of program accessibility when, "viewed in its entirety, [the program] is readily accessible and usable by individuals with disabilities."[38] State and local governments are not immediately required to make each of its existing facilities usable by individuals with disabilities, nor are they required to make structural changes in existing facilities where other methods are effective in achieving compliance with the ADA.[39] State and local governments are not required to make alterations that would fundamentally change the nature of a service or program or alter the significance of a historic building.[40]

Development of a transition plan. In the event that structural changes on existing state or local government facilities are needed in order to achieve program accessibility, public employers of fifty or more employees are required to develop a transition plan by 26 July 1992.[41] The purpose of the plan is to set forth the steps necessary to complete the structural changes. The transition plan should have the following characteristics:

1. The transition plan should address construction and alteration of existing facilities in order to achieve program accessibility. (If the state or local government has jurisdiction over streets and walkways, these must also be included in the plan.)
2. The transition plan should be publicly distributed for comment from individuals with disabilities and organizations representing people with disabilities.
3. The actual plan shall (a) identify physical obstacles in the public entity's facilities that limit access to its programs and activities to people with disabilities, (b) provide a detailed description of the methods used to make the facilities accessible, (c) specify the schedule for taking the necessary steps in order to achieve compliance, if need be on a year-by-year basis, and (d) identify the state or local government official responsible for implementation of the plan.[42]
4. By 26 July 1992, the transition plan must be developed by the state or local government. Construction performed on facilities under this section must be completed as expeditiously as possible, but not later than 26 January 1995.[43]

Employment Discrimination Prohibited by State and Local Governments

The regulations of Title II provide a specific definition of employment discrimination in the hiring and promotion of individuals with disabilities by state and local governments.

No qualified individual with a disability shall, on the basis of disability, be subjected to discrimination in employment under any service, program, or activity conducted by a public entity.[44]

Implications: The prohibition against employment discrimination under this section is patterned after Section 504 of the Rehabilitation Act, not Title I of the ADA. The difference is of little consequence, however, in that Title I and Section 504 are very similar in nature and in language. This section of the ADA will apply indefinitely to those local governments that employ less than fifteen employees. As noted, those local governments with fifteen or more employees must meet the requirements of Title I of the ADA on and after 26 July 1994.

As of 26 January 1992, all state and local governments that did not qualify in the past as recipients of federal financial assistance were required to comply with Title II, the ADA equivalent to Section 504 of the Rehabilitation Act of 1973. Many local governments and municipalities found themselves unprepared to adhere to the requirements of the ADA. An excellent first step in this process is to conduct a self-evaluation and one that is required by law of every state and local government, regardless of its size or its ties to federal funds.

Self-Evaluations by State and Local Governments

In addition to being required to disseminate sufficient information on the rights and protections provided by the ADA to individuals with disabilities, all state and local governments are required to conduct a self-evaluation to review and monitor their current policies and practices with regard to program access and employment opportunities of individuals with disabilities. The EEOC regulation specifically and clearly states the requirements of self-evaluation under Title II of the ADA.

A public entity shall [by 26 January 1993] evaluate its current services, policies, and practices, and the effects thereof, that do not or may not meet the requirements of this part and, to the extent modification of any such services, policies, and practices is required, the public entity shall proceed to make the necessary modifications.[45]

Implications: Self-evaluations conducted by state and local governments in the past have proven to be a valuable means of establishing a working relationship with people with disabilities and promote the effective and efficient implementation of Section 504. Similar results are expected when newly covered local governments implement the ADA. Only state and local governments with fifty or more employees are required to maintain the self-evaluation on file and make it available to the public for inspection for a period of three years.[46] The self-evaluation in this case should include a list of interested persons consulted, an examination of the problems identified and the areas examined, and a description of any modifications performed.[47]

The EEOC regulations establish that nothing in the ADA should be interpreted to apply a lesser standard than the requirements of the Rehabilitation Act of 1973 or its regulations. In addition, nothing in the ADA should be interpreted to invalidate or limit the remedies, rights, and procedures of any federal, state, or local law that provides greater or equal protections than the ADA.[48] The ADA specifically subjects states to liability for violations of its provisions. States are not immune to ADA lawsuits under the Eleventh Amendment and are subject to all of the available remedies to which other public and private entities are exposed.

CHAPTER 7

The Role of the Employer and Human Resource Manager

While the Congress and White House overwhelmingly supported, passed, and signed the Americans with Disabilities Act legislation into law, it is in the workplace where the new law is being applied and implemented. As in the Civil Rights Act of 1964 and Rehabilitation Act of 1973, after which the ADA is largely patterned, the role of the employer, supervisor, and human resource manager is of central importance to the success of the ADA mandate.

Millions of women and minorities have benefited from the employment provisions of the Civil Rights Act of 1964 and as a result, so has the productivity of the nation. But for people with disabilities, who have been last in line for full EEO legislation, the ADA represents that long-awaited turning point to become full-time members and participants in the national economy.

By the 1980s, America was turning its attention to people with disabilities as national polls disclosed a growing public interest in the aspirations of people with disabilities to become employed, independent, and have access to a full range of services that most citizens take for granted. In a 1986 public opinion poll by Louis Harris and Associates, Inc., 80 percent of the respondents felt that people with disabilities have an "underused potential" to contribute to the country by working and producing. In the poll, 85 percent of the respondents believed that making jobs, housing, transportation, and public places more accessible will be a benefit rather than a cost to society.[1] In essence, the broad bipartisan support in Congress and in the White House not only reflected a political consensus, but it reflected public opinion as well.

While all of the titles of the Americans with Disabilities Act affect America's businesses and commerce, Title I, the employment provisions, is one of the most central parts of the entire legislation to both employers and people with disabilities. The Americans with Disabilities Act provides new rights for people with disabilities, and it also provides new responsibilities and obligations for business. While there are new responsibilities for the employer, there are other aspects for employers to consider, such as tax credits and the protection of undue hardship when a reasonable accommodation cannot be afforded.

Paul G. Hearne, president of the Dole Foundation for Employment of People with Disabilities, noting the concerns of business, stated, "The fears that the ADA will add enormous costs are unjustified. More likely the ADA will provide opportunities for employers, employees, and public officials to work together to create a more productive and decent American workplace."[2]

Many of the underlying principles of the ADA are not completely innovative or untried by American business. As Senator Tom Harkin stated, "The provisions in the [ADA] bill regarding employment are not new; small employers doing business with the federal government or receiving federal aid have been complying with these provisions for almost fifteen years."[3] In addition, 49 percent of America's business establishments have experience with previous EEO legislation and in developing employment procedures and policies covering minorities and women, which began under the Civil Rights Act of 1964.

THE HUMAN RESOURCE MANAGER

Working with One of America's Largest Human Resources

People with disabilities are an increasingly important human resource today and will be throughout the early part of the twenty-first century because of America's shrinking labor force. Numerous federal government studies have found that during the 1990s and the early part of the twenty-first century America will experience a labor shortage. The baby boom is over. According to an article in *Businessweek*, "The U.S. work force throughout the 1990s will grow more slowly than at any other time in the past seventy years. Though the overall labor force will be larger, there will be nine million fewer people entering the job market in the 1990s than there were in the 1970s. . . . The number of workers age twenty to twenty-nine will fall by one-sixth over the 1990s."[4]

In addition, the Department of Labor has reported another trend: a shortage of skills in first-time job applicants. A 1988 Department of Labor survey found that 66 percent of the nation's employers were reporting severe deficiencies in the mathematical and literacy skills of first-time job applicants. Many businesses had to interview up to twenty entry-level applicants to find a single qualified candidate.[5] Economic experts agree that if these two simultaneous economic trends continue, the profitability and productivity of American business are bound to suffer because there will not be enough skilled and qualified workers to meet demand. One of the solutions for business in meeting these work force trends is to tap an underutilized resource—millions of educated, skilled, and qualified people with disabilities.

People with disabilities are an important human resource for American business in an era with a shrinking labor force compounded by a decline in the skills of first-time workers. For American business, people with disabilities represent a relatively untapped human resource—a human resource that, study after study shows, has low absenteeism, low turnover rates, and high motivation to prove themselves. For the human resource manager, working with both employees and applicants with disabilities, there are a number of new considerations in meeting the objectives and regulations of the ADA legislation.

The Human Resource Manager's Objectives

Susan R. Meisinger is vice president of government and public affairs for the Society for Human Resource Management. She has taken an active role in working with professionals from disability organizations, such as the Disability Rights Education and Defense Fund, Inc., and with her society's membership of 40,000 in promoting a better understanding of the ADA in the workplace:

Human resource professionals in corporations around the country will have primary responsibility for ensuring that their employers are in compliance with employment provisions of the Americans with Disabilities Act. Not only will they have to become familiar with the provisions of the new law, they will have to take steps to ensure that anyone with management responsibilities in the corporation is familiar as well.[6]

Meisinger also points out that the human resource management professional will also have to monitor two major areas of employment to ensure compliance with the new law, recruitment and placement and the return to work of existing employees who have had an accident or serious illness:

Human resource professionals engaging in recruitment and placement will be responsible for ensuring that recruitment efforts don't result in the exclusion of persons with disabilities. They must be sure they fully appreciate the requirements of the position for which they are recruiting, and insure that information sought during the interview process only relates to a person's ability to perform the essential functions of the position. All human resource professionals must also become more familiar with the concept of "reasonable accommodation," and recognize that such accommodation may not only be necessary for applicants, but may be necessary for existing employees who return to work after an accident or illness that leaves them disabled. Supervisors and managers will have to be counseled on the requirements of the new law, and understand that they may not be able to insist that the returning employee with a disability perform a function in exactly the same way as they had performed it in the past.[7]

Table 7.1
Five Key Areas for Employers and Human Resource Managers

1. Understanding the full impact of the ADA and fostering an understanding of the ADA among employees in the workplace
2. Utilizing appropriate interviewing procedures and testing for applicants and employees with disabilities
3. Utilizing a four-step procedure in determining a reasonable accommodation for an applicant or employee with a disability, if necessary
4. Ensuring that applicants and employees have access to the worksite and full utilization of workplace areas used by other employees, such as a lounge, cafeteria, and rest rooms
5. Implementing the job accommodation needs of employees with disabilities

SOURCE: Equal Employment Opportunity Commission

COMPLYING WITH THE NEW LAW

By July 1994, 2.6 million places of business in the United States will be affected by the employment provisions of the ADA when the law is fully implemented, according to the Small Business Administration.[8] Businesses covered include private employers and employment agencies. Also, over one million nonprofit associations, such as trade associations and professional associations are covered by the ADA, with the qualified exception of religious associations.[9] In addition, labor organizations and labor management committees are covered by the law.

All of these entities fall under Title I of the Americans with Disabilities Act and the regulations and enforcement of the Equal Employment Opportunity Commission. Employers with 25 or more employees must have been in compliance on 26 July 1992, and employers with 15 or more employees must comply by 26 July 1994. A business, such as a bank, that has a total of 25 or more employees in all three of its branches, would have to comply with the ADA at all of its locations by 26 July 1992. In the ADA, the term "employer" is interchangeable with "business" or "covered entity." An agent of a business includes any person or persons responsible for hiring, such as a supervisor, office manager, or staff of a human resources office or personnel office.

The ADA in many ways strikes a balance between the employment needs of people with disabilities and an employer's desire to obtain the best personnel possible for the job. The employer "is free to select the most qualified applicant available and to make decisions based on reasons unrelated to the existence or the consequence of a disability."[10] An example, which was explored during a Senate Committee on Labor and Human Resources hearing, has to do with two people applying for a typist position. One person with a disability accurately types 50 words a minute and the other person accurately types 75 words a minute. Under the ADA, the employer may hire the applicant with the higher typing speed, if typing speed is an essential function of the job.[11]

However, when disability itself comes into the decision-making process, the ADA provisions prevail. The Senate committee provided this example: If two job seekers seeking the typing position include an individual who requires a telephone headset with an amplifier and a person without a disability, and they both have the same typing speed, "the employer is not permitted to choose the person without a disability because of the need to provide the needed reasonable accommodation."[12] The obligation to make a reasonable accommodation only extends to qualified applicants with known disabilities.

Determining the Abilities of the Applicant

An applicant eligible under the EEO provisions of the ADA needs to be qualified for the position and, if hired, has a responsibility to the employer to perform the essential functions of the job. The balance between the employment needs of people with disabilities and the business needs of employers was stated by the EEOC:

The ADA thus establishes a process in which the employer must assess a disabled individual's ability to perform the essential functions of the specific job held or desired. While the ADA focuses on eradicating barriers, the ADA does not relieve a disabled employee or applicant from the obligations to perform the essential functions of the job. To the contrary, the ADA is intended to enable disabled persons to compete in the work place based on the same performance standards and requirements that employers expect of persons who are not disabled.[13]

But in the hiring process and with respect to current employees with disabilities, employers cannot discriminate on the basis of a disability. One of the most important rules in the entire ADA legislation is that an employer "shall not discriminate against a qualified individual with a disability because of the disability of such individual in regard to job application procedures, the hiring, advancement, or discharge of employees, employee compensation, job training, and other terms, conditions, and privileges of employment."[14]

George Gant, who has multiple sclerosis, is a manager for Dow Corning and is shown here checking plant improvements. Courtesy of the National Multiple Sclerosis Society.

The ADA provides specific rules in the employment process of individuals with disabilities. There are three basic obligations for employers during the hiring and promotion of people with disabilities:

1. Focus on the person's abilities, not disabilities.
2. The provision of reasonable accommodation when needed in pre-employment and employment.
3. Limited and specified use of pre-employment medical examinations.

EMPLOYMENT DECISIONS BASED ON ESSENTIAL JOB FUNCTIONS

Title I of the Americans with Disabilities Act protects qualified individuals with disabilities from employment discrimination. Employers will need to review their employment procedures and policies, and revise them if necessary, in order to comply with the ADA. In addition to satisfying the ADA definition of disability, the applicant or employee with a disability must be qualified for the position. According to the ADA, a "qualified individual with a disability" is "an individual with a disability who, with or without reasonable accommodation, can perform the essential functions of the employment position that such individual holds or desires."[15] Essential functions of an employment position are the fundamental duties of the job. This is a summary of the two-step process in determining whether the applicant or employee is a qualified individual with a disability.

The First Step

The employer must first decide whether the individual with a disability has the skill, experience, education, and other job-related requirements of the employment position that the person holds or desires. For instance, the employer must first decide whether a paralyzed individual who applies for an attorney position holds a license to practice law, or whether a blind individual who applies for a public teaching position is certified to teach. It is important to note that "other job-related requirements" may be considered in addition to one's skills, experience, and education.

The Second Step

Once the determination has been made that the individual meets the requirements for the position, the employer must then determine whether the individual can or cannot perform the essential functions of the position that is held or desired by the individual, with or without reasonable accommodation.

The purpose of the second step is to identify the essential functions or fundamental duties of the job. This ensures that individuals with disabilities, who cannot perform marginal or incidental aspects or tasks of a particular job, are not rejected if they can perform the essential functions of that position. Reasonable accommodation is "any modification or adjustment to a job or the work environment that will enable a qualified applicant or employee with a disability to perform essential job functions."[16] Essential job functions refers to the fundamental duties of a particular position of employment.

The appendix to the ADA regulations clearly explains that this two-step process to determine whether an individual with a disability is qualified must take place at the time of the employment decision. The determination should be based on the capabilities of the individual at that time and not based on speculation that the employee may become unable to perform functions in the future. The possibility that health insurance premiums or worker's compensation costs will increase due to the employment of an individual with a disability cannot be considered.

In summary, in order for a person with a disability to be qualified, the applicant or employee must be able to satisfy the following requirements:

1. The employer's job requirements for educational background, employment experience, skills, licenses, and any other qualification standards that are job related.
2. Be able to perform those tasks that are *essential* to the job, with or without reasonable accommodation.

(For more information on determining whether an applicant or employee is a qualified individual with a disability, see chapter 4.)

FURTHER PROTECTIONS FOR PEOPLE WITH DISABILITIES

The ADA adopts a framework for employment selection procedures that is designed to assure that persons with disabilities are not excluded from job opportunities unless they are actually unable to do the job. A House of Representatives report stated, "The requirement that job criteria actually measure the ability required by the job is a critical protection against discrimination based on a disability. As was made strikingly clear during the hearings on the ADA, stereotypes and misconceptions about the abilities, or more correctly inabilities, of persons with disabilities are still pervasive today."[17]

According to the EEOC, the employer should carefully examine each job to determine which functions or tasks are essential to carrying out the job. The EEOC notes that this is particularly important before making an employment action or decision such as recruiting, advertising, hiring, promoting, or firing. Factors to weigh when considering if a function of a job is essential include the following:

1. Does the position exist in order to perform that specific function?
2. Are there other employees available who could perform that function?
3. What is the degree of expertise or skill required to perform the function?

The EEOC considers the employer's judgment about which job functions are essential and a written job description prepared before advertising or interviewing for a job as "evidence of essential functions."[18] Other kinds of evidence of essential job functions include the following:

1. Work experience of present or past employees in the job.
2. Time spent performing a function.
3. Consequences of not requiring an employee to perform a function.
4. Terms of a collective bargaining agreement.[19]

REASONABLE ACCOMMODATION

The principal mandate of Title I, the employment provisions of the ADA, is that employers make reasonable accommodations to qualified individuals with disabilities if it is not an undue hardship. The EEOC has stated that reasonable accommodation enables a qualified individual with a disability "to participate in the application process, and to enjoy benefits and privileges of employment equal to those available to other employees."[20] The EEOC and the courts "may look at site-specific resources as well as the resources of the employer as a whole" in determining undue hardship on a case-by-case basis.[21]

To illustrate, suppose a large corporation based in St. Louis is hiring in Sacramento, which is one of its sixteen locations. The corporation needs to purchase a $9,000 reading machine for a blind engineer, who will use the automatic reader as a reasonable accommodation. This corporation would likely have adequate resources in both Sacramento and St. Louis, and be able to afford the reasonable accommodation because during last year the corporation made $15 million in profits. The corporation could not justify a claim of undue hardship because of the corporation's overall financial resources in comparison to the cost of the accommodation.

As former EEOC Chairman Evan J. Kemp, Jr. pointed out, "The guiding principle remains that larger employers have a greater duty to make accommodations than do smaller employers."[22] It is a violation of the ADA to fail to provide reasonable accommodation to the "*known* physical or mental limitations of a qualified individual with a disability, unless to do so would impose an undue hardship on the operation" of the business.[23]

Table 7.2
Examples and Factors of Undue Hardship

Examples of undue hardship include:
- Unduly costly
- Extensive
- Disruptive
- Fundamentally alter the nature or operation of the business

SOURCE: Equal Employment Opportunity Commission

Table 7.3
Specific Factors in Determining Undue Hardship

Factors for a specific business:
- Cost of the reasonable accommodation
- The size of the business
- Financial resources of the business
- Nature and structure of the business

SOURCE: Equal Employment Opportunity Commission

Because an employer must have knowledge of an applicant's disability in order to be required to comply with the ADA, it is essentially the responsibility of an applicant or employee to make a request for reasonable accommodation.

As already noted, the ADA legislation clearly states that employers are obligated to make reasonable accommodations only to the known physical or mental limitations of a qualified individual with a disability. As a result, the duty to accommodate is generally triggered by a request from an applicant for employment or an employee. Of course, if a person with a known disability is having difficulty performing his or her job, it would be permissible for the employer to raise the possibility of a reasonable accommodation with the employee.[24]

While it is not necessary for an employer to provide a reasonable accommodation if it would cause an undue hardship, an employer is still responsible for identifying an alternative reasonable accommodation that poses less of a hardship. But Evan Kemp, Jr. stated, "an employer's reasonable accommodation responsibility is not limitless" and has noted what those limitations are.[25] First, an applicant or employee must request a reasonable accommodation, according to Kemp. Second, the obligation to provide a reasonable accommodation only extends to qualified people with disabilities. Third, if "an employer can show that the accommodation would impose an undue hardship on the operation of the business," said Kemp, "the employer is relieved of the obligation to provide that accommodation."[26]

AFTER A JOB OFFER IS MADE

An employer may request an applicant, who has been offered a job, to take a medical examination prior to starting the new job, but only if all other employees in the same job category are also required to take the medical exam. An employer may condition the job offer on the results of the exam as long as the employer does not use the exam results, uncovering the disability, against the applicant based on the disability. However, if an individual with a disability is not hired because the exam reveals the existence of a disability, the employer must be able to demonstrate that the reasons for exclusion are job related and necessary for the conduct of business.[27] In addition, the employer must be able to demonstrate that there was no reasonable accommodation that would have made it possible for the individual with a disability to perform the essential job functions.

After an employer has hired a new employee, the employer cannot require a medical exam or ask an employee questions about the employee's disability unless it can be demonstrated that the questions are job related and necessary for the conduct of business. Employers may conduct voluntary medical exams that are a part of an employee health care program. The results of all medical examinations and other information regarding an individual's disability must be kept confidential and maintained in separate medical files.

Examples of What Employers Cannot Do

1. An employer cannot use an application form that lists a number of disabilities, ask how a individual became disabled or the prognosis of the disability, or how often the individual will need treatment or leave as a result of the disability. However, the employer may state the attendance requirements of the job and ask the applicant if this requirement can be met.[28]

2. An otherwise qualified person with a disability cannot be disqualified for a position because of the individual's inability to perform non-essential or marginal functions of the job.[29]

3. Employers are required to make employment decisions based on facts applicable to individual applicants or employees, and not on the basis of presumptions as to what a class of individuals with disabilities can or cannot do.[30]

4. An employer cannot limit the duties of an individual with a disability

based on a presumption of what is best for the individual or based on a presumption about the ability of the individual to perform certain tasks.[31]

5. Employers cannot deny employment to an applicant based on generalized fears about the safety of the applicant or higher rates of absenteeism.[32]

6. An employer cannot deny a qualified individual with a disability equal access to health and life insurance, and may not subject the person to different terms of insurance based on the disability alone, if the disability does not impose increased risks.[33]

7. Employers cannot administer employment tests to eligible applicants or employees who have sensory, manual, or speaking impairments in test formats that require the use of the impaired skill.

8. It is unlawful for an employer to use standards, criteria, or methods of administration that are not job related and consistent with business necessity and have the effect of discriminating or perpetuating discrimination.

9. Employers cannot restrict the employment opportunities, or segregate into separate work areas or into separate lines of advancement, qualified individuals with disabilities based on stereotypes and myths about an individual's disability.

10. An employer cannot deny an employment opportunity to an individual with a disability because of a slightly increased risk to the health or safety of the individual or others. The risk can only be considered when it poses a significant risk—high probability of substantial harm. A speculative or remote risk is insufficient.

IMPLEMENTING VOLUNTARY COMPLIANCE

Developing an ADA Employment Compliance Plan

While developing an ADA employment compliance plan is not required under the law, many businesses will find it helpful as a means to ensure that specific steps have been taken within a business to voluntarily comply with the employment provisions of the ADA. An ADA employment compliance plan can be utilized as a checklist to ensure that a business or nonprofit association has taken the appropriate and specific actions to meet the requirements of the new law. As a document, it can be placed on bulletin boards within a business or nonprofit association to assist employees and applicants better understand the ADA and how the employer is meeting the ADA's employment provisions.

Dissemination of the provisions of the ADA is mandated by the law. According to the ADA, "Every employer, employment agency, labor organization, or joint labor management committee covered by this title [Title I] shall post notices in an accessible format to applicants, employees, and

Table 7.4
The ADA Employment Compliance Plan

---

1. A Policy Statement
2. Education and Training of Management
3. Education and Training of All Employees
4. Review of Employment Procedures
5. Review Employment Positions and Job Descriptions
6. Develop Written Job Descriptions
7. Review Architectural and Communications Barriers
8. Develop Plan to Remove Barriers, Make Accommodations
9. Disseminate the ADA Employment Compliance Plan
10. Develop and Implement an ADA Awareness Program

SOURCE: Equal Employment Opportunity Commission and previous federal
legislation affecting employment

members describing the applicable provisions of this Act, in a manner
prescribed by [the Civil Rights Act of 1964]."[34]

The following procedures will assist employers in complying with the
regulations of the Americans with Disabilities Act.

Develop Written Job Descriptions

Two experts in vocational rehabilitation, Joyce Couch Cole and Ruth
Bragman, have found that the interview process of people with disabilities
can be improved by having a written job description. According to Cole
and Bragman, the employer's "questions should be developed so that the
individual is encouraged to communicate his or her true qualifications."
They conclude, "If an applicant is not suitable for the position, the employers have documented evidence for his or her rejection, in addition to
verified attempts at trying to accommodate the individual. If no accommodations are necessary, and/or reasonable accommodations can be met
without undue hardship, the employers may have just interviewed the *most*
qualified person for the job."[35]

Develop Sensitivity Training Programs

The *New York Times* reported in 1991 on how Honeywell Inc. initiated
a sensitivity training program for nondisabled managers. In 1990 the company sent 60 nondisabled managers from its various human resources and
training departments to take the "Windmills" program offered by the California Governor's Committee on Employment of People with Disabilities.
Angela Johnson, an engineer with Honeywell, stated, "One of the biggest
problems disabled people encounter is the stigma, the discomfort, that

non-disabled people feel around them. Any program that helps non-disabled people explore their own negative attitudes is going to help."[36]

Chairman Kemp in an interview with *Businessweek* was asked what will be the biggest challenge in implementing the ADA. Kemp responded, "Attitudes are going to be the biggest problem. And all of the lawyers in the world won't be able to change attitudes."[37] (For more information on developing a sensitivity or awareness program about the ADA and workers with disabilities, see chapter 8.)

CONCERNS FOR THE EMPLOYER

Testing for Discrimination

In an article in the *National Journal*, it was reported that the EEOC intends to use phony job applicants, called testers, to monitor how much job discrimination is taking place. "Widespread use of testers has been a valuable tool in fighting housing discrimination. But employers are cool to its use in the employment area, where, they say, subjective judgments are made in many hiring decisions and companies often decide between several highly qualified applicants."[38] The use of testers, according to the article, is the "EEOC's latest enforcement tool" and "a controversial way of ferreting out job bias."[39] While employment rights groups have supported the tester initiative, the most controversial aspect of the program is whether EEOC employees should be the testers.

Health Insurance and Other Benefits

According to the interpretive guidance for the ADA regulations published by the EEOC, an employer "cannot deny a qualified individual with a disability equal access to insurance or subject a qualified person with a disability to different terms or conditions of insurance based on disability alone, if the disability does not pose increased risks."[40] According to the EEOC, an employer can offer health insurance policies that exclude coverage for pre-existing conditions, even though such clauses may adversely affect employees with disabilities more than others.

Lex Frieden, a former executive director of the National Council on Disability, who helped draft the ADA legislation, stated "It is in the area of health insurance that the ADA is the weakest."[41] Frieden said, "Health insurance for people with disabilities and other forms of insurance, in my opinion, are sadly left out of the ADA. It happens to be the biggest, most awesome gap in the legislation."[42] The reason for this lack of focus on insurance, according to Frieden, was due to members of Congress who did not want insurance to be a stumbling block to the passage of the ADA legislation.[43]

According to expert opinion, significant litigation may arise with respect to the issue of the ADA's effect on health insurance. Under Titles I, II, and III, legitimate arguments can be made that bring private and public health insurance programs under the ADA's nondiscrimination mandate. It will be the responsibility of the courts and Congress to further determine the ADA's effect on health insurance. (For more information on health insurance, see chapters 5, 10, and 11.)

Direct Threat to the Safety and Health of Oneself or Others

According to the EEOC regulations, an employer can, as a qualification standard, require that an individual with a disability not pose a direct threat to the health or safety of "oneself or others." However, as already noted, this is a controversial regulation because the specific wording goes beyond the ADA legislation. The ADA itself defines a direct threat as *not* including a direct threat to oneself, but confines it to the health or safety of others.

Reginald Welch, spokesperson for the EEOC, defended the regulation, stating that it would be difficult for employers to abuse and that employers would have to prove a person had a "high probability of harming himself or others."[44] Welch added that employers would also have to attempt to find a reasonable accommodation to alleviate the safety threat.[45] The Associated Press reported, "Under the rule . . . employers can turn away people who might pose a direct threat to themselves or others. The text of the [ADA] law mentioned only harm to others."[46] Many experts think that the courts will become the eventual interpreters of the issue of direct threat to oneself.

In the EEOC regulations, direct threat means a significant risk of substantial harm to the health or safety of the individual or others that cannot be eliminated or reduced by reasonable accommodation. However, an employer is not permitted to deny employment to an individual merely because of a slightly increased risk—the risk needs to be significant. In determining whether an individual would pose a direct threat, the regulations require a decision based on objective, factual evidence, including: (1) the duration of the risk, (2) the nature and the severity of the potential harm, (3) the likelihood that the potential harm will occur, and (4) the imminence of the potential harm.[47]

An example of an employer successfully challenging an applicant as a direct threat to oneself occurred in 1989 when a federal appeals court agreed that the Federal Bureau of Investigation did not have to hire a man with diabetes because of the possibility of insulin shock while on duty.

Christopher Bell, the attorney-advisor to the EEOC chairman, has acknowledged that the direct threat to oneself language is not included in earlier federal legislation. Bell said that the EEOC included the direct threat language in the regulations as "added protection" and that it was important to the EEOC to "establish a direct threat standard that was stringent" rather than leave it to the courts.[48]

People with disabilities voiced their concern over this controversial regulation in letters to the EEOC during the comment period before the regulations became final. In publishing the final regulations, the EEOC recognized the views of concerned people with disabilities. As stated in the introduction to the EEOC's guidelines to the ADA, "Many disability rights groups and individuals with disabilities asserted that the definition of direct threat should not include a reference to the health or safety of the individual with a disability. They expressed concern that the reference to 'risk to self' would result in direct threat determinations that are based on negative stereotypes."[49]

A *New York Times* article described the ADA direct threat regulation as a "setback for the disabled and their advocates."[50] The news story stated, "Advocates for the disabled denounced the plan, saying that under the regulations it could be easier for businesses to avoid hiring the physically or emotionally impaired."[51] It concluded, "While the regulations are intended to clarify the law, questions remain on the extent of a disabled worker's rights and on the limits of an employer's responsibilities under the act. Many of those questions will be answered on a case-by-case basis as the federal courts hear job discrimination suits under the law."[52]

Food Handling Jobs

To control and prevent the spread of infectious and communicable diseases through the handling of food, the ADA legislation has specific employment provisions for these jobs. First, the secretary of the Department of Health and Human Services is required to disseminate a list, updated annually, of all infectious and communicable diseases transmitted through the handling of food. An employer can refuse to assign or continue to assign a job involving food handling to an individual disabled by an infectious or communicable disease, if the risk cannot be eliminated by reasonable accommodation. According to the EEOC guidelines for the ADA, "If the individual is a current employee, the employer would be required to consider the accommodation of reassignment to a vacant position not involving food handling for which the individual is qualified."[53] (For more information on food handling, see chapter 11.)

Employer Assistance from Vocational Rehabilitation Agencies and Governor's Committees

For employers, supervisors, and human resource managers who are interested in hiring persons with disabilities or need technical assistance with reasonable accommodation, there are a number of federal, state, and local

Table 7.5
Alternative Funding for Reasonable Accommodation

- Obtaining funding from an outside source, such as a vocational rehabilitation agency
- State and federal tax credits or deductions may offset cost
- Applicant or employee must have the opportunity to pay for the portion of the reasonable accommodation that constitutes an undue hardship

SOURCE: Equal Employment Opportunity Commission

government agencies and national associations that provide assistance to employers at no cost. The ADA has no requirement that people with disabilities be recruited. However, state and city vocational rehabilitation programs can provide employers with qualified applicants for employment in entry-level to management positions. These programs include state vocational rehabilitation agencies, commissions, or departments of rehabilitation services for the blind, and governor's committees on employment of people with disabilities. These vocational rehabilitation and employment programs can also be useful for obtaining technical assistance, information on city and local programs, and consultation on worksite accommodations. (For listings of organizations providing information to employers and people with disabilities on the ADA, see the appendix.)

Tax Credits for the Employer: The Access Credit

According to the EEOC, other recently enacted legislation will facilitate compliance with the ADA.[54] As amended in 1990, the Internal Revenue Code allows a deduction of up to $15,000 per year for expenses associated with the removal of qualified architectural and transportation barriers. The 1990 amendment also permits eligible small businesses to receive a tax credit for certain costs of compliance with the ADA. The definition of a small business is one whose gross receipts do not exceed $1 million or whose work forces does not consist of more than 30 full-time workers. A qualifying small business may claim a credit of up to 50 percent of eligible access expenditures that exceed $250 but do not exceed $10,250.

Examples of eligible access expenditures include the necessary and reasonable costs of removing barriers, providing auxiliary aids, and acquiring or modifying equipment or devices. As Daniel C. Schaffer, a professor at Northeastern University School of Law and an expert on tax law, has pointed out: "Congress has often used the Internal Revenue Code as a means of promoting social and economic goals. Since 1976 Congress has reduced the tax burden of businesses that remove barriers to persons with disabilities (Section 190 of the Revenue Code). . . . In 1990, shortly after the enactment of the Americans with Disabilities Act, a new tax credit, the 'access credit,' was enacted to provide tax relief to small businesses that incur eligible costs when complying with the ADA."[55]

An overview of the different types of access credits available to employers as tax credits includes the following:

1. In 1990, Section 190 of the Tax Reform Act was amended to allow a $15,000 tax deduction annually for the removal of architectural and transportation barriers.

2. Congress also adopted the Disabled Access Credit (amending Section 44 of the Internal Revenue Code), which is available to an "eligible small business" and is equal to 50 percent of the "eligible access expenditures" that do exceed $250 but do not exceed $10,250. Businesses will have to pay the first $250 of any accommodation cost.[56]

This access credit is allowed only to small businesses. A small business with less than $1 million in gross receipts or with fewer than 50 full-time employees will be eligible for a tax credit.

3. The limit on the Section 190 deduction was reduced from an annual $35,000 deduction to a $15,000 annual deduction. As a result, for larger firms, the 1990 legislation lowered the Section 190 deduction and does not add a credit as it did for small businesses.[57]

4. If a business spends more than $250 on an accommodation, the business qualifies for a 50 percent nonrefundable credit of up to $5,000. Costs above $5,000 qualify for a tax deduction of up to $15,000.[58]

In general, all members of a group or corporation will be treated as one person for the purposes of the credit and the dollar limitation among the members of any group will be determined by regulation. In the case of a partnership, the requirements will apply to the partnership and to each partner. Eligible access expenditures are defined as amounts paid or incurred by an eligible small business for the purpose of enabling small businesses to comply with applicable requirements of the ADA.

The access credit became effective on 5 November 1990 and applies to the expenditures paid or incurred after that date. The access credit has been included as part of the general business credit and is subject to the rules of current law that limit the amount of general business credit. Claims for the access credit cannot be carried back to a taxable year prior to the date of the enactment of the credits.

The enactment of the new access credit in Section 44 of the Internal Revenue Code was specifically intended by Congress to assist small business, which is widely viewed as having a larger economic burden compared to larger business in complying with the ADA. The secretary of the Department of the Treasury is required to publish regulations to implement the access credit.

CHAPTER 8

Gaining a Better Awareness of the Applicant and New Employee

When EEOC Chairman Evan J. Kemp, Jr. was once asked why attitudinal barriers persist regarding people with disabilities, he answered, "Because some people are terrified of getting old or becoming disabled themselves. They're afraid that knowing people with disabilities in normal settings will make them even more uncomfortable about those possibilities." When asked if sensitivity training could be of value in that type of situation, he responded, "It's the *most* important thing businesses can do."[1]

The Americans with Disabilities Act created a mandate to mainstream people with disabilities into millions of America's workplaces. During the application, hiring, and employment stages, information on the ADA and disability in general will be useful to managers and co-workers. Informed and aware managers and employees can generate the acceptance and understanding necessary for the ADA to become successful legislation—the full inclusion of qualified people with disabilities into the nation's work force. This "last great inclusion," as George Will put it, cannot take place through the employment alone of people with disabilities.

A number of employees at a worksite may have little direct contact or experience with a person with a disability or a specific type of disability, such as multiple sclerosis, epilepsy, or cerebral palsy. Co-workers play an important role by creating a work environment that effectively and appropriately interacts with employees with disabilities. For these reasons it is important for employers, human resource managers, and all employees and co-workers to better understand people with disabilities. This is an important key in creating the mutual cooperation and teamwork necessary in any effective business enterprise.

These suggestions can be utilized in creating an awareness program for all employees tailored to the specific needs and objectives of a small or a medium-sized business or a section or division of a company. Among the basics of an awareness program is understanding some of the "do's and don'ts" when interviewing, interacting, communicating, and working with an individual with a disability. These pointers do not apply to all people with disabilities, but they can be the basis for a better understanding and more effective two-way communication. One of the most important concepts is to separate the individual from the disability.

For starters, there are a number of terms that can be derogatory—just as there are a number of disparaging, unkind, sexist, or even hateful terms for members of other religious groups, nationalities, minority groups, and women. As noted earlier, the term "handicap" is derived from a seventeenth-century English game of chance and has been outgrown and discarded. Most people with disabilities consider it antiquated and derogatory.

Federal agencies using "handicapped" in their agency name replaced "handicapped" for the more neutral terms "disabled" and "disability" in the 1980s. For example, beginning in 1947 as the President's Committee on Employment of the Handicapped, this federal agency is now the President's Committee on Employment of People with Disabilities. Other buzzwords for disability such as "physically challenged' are "too cute" according to John Kemp, executive director of the United Cerebral Palsy Associations, Inc.[2] Kemp, an attorney who keeps a busy schedule, is often seen walking hastily from one of his association's offices to another, reading new regulations and signing correspondence. He was born without complete arms or legs and uses four prostheses. He would not describe himself as challenged. Along with "handicapped," phrases such as "afflicted with," "suffering from," "a victim of," and "crippled by," have also been discarded. A person *has* epilepsy, for example, and *is not* afflicted with or suffering from epilepsy. As with John Kemp and millions of other individuals with disabilities, these phrases and adjectives are inappropriate and demeaning.

One of the objectives of the ADA, in terms of creating equal employment opportunity for people with disabilities, is to remove these stereotypes, myths, and baggage-laden terms that tend to both reflect and foster prejudice and discrimination. The International Association of Business Communicators provides an excellent summary of how to interact with people with disabilities:

1. Separate the person from the disability.
2. Recognize that persons with disabilities have rights, among them the right to privacy.
3. Treat people with disabilities with respect.
4. Avoid stereotyping persons with disabilities by occupation or attribute; for example, "that's a disabled job" or "the mail room is the mentally retarded office."[3]

Also, while discrimination in a legal sense may not be taking place, there are of course certain actions by nondisabled people that can be demeaning and certainly inappropriate. Senator Tom Harkin defines discrimination to include actions that are not always overt or thought out. "Discrimination is sometimes the result of prejudice; sometimes it is the result of patronizing attitudes; and still other times it is the result of thoughtlessness or indifference."[4] Employers, human resource managers, supervisors, job interviewers, and co-workers should take this perspective into account during the interview stage and in the future working relationship with persons with disabilities. This is certainly the spirit and intent that underlies the ADA legislation.

THE JOB INTERVIEW

The ADA regulations go far beyond traditional civil rights legislation by spelling out with great specificity what can and cannot be said and done during the interview process to and with people with disabilities. An interview is an opportunity to ask questions and seek answers that will reflect the applicant's or employee's ability to perform the essential functions of the particular job in question, with or without a reasonable accommodation. While in the majority of cases reasonable accommodation is not necessary, if it is needed, it provides in effect a level playing field for people with disabilities.

However, one of the quickest ways to place a barrier between an employer or co-worker and an individual with a disability is to excessively cater to or overreact to a person with a physical or mental impairment. People with disabilities want, and should be afforded, the same courtesies given to people without disabilities, no more and no less.

Creating a "Two-Way Street" in Communication

Interviewers should know how to communicate with people with disabilities and understand that there are some specified limitations to questions and examinations that tend to discriminate against an individual. According to the Society for Human Resource Management, "Since the ADA prohibits certain pre-employment inquiries, such as 'What happened to your arm?' or 'Have you ever had a back problem?', interviewers should be trained to only ask questions about a person's ability to perform the functions of the job in question. Interviewers will also need training on subjects they should avoid during an interview."[5]

In the job interview, the employer, manager, or supervisor who is conducting the interview must refrain from asking specific questions that are phrased in terms of the individual's disability. As EEOC Chairman Kemp stated, "In addition, an employer may not make pre-employment inquiries as to the existence, nature, or severity of an applicant's disability, but may ask questions as to an applicant's ability to perform job-related duties."[6]

Once the existence of a disability has been raised by the person with the disability, however, it does not have to be treated as a taboo subject. The employer can ask the applicant to describe or demonstrate how, with or without reasonable accommodation, the applicant will perform job-related functions. The employer can ask questions in order to determine whether the applicant has the appropriate educational background, employment experience, skills, and licenses necessary to satisfy the prerequisites for the position. An employer cannot require the applicant to take a medical examination before making an employment offer, but the employer can require a medical examination after making a job offer. An employer may condition an offer of employment based on the results of the medical examination, but only if all entering employees in the same job category are subjected to the medical examination.

Creating Awareness with the Interviewer and the Co-Worker

Perhaps the major fault with the term "people with disabilities" is that it does not do justice to the wide range of diversity in America's largest minority group. For the employer, an interview is an important opportunity to learn more about a prospective employee. While each interview is with an individual, and certainly no two persons are the same, there are some pointers for effective communication with people with specific types of disabilities. These strategies can further the vitally important "two-way street" of effective communication between applicant and interviewer.

People Who Use Wheelchairs

People who use wheelchairs can and often do hold physically demanding and stressful jobs. There are as many as one million Americans who use wheelchairs, and they need not be confined to desk jobs. People who use wheelchairs need space for their chairs to enter and exit their specific workplace. The workplace can be modified by simply raising an ordinary desk or worktable on blocks. There are tax deductions available for providing the wheelchair user with specially designed workstations, accessible parking spaces, or rest room facilities.

Do's	Don'ts
Find a wheelchair accessible location for an interview.	Do not make contact with a person's wheelchair unless asked to do so.

If possible, place yourself on the same eye level with the person in a wheelchair.

Do not grab or push a person's wheelchair unless asked to do so.

Assistance may be offered, but don't insist upon it.

Don't be sensitive to words like "running" and "walking."

Keep accessibility in mind. Is the hallway blocked?

Don't use terms like "wheelchairbound," "confined to a wheelchair," or "crippled."

People Who Are Mobility Impaired

Like individuals who use wheelchairs, people who are mobility impaired often have physically demanding jobs. A person with this type of impairment may use a mobility aid, such as a cane, braces, crutches, or artificial legs. There are over 7.7 million people who use some type of mobility aid according to the National Center for Health Statistics. Some of the many famous persons with a mobility impairment include Sarah Bernhardt, Peter Stuyvesant, Henri de Toulouse-Lautrec, and President Woodrow Wilson who was partially paralyzed as the result of a stroke.[7] (For more information on issues relating to persons with mobility impairments, see contributed article by the National Multiple Sclerosis Society, chapter 12.)

Do's

When accompanying a person with a mobility impairment, try to walk alongside the person, not in front.

Assume people who use artificial legs, canes, and crutches can use the stairs in addition to elevators, unless they inform you otherwise.

Be aware of distances. Even a two to three block walk to a lunch interview could be tiresome to some individuals with a mobility impairment.

Don'ts

Don't use terms such as "deformed," etc.

Don't move someone's crutches, walker, cane, or other mobility aid without permission.

Don't make assumptions about what a person with a mobility impairment or other type of physical disability can do or cannot do. People with disabilities are the best judge of their own capabilities.

People Who Are Blind or Visually Impaired

A legally blind person has less than 10 percent of normal vision. "Visually impaired" is the generic term preferred by some individuals to refer to all degrees of vision loss. Relatively inexpensive accommodations for blind people in the workplace include raised lettering or braille symbols on signs and elevator buttons. Famous persons in history who were blind include Homer, Louis Braille, and Thomas Gore, one of the first senators from Oklahoma. Famous persons with a visual impairment include President Andrew Jackson, Lord Nelson, Charles Dickens, James Thurber, and Joseph Pulitzer. (For more information on reasonable accommodations for people who are blind or visually impaired, see chapter 9.)

Do's	Don'ts
Use verbal cues extensively in giving directions and be as specific as possible in giving directions ("the door is ten steps directly in front of you").	Resist the temptation to speak louder or slower.
Identify yourself and others present.	Don't pet or distract a guide dog unless the owner has given permission.
Cue a handshake (by saying "I'd like to shake your hand").	Don't leave without saying that you are leaving.
Ask whether the visually impaired person would like to take your elbow (if you need to walk down a series of corridors, and point out obstacles).	
Use the words "look" and "see" freely: there are no reasonable alternatives.	
Be prepared to read aloud information that is written, or ask the person if a reader is needed.	

People Who Are Deaf or Hearing Impaired

When speaking with a person who is deaf or hearing impaired, face the person directly. Not all people who are hearing impaired can lip-read, but many are proficient. If a sign language interpreter is involved in the conversation, speak directly to the person who is hearing impaired, not the interpreter. The interpreter is not a participant in the job interview or conversation. If you cannot easily understand the person with a hearing impairment, do not be afraid to ask the person being interviewed to repeat.

Assisting in accommodating individuals with hearing impairments may be no more complicated than turning a receptionist's desk to face the door. A variety of devices are available for telephones to amplify hearing and speech. Devices that flash lights instead of ring can be provided for telephones and alarm systems. People who are deaf or have a hearing or speaking impairment use telephones called TDDs (telecommunications device for the deaf) or TDYs. Under the ADA, telecommunications relay systems make it possible for deaf and hearing-impaired persons to communicate, using a TDD, with a hearing person using a telephone. In fact, the telephone was originally invented for use by the deaf—Alexander Graham Bell was working on an assistive device for his wife—over one hundred years ago. (For more information on reasonable accommodations for the deaf and hearing impaired, see chapter 9, and for information on the impact of the ADA on the deaf see contributed article by I. King Jordan, chapter 12.)

Do's	Don'ts
When speaking to someone who is hearing impaired, face the person directly.	Do not shout. Use a normal tone of voice.
Keep your hands from covering your mouth when talking.	Do not resort to the use of monosyllabic words, but do not use wild gestures either.
Use meaningful facial expressions and gestures while you are talking.	Do not create a silhouette effect by positioning yourself so that you are directly in front of a harsh light or window. Your face will be difficult to see.
Investigate the availability of sign language interpreters for future reference, if needed.	

People with Epilepsy

There are over two million Americans with epilepsy. The majority of Americans with epilepsy, 80 percent, control their seizure disorder with prescription medication.[8] People with epilepsy have the same range of intelligence as any other segment of society, and studies by the Epilepsy Foundation of America (EFA) reveal that people with epilepsy have *fewer* sick days than the average worker. Employers who deny employment to an individual with a seizure disorder "must establish that, in light of the employee or job applicant's work and medical history, employment of that individual would pose a reasonable probability of substantial harm."[9]

According to a 1991 EFA report, "It is not enough [for the employer] to demonstrate that the individual is likely to suffer another seizure. The employer must also demonstrate a connection between the likelihood of another seizure and likelihood that substantial harm will occur on the job to the employee or others."[10] Because the majority of people with epilepsy effectively control seizures, the possibility of an individual being a threat to oneself or others is insignificant, especially given the fact that for people with epilepsy "absenteeism and accidents are no greater than in the work force in general."[11]

A number of people with a seizure disorder experience a warning called an "aura," which can caution the advent of a potential seizure. Those who successfully control their seizures with prescription medications usually have a drivers license. Most people with a seizure disorder would probably agree that the way members of society sometimes react to a person with epilepsy is often worse than the seizure disorder itself. Despite these attitudinal barriers there have been a number of people with epilepsy who have made their mark in the historical record: Alexander the Great, Fyodor Dostoyevsky, Louis Hector Berlioz, Peter I. Tchaikovsky, and first lady Ida McKinley, wife of President William McKinley.

As long ago as 400 B.C., Hippocrates repeated the popular folklore myth that epilepsy was a "visitation of the gods," but he correctly suspected that it was a disorder of the brain.[12] Over 2,300 years later in an age of medical advances and breakthroughs, when medicine has established that epilepsy is a neurological disorder and not a disease, American society is beginning to overcome the superstitions, stigma, and prejudice long associated with epilepsy.

The Training and Placement Program (TAPS), run by the EFA and its affiliates around the country, has assisted over 12,000 individuals with epilepsy find employment.[13] Individuals with a seizure disorder have successfully utilized state and federal antidiscrimination laws to obtain jobs once considered off limits, such as employment as nurses, welders, and police officers. As a result of expanded training and employment opportunities, people with epilepsy are working as physicians, engineers, managers, administrative assistants, urban planners, government officials, teachers, and professors. People with a seizure disorder have also become professional players on major league baseball, basketball, and hockey teams, as well as leading movie actors and actresses.[14]

Do's	Don'ts
Jill Rodriguez has a seizure disorder.	Jill Rodriguez has fits. Do not use the term "fits."
Peter Williams has epilepsy.	Peter Williams is epileptic. Do not use the term "epileptic."

People with Mental Retardation

The vast majority of individuals with mental retardation, nine out of ten, have a mild form of mental retardation. There are more than six million children and adults with mental retardation in the United States, and the vast majority of people with mental retardation are employable. However, according to The Arc (formerly the Association for Retarded Citizens of the United States), when people with mental retardation have been able to achieve employment, it has been limited to "entry level, low-paying, no benefit jobs involving what has traditionally been called the three 'Fs,' food (typically fast food restaurants), filth (janitorial jobs), and flowers (nurseries or landscaping)."[15]

There are a number of myths and misunderstandings about people with mental retardation. Employees with mental retardation have been found to be careful in their work, stable, dependable, and hard working, with no increase in the rate of accidents or in the cost of insurance rates, according to the President's Committee on Mental Retardation.[16] People with mental retardation have proven themselves in jobs that include a range of responsibility and technical proficiency, such as working as an ambulance attendant or managing photocopying and mail room activities for a small company.

Alan Abeson, executive director of The Arc, believes that the ADA is an important opportunity for people with mental retardation to find secure employment in a full range of jobs:

Fortunately, eliminating discrimination against people with mental retardation as called for in Title I of the ADA is not beginning in the absence of a body of experience and know how. In fact where workers with mental retardation have been given opportunity, there now exists a solid although too brief a history of capability and achievement. Today, the stories of many men and women with mental retardation obtaining and succeeding as workers are legion. . . . While these workers tended to be those with mild mental retardation, in more recent years with the expansion of education, training, and supported programs, a whole new population of people with more significant mental retardation, who formerly spent their time at home or day activity centers or resided in large congregate institutions, have also become successfully employed.[17]

The Arc has developed a partial list of the types of jobs in which workers with mental retardation have proven themselves: animal care-takers, laundry workers, maintenance workers, library assistants, card punch operators, mail clerks, photocopy machine operators, clerical aides, office machine operators, carpenters, medical technicians, store clerks, messengers, cooks, engineering aides, printers, factory workers,

A young man with mild mental retardation employed as a forklift operator. Photograph by Rick Berkobien, The Arc.

grocery clerks, and sales personnel. The Arc's National Employment and Training Program, funded by the Department of Labor since 1966, has assisted more than 45,000 workers with mental retardation locate and maintain employment.[18] (For more information on the impact of the ADA on persons with mental retardation, see contributed article by Alan Abeson, chapter 12.)

Do's	Don'ts
Use understandable language, shorter sentences, and basic sentence structure.	You don't have to speak louder to be understood.
If it is necessary to describe the condition, use the term "mental retardation."	Do not describe the person or condition as "retarded."
Allow ample time to learn. A "job coach" may be necessary during the training period, free of charge to the employer. A reasonable accommodation, such as job restructuring, may be useful in a situation where an individual can perform, for example, 10 of 12 essential functions of a job. By having another employee take on the two job functions, and switch other functions, the individual with a disability is accommodated.	The capabilities of individuals with mental retardation are diverse. Do not prejudge the level of skills or abilities of an individual with mental retardation.

People with a Speech Impairment

There are an estimated 2.1 million people in the United States who can hear but have difficulty with expressive communication.[19] Stuttering, which is not a nervous or personality disorder, is one of the most common forms of speech impairment, affecting 1 percent of the adult population. Among the more notable persons in history who stuttered are Aristotle, Charles Darwin, Clara Barton, and Winston Churchill.

Other communication impairments can result from disabilities, such as cerebral palsy, mental retardation, traumatic brain injury, and stroke. Speech impairments can also be caused by specific neuromuscular disorders, such as amyotrophic lateral sclerosis (also known as Lou Gehrig's disease), dystonia, Huntington's disease, multiple sclerosis, muscular dystrophy, and cancer of the larynx. To express themselves to others, people with communication disabilities may use an interpreter or a message board, or use telecommunications, such as a TDD. (For more information on reasonable accommodation for persons with a speech impairment, see chapter 9.)

Do's	Don'ts
Talk as you would to any person.	Don't pretend to understand when you do not.
Be patient.	Unless you know the person well, don't attempt to finish sentences.
Provide your undivided attention and maintain normal eye contact.	If a person is stuttering, don't say "relax" or "slow down."
If you don't understand, ask to have the message repeated.	

People with Mental Illness or a History of Mental Illness

One in four Americans will have some form of mental illness during their lifetime, according to the Department of Education. *The Washington Post* reported, "Of the estimated three million Americans who suffer from serious mental illness, only about 10 percent hold jobs."[20] However, many people who have had a mental illness or control a mental illness with prescription medication are in America's work force.

What is important from the standpoint of people with mental illness who are willing and able to work is that the ADA represents a significant breakthrough. In a front-page article in the *New York Times* in 1991, it was reported that the ADA will provide "far-reaching employment rights to the mentally ill, requiring most businesses to alter hiring practices and workplace conditions."[21] The ADA prohibits an employer from asking a job applicant whether the applicant has a history of mental illness or if the applicant is mentally ill. People with a mental illness have very frequently been fearful of making the full truth known to an employer for fear of either not getting a job or losing a job. While people with a mental illness may continue to not reveal their past or current condition to an employer, the ADA does provide new protections. Mental illness is a disability and discrimination on the basis of a disability is against the law.

One of the first people to work as an advocate for the mentally ill and to confront this issue was Clifford Beers in the late nineteenth and twentieth century. Beers, who as a young man learned to cope with a mental illness, best sums up the problem of a job applicant with a history of a mental illness attempting to land a new job. In his autobiography, *A Mind That Found Itself*, published in 1908, Beers reveals much of what is still true about people who have overcome mental illness and are seeking employment.

Beers wrote, "Though a former patient receives personal consideration, he finds it difficult to obtain employment. No fair-minded man can find fault with that condition of affairs, for an inherent dread of insanity leads to distrust of one who has had a mental breakdown. Nevertheless, this attitude is mistaken." Beers obtained employment with a "broad-minded" man in banking. Beers spoke of his work "as one of those rare compensations which Fate sometimes bestows upon those who survive unusual adversity."[22]

Nearly a half century after Beers, as the result of pharmaceutical research in the 1950s, new prescription drugs have become available that can treat and control a number of types of mental illness. The development of these prescription drugs has had the effect of unshackling many persons with mental illness for the first time. The actress and author Patty Duke, who has overcome a disability, manic depression, is one of many tens of thousands of individuals with a mental illness or who have overcome a mental illness, who lead very useful lives and have successful careers.[23] Now that medical science has made a number of revolutionary breakthroughs in the treatment and control of mental illness, the Americans with Disabilities Act provides far-reaching employment rights for qualified individuals with mental illness or a history of mental illness in American society.

Do's	Don'ts
Jack Smith has a history of mental illness. Jack Smith has been (or is currently being) treated for a mental illness.	Jack Smith is crazy, etc.
Talk to the individual as you would anyone else.	

People Who Have Cerebral Palsy

Public awareness of cerebral palsy and the ability to overcome the most severe cases of this neuromuscular disorder was heightened by the movie *My Left Foot*, based on the autobiography of the Irish artist Christy Brown. Cerebral palsy may affect motor ability and/or speech, but it does not affect intelligence. The severity and functional effects of the disability vary from person to person. Some people with cerebral palsy, who have difficulty with speech, find it more effective to communicate in writing, by typing, or by using communication boards or electronic devices. People with cerebral palsy work in all types of positions, for example, as writers and editors, supervisors and managers in government, vice-presidents of banks, ministers, bookkeepers, physicians, and computer-assisted drafters, to name a few.[24]

Do's	Don'ts
Gwen Peterson has cerebral palsy.	Gwen Peterson is "lame" or "spastic."
If an individual's speech is difficult to understand, do not be afraid to ask that a statement be repeated.	

People with a Learning Disability

Learning disabilities are disorders that affect an individual's ability to learn language skills. In some instances they can interfere with effective muscle control in speech and writing, or affect a person's sense of orientation and the ability to concentrate. Perhaps the most well-known learning disability is dyslexia, which affects an individual's capacity to understand printed or written words. There are a number of types of learning disabilities, and learning disabilities are thought to affect over 10 percent of the population.

Different types of learning disabilities affect specific types of skills and functions, such as reading, writing, spelling, listening, thinking, speaking, and doing arithmetic. People with learning disabilities, although they may be average or above in intelligence, may have difficulty with direction, coordination, spatial orientation, or distinguishing left from right. Some people with a learning disability may be clumsy and awkward. Scientific researchers have not been able to find the causes of specific learning disabilities but have linked a number of factors, including minor brain or nerve damage, accidents, childhood illness, and poor nutrition.[25] Famous persons with a learning disability include Thomas Alva Edison, Albert Einstein, General George S. Patton, and actors Cher and Tom Cruise.

Do's	Don'ts
For many people with a learning disability some types of learning may be difficult.	Do not mistakenly form an opinion that a person with a learning disability has an "attitude problem."
People with learning disabilities are not illiterate and understand what is being discussed.	Do not call an individual with a learning disability "stupid" or "dumb." People with a learning disability are not mentally retarded.
	Do not use timed exams, unless speed in performing essential job functions is necessary and is a purpose of the test.

People Who Are HIV Positive or Have AIDS

The Americans with Disabilities Act specifically identifies people who are HIV (human immunodeficiency virus) positive or who have AIDS as individuals with disabilities, and they are covered by the same protections as persons with any other type of disability. The vast majority of the estimated one million Americans who are infected with the AIDS virus are of working age. According to Chai R. Feldblum, a visiting professor of law at the Georgetown University Law Center and one of the drafters of the ADA legislation:

People with HIV disease (which includes individuals who have any form of human immunodeficiency virus [HIV] illness, from asymptomatic HIV infection to full-blown AIDS) are included within the first prong definition of disability. People with HIV disease have been covered under the Rehabilitation Act for years. In order to receive protection under the [ADA] law, such individuals, just like people with any other disability, may not pose a "direct threat" to the health or safety of others.[26]

An analysis of employment discrimination of workers with AIDS in the *Wall Street Journal* stated, "Attorneys agree that under the Americans with Disabilities Act . . . it will be illegal for most companies to fire or even reassign an employee solely because the person is HIV positive. But many states have had such laws for years, and HIV positive workers still face job discrimination."[27] The *Wall Street Journal* article points out that the U.S. government and companies that receive federal funds also cannot discriminate. For people with AIDS, "The Americans with Disabilities Act will extend those protections."[28] According to Jim Graham, director of Washington, D.C.'s Whitman-Walker Clinic, "There's a difference between being infected with HIV, which is asymptomatic, and having AIDS. For virtually everyone who is HIV-infected and without symptoms can work as anyone else for up to 10 years after being infected."[29]

The Public Health Service's Centers for Disease Control and Prevention (CDC) has stated, "There is no reason to avoid an infected person in ordinary social contact."[30] AIDS is not spread through casual contact in the workplace. There are three ways adults can become infected with AIDS, according to the Public Health Service: sexual contact with someone who is infected, sharing intravenous needles with an infected person, and by receiving infected blood products or transfusions. In December 1992 the CDC began a national AIDS in the workplace awareness program, Business Responds to AIDS, to better inform employers and employees about AIDS in the work environment.

The *Wall Street Journal* stated that a "critical but unanswered question in discrimination cases is whether courts will exempt certain jobs, mainly in the health care field, from the act. The law doesn't apply if the worker's illness poses a significant threat to others and if the employer can't find a reasonable way of eliminating that risk."[31]

Surveys taken over the last several years indicate that 68 percent of business employers have not seen any need to establish specific policies regarding AIDS in the workplace.[32] But for the manager who has not worked with employees who are HIV infected before, there may be a number of unanswered questions. Charles J. Nau is senior counsel to Syntex Laboratories Inc. and has served as a member of the National Leadership Coalition on AIDS:

The several challenges presented to employers by the ADA will be particularly seen in the context of HIV-infected employees. . . . [Those who are] HIV-positive, or recently diagnosed with milder infections concomitant with an ARC [AIDS related complex] diagnosis, might well appear to be fully healthy. Yet the respective rights of such persons under the ADA (and more importantly, the employers' obligations toward them) would be precisely the same as those owing to employees more obviously disabled. . . . It is important, then, that employers establish policies which allow employees to easily come forward and self-identify as regards their disability status. Because of the special stigma which often attaches to AIDS and HIV, this will be a difficult goal to achieve, making it all the more important that managers and human resource personnel be trained regarding the importance of strict confidentiality and sensitivity.[33]

Do's	**Don'ts**
Shake hands as you would with anyone, without fear of becoming infected. Respect the applicant or employee as any other person.	Just as with other types of disabilities, it is illegal to ask whether an applicant or employee is HIV positive or has AIDS.
Become familiar or assist in developing a worksite education and prevention program that includes supervisor training, employee education, and education in the community.[34]	

AN INFORMED WORKPLACE

The employment and advancement of people with disabilities in the work force and the fostering of a better understanding of people with disabilities has been a central objective of Bernard Posner, who is a consultant to the National Organization on Disability and was executive director of the President's Committee on Employment of People with Disabilities from 1972 to 1985. Posner's experience and leadership in advancing the employment aspirations of people with disabilities provides a perspective on the importance of an informed and sensitized workplace:

For years the President's committee on Employment of People with Disabilities has been trying, through a number of different voluntary programs, to inform employers and sensitize human resource people in businesses large and small. We had some successes. But the Americans with Disabilities Act creates an entirely new focus by making the employment of people with disabilities, not just "good business," or the "nice thing to do," but the law of the land. It is more than a law. It is a means of encouraging employers to inform, educate, and sensitize their staffs about the ADA and about employees and applicants with disabilities.[35]

An informed workplace is in many ways a cornerstone to the advancement of two of the most central principles of the ADA: providing people with disabilities with the opportunity to become full participants in the American economy as employees, consumers, and taxpayers *and* to be included as full members of American society. Reflecting on the potential of the ADA beyond the workplace, Posner said, "One of the most important results to come out of all this is the achievement of a better understanding and better communication between co-workers and people with disabilities in the workplace . . . indeed, between this entire country and the disabled people who live in it."[36]

CHAPTER 9

The Age of Reason—Reasonable Accommodation

Reasonable accommodation—probably the two most important words in the Americans with Disabilities Act. The concept of reasonable accommodation, while being one of the most central principles in the Americans with Disabilities Act, is one of the most poorly understood. A reasonable accommodation is an action by an employer, mutually determined with an applicant or employee with a disability, that assists that individual in performing the essential functions of a specific job. For the employer, a reasonable accommodation includes a range of services, equipment, or modified policies that an employer must provide to a *qualified* applicant or employee with a disability, if it does not cause an undue hardship on the employer.

For an individual with a disability to be protected under the employment provisions of the ADA, including reasonable accommodation, that individual must be *qualified*. (For the definition of "qualified individual with disability," see chapter 4.) The term "reasonable accommodation" is not new; it was first used in the Rehabilitation Act of 1973, when it applied to the federal government and programs and contracts in the private sector funded by the federal government. These federally funded programs and contracts affect only about 1 percent of the economy. The provision of reasonable accommodation is what makes the ADA unique in comparison to other laws enforced by the Equal Employment Opportunity Commission. As a result of the ADA, reasonable accommodation is now applied to almost the entire private sector economy.

The EEOC final regulations define reasonable accommodation as "any change in the work environment or in the way things are customarily done that enables an individual with a disability to enjoy equal employment opportunities."[1]

The underlying goal of reasonable accommodation is to create a level playing field where qualified people with disabilities have the same opportunity to perform essential job functions as persons without disabilities. Most reasonable accommodations do not require costly renovations but may involve shifting schedules for an employee, changing or modifying work duties, modifying equipment, or acquiring assistive devices. A highly motivated worker with low absenteeism is a valuable worker, and a reasonable accommodation is like a tool that assists that worker to produce and perform well on the job.

Richard C. Douglas brought his corporate career experience to his position as executive director of the President's Committee on Employment of People with Disabilities. He summed up the many ways in which reasonable accommodation can be implemented in the workplace:

The goal of making reasonable accommodations is to enable individuals with disabilities to reach their full potential as employees, as taxpayers, and as users of services in the marketplace. There are many aspects of reasonable accommodation, in which the use of adaptive technology plays a highly publicized but relatively limited role. Use of technology by skilled people has increased the potential of millions of workers, both disabled and non-disabled, but adjustments in work schedules and flexibility in the manner of doing a job are equally important. The Job Accommodation Network, a clearinghouse of information established by the President's Committee, emphasizes practical rather than theoretical accommodation at the worksite or in places of public use.[2]

CREATING A LEVEL PLAYING FIELD

Reasonable accommodations cover a broad range of modifications in the work environment, from equipment to modified work schedules. Studies indicate that most qualified individuals with disabilities *do not* need a reasonable accommodation in order to perform their jobs. When it is needed and does not pose an undue hardship on an employer, a reasonable accommodation can make a significant difference for the applicant or worker by creating a level playing field. An example of the level playing field principle is when an employer, such as a hospital, provides a modified schedule for one of its nurses who has epilepsy. The nurses in the hospital work a rotating shift of 7:00 A.M. to 3:00 P.M., 11:00 A.M. to 7:00 P.M., and 4:00 P.M. to 11:00 P.M.. Because the nurse with epilepsy, who normally has good control of her seizure disorder with prescription medication, can experience a seizure due to dramatic changes in her sleep cycle, a reasonable accommodation could be made by her employer to allow her a steady work schedule of 7:00 A.M. to 3:00 P.M.

In another example of reasonable accommodation, a young man who is an applicant for a position that requires taking a written examination, informs the interviewer that he has dyslexia. Because of the young man's disability, written tests do not accurately reflect his skills. The interviewer

Table 9.1
The Ten Types of Reasonable Accommodation

1. Making facilities accessible and usable, creating a modified workplace
2. Job restructuring
3. Modified work schedules
4. Flexible leave policies
5. Reassignment to a vacant position
6. Acquisition or modification of equipment and devices, such as assistive devices
7. Adjusting and modifying examinations, training materials, and policies
8. Providing qualified readers
9. Providing qualified interpreters
10. Other accommodations

SOURCE: Equal Employment Opportunity Commission

tells the applicant that the test will be read aloud to him and not timed, as a form of reasonable accommodation.

In a final example, a woman who is an electrical engineer and uses a wheelchair has just been hired by a firm. All areas of the firm including her office are accessible except the conference room, which has a four inch step up from the hallway. Her employer agrees to build a ramp leading from the hallway to the conference room as a reasonable accommodation.

The difference that reasonable accommodation can make in these three instances is significant. In the first case, the nurse can continue to work without compromising the control of her seizure disorder. In the second case, the young man with dyslexia is provided with a reasonable accommodation to the written examination, allowing him a fair test of his skills and abilities. In the third case, an employer has modified the workplace as a reasonable accommodation, providing the new employee with access to the firm's conference room. By creating a level playing field, the provision of reasonable accommodation is a key factor in enabling a qualified individual with a disability to continue with a job, start a new job, or when applying for a job, to be tested in an equitable manner.

What Is a Reasonable Accommodation

The EEOC further defines a reasonable accommodation under three conditions:

For the Applicant. Modifications or adjustments to a job application process that enable a qualified applicant with a disability to be considered for a position such a qualified applicant desires.

For the Applicant and Employee. Modifications or adjustments to the work environment, or to the manner or circumstances under which the position held or desired is customarily performed that enable a qualified individual with a disability to perform the essential functions of that position.

For the Employee. Modifications or adjustments that enable an [employer's] employee with a disability to enjoy equal benefits and privileges of employment as are enjoyed by its other similarly situated employees without disabilities.[3]

Some Principles of Reasonable Accommodation

According to the EEOC, which developed the ADA employment regulations and is responsible for enforcing them, these are the overriding principles governing reasonable accommodation:

1. A reasonable accommodation must be an effective accommodation.

2. The reasonable accommodation obligation applies only to accommodations that reduce barriers to employment related to a person's disability.

3. A reasonable accommodation need not be the best accommodation available, as long as it is effective for the purpose.

4. An employer is not required to provide an accommodation that is primarily for personal use.

5. Equipment or devices that assist a person in daily activities on and off the job are considered personal items that an employer is not required to provide. (In some instances, however, equipment or devices that would be considered personal may be required as an accommodation if it is specifically designed or required to meet job-related rather than personal needs. An example would be an employer who might be required to provide an employee who has a visual impairment with specially designed glasses for use with a computer monitor.)

6. If an employer can show that the cost of the accommodation would impose an undue hardship, the employer would still be required to provide the accommodation if the funding is available from another source, such as a state vocational rehabilitation agency or the applicant or employee who needs the accommodation.

Reasonable Accommodation Begins with an Accessible Work Environment

The ADA provides that employers should make reasonable accommodations in order that facilities are accessible to and usable by applicants and employees with disabilities. However, the manner and the degree of accessibility and utilization for people with disabilities depends on whether the facility is used as a worksite by a private employer, a state or local government, or a place of public accommodation, such as a bank, a retail store, or a restaurant. These entities are covered by different sections of the Americans with Disabilities Act, Titles I, II, and III, respectively.

An employer's obligation under Title I of the ADA is to provide an individual employee with a disability with access to all facilities used by employees and needed equipment or modifications to perform the essential functions of the job. According to the EEOC, "An employer must provide this access unless it would cause an undue hardship."[4] In addition, a private employer under Title I is not required to make its existing facilities accessible until a particular applicant or employee with a disability needs an accommodation, and then the modifications should meet the disabled individual's work needs.

Under Title II of the ADA, state and local governments have the obligation to provide "program accessibility" in their programs and procedures, as well as in their facilities. These responsibilities differ from their obligations as employers under Title I. According to the EEOC, "Title II requires that these governments operate each service, program or activity in existing facilities so that, when viewed in its entirety, it is readily accessible to and usable by a person with disabilities, unless this would cause a 'fundamental alteration' in the nature of the program or service, or would result in 'undue financial and administrative burdens.' "[5]

Under Title III of the ADA, however, it is required that places of public accommodation "make their goods and services accessible generally, to all people with disabilities."[6] Under Title III, existing buildings and facilities of public accommodation must be made accessible by removing architectural or communications barriers that are structural in nature, if this is "readily achievable." If this is not readily achievable, services must be provided to people with disabilities in some alternative manner that *is* readily achievable.[7]

The Ten Types of Reasonable Accommodation

1. Making Facilities Accessible and Usable

A workplace should become a *modified workplace* by "making the existing facilities used by an employee in general, readily accessible to and usable by individuals with disabilities."[8] According to the EEOC interpretive guidance, reasonable accommodations include modifications to nonwork areas that must be accessible for a disabled employee to perform essential job functions and related activities. These nonwork areas of the job include break rooms, lunch rooms, training rooms, and rest rooms.[9]

Example 1: A young woman who uses a wheelchair has just obtained employment as a public information specialist in the state office of a national association. As a reasonable accommodation to the woman, the

Walt Shinault, who has quadraplegia, is a financial consultant with Merrill Lynch in Jackson, Mississippi. He is shown here using a mouthstick to enter data on his computer. Courtesy of the National Easter Seal Society.

worksite has been modified by placing blocks under the legs of her desk and installing grab bars in the women's rest room.

Example 2: A young man with cerebral palsy needs to keep his hands free while using the telephone in an accounting firm. A headset attached to the telephone is provided to him by his employer as a reasonable accommodation.

2. Job Restructuring

The Senate Committee on Labor and Human Resources defines restructuring a job as "modifying a job so that a person with a disability can perform the essential function of the position. Barriers to performance may be eliminated by removing nonessential elements, redelegating assignments, exchanging assignments with another employee, and redesigning procedures for task accomplishment."[10] The EEOC has noted that job restructuring as a reasonable accommodation may involve reallocating or redistributing the marginal functions of a job. However, an employer is not required to reallocate essential functions of a job as a reasonable accommodation.[11]

Example 1: At the New England Medical Center in Boston, a human resource manager interviews an individual who wants a full-time job as a file clerk. There are no full-time filing positions, but the human resource manager restructures work in several departments, creating a full-time filing position that encompasses several departments.[12]

Example 2: A man who works in the accounts payable section of a department store has sustained a serious back injury. Part of his job is to transfer computer documents to another office by walking up two flights of stairs. Having another employee make the transfer of computer documents each day is considered a reasonable accommodation.

Example 3: A young man is a clerk in a real estate office. Part of his job on the way to work each day is to pick up the morning mail at the post office on the other side of town. The young man has a mobility disorder that increasingly makes it difficult for him to pick up the mail at the post office. The employer decides, as a reasonable accommodation, that she can wait for the afternoon mail delivery and that the early morning mail pickup is not necessary.

3. Modified Work Schedules

Part-time or modified work schedules can be a no-cost way of accommodation. Some people with disabilities are denied employment opportunities because they cannot adhere to a standard work schedule. As stated by the EEOC, "An employer should consider modification of a regular work week schedule as a reasonable accommodation unless this would cause an undue hardship. Modified work schedules may include flexibility in work hours or the work week, or part-time work where this will not be an undue hardship."[13]

Example 1: A graphic artist in her thirties who has multiple sclerosis frequently becomes fatigued in the late afternoon. As a form of reasonable accommodation, her employer changes her work schedule to 9:00 A.M. to 5:00 P.M..

Example 2: A mail clerk in his forties who has diabetes is granted greater flexibility in his work schedule as a reasonable accommodation so he can take short breaks for food.

Example 3: A young man is assistant manager of a convenience store. He has experienced a significant loss in night vision and is unable to drive a car at night. As a reasonable accommodation the employer reassigns his schedule to the day. As noted by the Senate Committee on Labor and Human Resources, "Allowing constant shifts or modified work schedules are examples of a means to accommodate the individual with a disability to do the same job as a non-disabled person."[14]

4. Flexible Leave Policies

Flexible leave policies should be considered as a reasonable accommodation when qualified employees with disabilities require time off from work due to their disabilities. According to the EEOC, an employer is not required to provide additional paid leave as an accommodation but should consider allowing the use of accrued leave, advanced leave, or leave without pay, where this will not cause an undue hardship.[15]

Example 1: A young woman who has spina bifida and uses a wheelchair requests leave for one hour each week for physical therapy.

Example 2: A man who has cancer that is in remission requests leave for two hours, twice a month, for three months in order to receive needed chemotherapy treatments.

5. Reassignment to a Vacant Position

As the Senate Committee on Labor and Human Resources report stated, "If an employee, because of disability, can no longer perform the essential functions of the job that she or he has held, a transfer to another vacant job for which the person is qualified may prevent the employee from being out of work and the employer from losing a valuable worker."[16] An employer may reassign an individual to a lower paying position if there are no accommodations that would enable the employee to remain in the current position and there are no vacant equivalent positions.

An employer is not required to maintain the reassigned individual at the salary of the higher graded position.[17] Reassignment may not be used to limit, segregate, or otherwise discriminate against individuals with disabilities by forcing reassignments to undesirable positions or to designated offices or facilities.[18] Reassignment as a reasonable accommodation is not available to an applicant.

Example 1: A warehouse worker injures his back lifting boxes, and there are no other possible accommodations or devices available to assist him with his job. The employer must consider him for the next available job that he is qualified for, including providing the warehouse worker with training, but does not have to give the warehouse worker that job. The warehouse worker may be offered the new job, but it is up to the worker to take a pay cut if the new position has a lower salary.

Example 2: A salesperson in a department store stands on her legs most of the day. As the result of an automobile accident, a chronic knee injury now makes long periods of standing uncomfortable. Her manager transfers her to a different job in the customer convenience office, which involves significantly less standing.

6. Acquisition or Modification of Equipment and Devices

Employers are required to provide a qualified applicant or employee with modified equipment or an assistive device if it poses no undue hardship on the employer. While the term "assistive device" is not used in the ADA legislation, the term has had widespread use in government, science, and industry to describe both low- and high-tech equipment and devices that have been developed and designed for use by people with disabilities.

Example 1: Reasonable accommodation in this area includes an amplified telephone for a person who is hearing impaired or a voice synthesizer attached to a computer for a blind person or an individual with a learning disability who has difficulty reading.

Example 2: A young woman who is a computer programmer is hearing impaired and can use a telephone but needs both a visual and an audible alert for the phone. Because she spends so much time using the computer, she is paged to the phone by a visual signaling device on the monitor of her computer. This will be a reasonable accommodation unless the installation of this system creates an undue hardship for the employer.

7. Adjusting and Modifying Examinations, Training Materials, and Policies

An employer may be required to modify, adjust, or make other reasonable accommodations in the methods and administration of tests and training in order to provide equal employment opportunities for qualified applicants and employees with disabilities, according to the EEOC.[19] Accommodations may be needed to assure that tests or examinations measure the actual *ability* of an individual to perform job functions, rather than reflecting limitations caused by a disability.[20] Equal Employment Opportunity Commission regulations provide that modifications or adjustments should be made to the job application process so as to create a level playing field for the qualified applicant with a disability.

During the employment testing process, individuals who have a visual or a learning disability may be read the test. For individuals with limited use of their hands, as in some cases of cerebral palsy or amputation, a recorder may write down the answers to the test. There is some flexibility with regard to reasonable accommodation in testing. A person who is hearing impaired and can lip-read should be tested in proximity to the tester and be able to clearly see the person giving the test. In addition, the tester should be informed beforehand so that the tester is facing the applicant to facilitate lip-reading.

Example 1: A man who is blind is required to take an employment application test to be considered for a particular job. The human resource manager makes arrangements to have the test read to him as a reasonable accommodation.

Example 2: A woman with multiple sclerosis is a candidate for a position with an advertising firm. She needs to take a test but has limited control of her hands. A reasonable accommodation is made to have an individual from the human resource management office write down the applicant's test answers.

8. Providing Qualified Readers

The ADA legislation provides for "qualified readers, taped texts, or other effective methods of making visually delivered materials available to individuals with visual impairments."[21] An alternative to a reader is a reading machine, and there are computer systems that have voice output from a computer disk. For more information contact the National Federation for the Blind or state commission for the blind. (See the appendix.)

Example: A woman who is blind is employed as a counselor for a city-sponsored graduate equivalency program for young adults who never finished high school. As a reasonable accommodation, a member of the staff reads her mail and other print materials for one half-hour each day.

9. Providing Qualified Interpreters

To accommodate individuals who are hearing impaired and communicate using American Sign Language, or need an oral interpreter, professional interpreters are available on a contractual basis. Hearing-impaired individuals and their employers or supervisors should develop a plan to ensure that interpreter services are available when necessary. Interpreters should be available on site for interpreting at meetings, conferences, and training courses. According to the National Center for Access Unlimited, the fees for interpreters range from $25 to $40 per hour with a two-hour minimum fee.[22] The ADA legislation provides definitions of an interpreter and reader and other methods for making materials available to persons with sensory disabilities.

The ADA legislation provides for "qualified interpreters or other effective methods of making aurally delivered materials available to individuals with hearing impairments."[23] Sign language interpreters can use American Sign Language or other varieties of signed English. Information on fees for interpreters is available from state vocational rehabilitation agencies.

10. Other Accommodations

The ADA regulations do not require employers to obtain the services of personal attendants. However, the EEOC interpretive guidelines recommend the use of personal assistants, when necessary, if it does not create an undue hardship for the employer. According to the EEOC, "Providing personal assistants, such as a page turner for an employee with no hands or a travel attendant to act as a sighted guide to assist a blind employee on occasional business trips, may also be a reasonable accommodation."[24]

How an Assistive Device Can Make a Difference

For people with disabilities, reasonable accommodation often means being able to use assistive technology in their daily jobs. Assistive devices such as eyeglasses, speaker telephones, and TV remote control are used by persons with and without disabilities every day. Technology is continually producing new state-of-the-art assistive devices that provide convenience in everyday life, but with such devices people with disabilities are able to overcome barriers in the workplace. In 1990 over 13 million Americans were using assistive devices to overcome a physical impairment. Lawrence A. Scadden, a former acting director of the National Institute on Disability and Rehabilitation Research, who conducts research on high-technology assistive devices for people with disabilities for the Electronic Industries Foundation, has stated:

Assistive devices are tools. Like all other tools, they increase the worker's productivity, independence, strength, or they reduce the energy needed to perform a task. All workers have used tools. . . . Persons with disabilities may need different tools than their peers, but these tools also permit them to be productive. When employers provide qualified employees the tools needed to improve performance, they are making reasonable accommodations. Similarly, employers can accommodate employees who have disabilities by providing appropriate environments, schedules, and tools that make them fully productive workers.[25]

The TDD (telecommunications device for the deaf) is an excellent example of how assistive technology, used as a reasonable accommodation, is making a dramatic impact in the workplace. The TDD has a typewriter style keyboard, a readout display, and a phone line connector or an acoustic coupler for a standard telephone handset. Modems compatible with TDDs can also be added to personal computers. For Frank Bowe the assistive technology of the TDD has made a profound difference in his ability as a professor to communicate with students and faculty:

My life has changed dramatically during the last two years. . . . For some forty years, I've been unable to understand speech. Growing up, I just assumed that the telephone was not for me: it was part of "their" world. . . . And here I am, just as deaf as I was then. I'm a university professor with several hundred hearing students every year. They call me—usually to request postponements of due dates for term papers or to report that they'll miss class. I call them—to schedule an exam, to answer their questions. It happens every day. . . . All of this is very strange upon reflection. I never expected to be living a life like this. And without technology, I'm not sure I would be. . . . Deafness used to mean the inability to understand speech. Yet I do, every day. And all I use is the telephone and a low-cost terminal, the TDD.[26]

Costs of Reasonable Accommodation Are Frequently Reasonable

Harold Russel, former chair of the President's Committee on Employ-ment of People with Disabilities, who lost both hands during World War II, told senators during a hearing on the ADA legislation that for a majority of employees with disabilities no reasonable accommodation is necessary. For many others, the cost of reasonable accommodation can be less than $500. These types of reasonable accommodations are assistive devices, technology that can greatly affect the ability of a qualified person with a disability to perform a job. Russell provided the following examples of low-cost assistive devices:

A timer costing $26.95 with an indicator light which allowed a medical technician who was deaf to perform the laboratory tests required for her job. A receptionist who was visually impaired was provided with a light probe, costing $45, which allowed her to determine which lines on a telephone were ringing, on hold, or in use at her company. Obtaining a headset for a phone costing $49.95 allowed an insurance salesperson with cerebral palsy to write while talking.[27]

Other examples of effective low cost assistive devices include:

- A telephone amplifier designed to work with a hearing aid allowed a plan worker to retain his job and avoid being transferred to a lower paying job. Cost $24.
- A clerk with limited use of her hands was provided a "lazy susan" file holder, enabling her to reach all materials needed for her job. Cost $85.
- A person who had use of only one hand, working in a food service position,

could perform all tasks except opening cans. She was provided with a one-handed can opener. Cost $35.

An example of how a company can make reasonable accommodations, including worksite modification, at a relatively low cost is when Sears and Roebuck made their whole national headquarters accessible for $7,600 with TDDs and ramps. Remarking on these accommodations in testimony before Congress, Evan J. Kemp, Jr., former chairman of the Equal Employment Opportunity Commission, who uses a wheelchair, said, "It is hard to believe [Sears and Roebuck] could do it for that price. But if a person wants disabled people, the accommodations really don't become a burden."[28] According to surveys, 81 percent of the accommodations recommended by the Job Accommodation Network, a federal clearinghouse on reasonable accommodation, cost $1,000 or less, and of those, 31 percent cost nothing.

John C. DeWitt, president of a consulting firm and a member of AT&T's Consumer Advisory Panel, emphasized that assistive technology is a working investment:

The development of assistive technology in the workplace and places of public accommodation will not be a burden on American business and public institutions. The cost of assistive technology is frequently quite small. Offsetting tax and accounting treatments might reduce its impact upon tight budgets. Most important, the economy benefits as Americans with disabilities become integrated more fully into society as employees, customers, taxpayers.[29]

THE JOB ACCOMMODATION NETWORK

The Job Accommodation Network (JAN), provides no-cost consulting services on reasonable accommodation to employers and people with disabilities. The Job Accommodation Network was established in 1983 by the President's Committee on Employment of People with Disabilities. Its purpose is to help employers and people with disabilities stay informed and up-to-date with the growth of assistive devices and accommodations for the workplace. Its services are free of charge to employers and people with disabilities. The Job Accommodation Network's computer network contains a data base with over 20,000 accommodations to people's limitations and resource information on accommodations from over 3,000 manufacturers around the world. The majority of these accommodations, 70 percent, range from no cost to $500, and only 11 percent of JAN's accommodations cost over $1,000.

The following examples are some of the recommendations for reasonable accommodations made by JAN for employers and employees around the country:

- In Iowa, an engineer with multiple sclerosis began having difficulty reading her computer monitor due to diminishing eyesight. By installing a special lens covering the screen, which enlarged the print and reduced glare, the engineer was able to continue her work while she received special training.

- A truck driver in Montana was having difficulty continuing his job due to carpal tunnel syndrome, which limited his wrist movement and caused great discomfort in cold weather. By using a special wrist splint in conjunction with a glove designed for skin divers, he was able to continue driving the truck, even during the coldest months.

- In New Jersey, a telephone amplifier was supplied to a computer programmer with a hearing impairment. (For more information on JAN, see listing under President's Committee on Employment of People with Disabilities, in the appendix.)

THE EMPLOYER'S OBLIGATION TO PROVIDE REASONABLE ACCOMMODATION

In addition to making reasonable accommodation available to an employee, reasonable accommodation must be provided to an individual with a disability to participate in the application process. According to the EEOC, "It is a violation of the ADA to fail to provide reasonable accommodation to the *known* physical or mental limitations of a qualified individual with a disability, unless to do so would impose an undue hardship on the operation of your business. Undue hardship means that the accommodation would require significant difficulty or expense."[30]

Frequently when a qualified individual with a disability requests a reasonable accommodation, the appropriate accommodation is obvious because the individual has used a similar worksite accommodation in the past. However, when an appropriate accommodation is not readily apparent, it is the responsibility of the employer, as the EEOC points out, "to make a reasonable effort to find one."[31] The EEOC states, "The best way to do this is to consult informally with the applicant or employee about potential accommodations that would enable the individual to participate in the application process or perform the essential functions of the job."[32]

Determining the Appropriate Reasonable Accommodation

The EEOC has developed a four-step process that assists the employer to determine a specific reasonable accommodation and in so doing comply with the ADA. The process of obtaining a reasonable accommodation starts with the applicant or employee initiating the request. As pointed out in the regulations, an employer cannot be responsible for making an accommodation if the employer is unaware that an accommodation is needed. According to the EEOC, "Once a qualified individual with a disability has requested the provision of a reasonable accommodation, the employer must make a reasonable effort to determine an appropriate accommodation. The appropriate reasonable accommodation is best determined through a flexible, interactive process that involves both the employer and the qualified individual with a disability."[33] Employers should be responsive to applicants or employees who request reasonable accommodation.

When an applicant or employee requests a reasonable accommodation from the employer to assist in the performance of a job, the EEOC states that an employer should use "a problem solving approach"[34] that includes four steps:

1. Analyze the particular job involved and determine its purpose and essential functions.

2. Consult with the individual with a disability to ascertain the precise job-related limitations imposed by the individual's disability and how those limitations could be overcome with a reasonable accommodation.

3. In consultation with the individual to be accommodated, identify potential accommodations and assess the effectiveness each would have in enabling the individual to perform the essential functions of the position.

4. Consider the preference of the individual to be accommodated and select and implement the accommodation that is most appropriate for both the employee and employer.[35]

It is important to bear in mind that a reasonable accommodation often makes common sense and is obvious, making the determination process unnecessary. As Richard C. Douglas, executive director of the President's Committee on Employment of People with Disabilities stated, "Reasonable accommodations achieve an important goal: making a good match between a qualified worker and the right job. Reasonable accommodations reflect common sense combined with creativity and knowledge of what is available, and identification of what are the *real* needs of people with disabilities."[36]

Employees with Mobility Impairments

While there are a number of assistive devices available to people with varying degrees of mobility impairment that improve mobility and dexterity, it is important to recognize that the entire worksite needs to be considered for accessibility. For persons using wheelchairs this includes modifying narrow aisles, workstation surfaces that are too high or too low, or doors that are too heavy to be opened.

People Who Are Deaf or Hearing Impaired

There is a wide range of devices available that are specific to the needs of those individuals with impaired hearing and those individuals who need devices such as a TDD or an interpreter.

Speech amplification. For hearing-impaired individuals, there are several telephone devices that are available. For persons who use or do not use hearing aids, there are portable handset amplifiers. There are also portable speech amplification devices that may be easily set up for use in a meeting, training course, or lecture.

Hearing aid compatible phones. A high pitched background sound is often heard by a person wearing a hearing aid when using a telephone. Individuals with hearing aids should be provided with hearing aid compatible telephones.

TDD. For an employee who cannot use an amplified telephone, a telecommunications device for the deaf or TDD-compatible device may be a reasonable accommodation. A TDD permits a hearing-impaired individual to communicate over a standard telephone line with another TDD user or through a relay operator to reach a non-TDD user. The TDD enables the sender to type a message that is displayed as text for the receiving party to read and respond to just as in a telephone conversation. A personal computer can also be configured to function as a TDD by adding a special modem. Because the TDD assists individuals in direct and interactive communications, it cannot be substituted for by a facsimile machine, which is not interactive.

TDD with braille display. Individuals who are both blind and deaf may need a specialized TDD that also has a "refreshable" braille display unit attached. This assistive device allows a person who is both blind and deaf to communicate with hearing and sighted individuals.

Signaling system. For a person who is hearing impaired or deaf, a transmitter can be attached to a telephone that causes a light to flash as an alternative to the phone ringing.

Captioning. Any video that is produced for training, instruction, and information can be captioned for the hearing impaired.

Electronic mail. Because electronic mail is essentially a visual process, it presents few barriers to hearing-impaired people. The "chat mode" system of electronic mail can greatly expand the communications possibilities. The electronic mail system should include a feature that provides a visual indicator of message status. Access to an electronic bulletin board system may be useful as a supplement to electronic mail.

People with Impaired Vision or Who Are Blind

Large monitor with high resolution. This monitor, which ranges in size from 19 to 25 inches, increases the character size of words and provides a clear, sharp image.

A gentleman who is blind scans and listens as a Kurzweil Reading Machine "reads out loud" from a book or typewritten letter. Courtesy of Xerox Imaging Systems.

Magnified display of computer screen. Both software and hardware systems are available to magnify the image on a monitor.

Speech synthesizer. A computer hardware device is available that, in conjunction with a screen reader, can convert screen contents into spoken words by using synthetic speech. An example of this technology is the Kurzweil Reading Machine. About the size of a large briefcase, it converts text to synthetic speech at the rate of 550 words per minute or more than twice the speed that people talk. The Kurzweil Reading Machine "reads out loud" to people who are blind, have low vision, retinitis pigmentosa, or who have had a stroke, or have a learning disability that impairs reading. These reading machines were invented and introduced by Ray Kurzweil in 1976.

Eye-operated computers. New infrared systems are being developed and are on the market that allow the eye to operate a computer. These specially designed computer systems are sensitive to the infrared rays that are reflected off the corneas of the eyes of the computer user. These infrared computer systems "know" precisely where on the computer screen the eyes are being directed. The user can create sentences, write letters, or pull up files by selecting letters on the screen. This type of computer system can be used by individuals with quadriplegia or other severe mobility impairments, such as stroke.

Whether an assistive device is low-tech, like a "lazy susan" or high-tech, like a Kurzweil Reading Machine, the objective is essentially the same:

to provide an accommodation for the worker with a disability so that the essential functions of a job can be performed. In many of the cases cited, the provision by the employer of reasonable accommodation to an employee or applicant made the difference in whether the employee could keep a job or whether the applicant could be seriously considered for a position. Unlike other equal employment laws enforced by the EEOC, the ADA is fundamentally connected to the provision of reasonable accommodation. The process of determining reasonable accommodations is vital in meeting the ADA's overall commitment to the inclusion of people with disabilities in the nation's work force.

CHAPTER 10

New Rights of People with Disabilities

The Americans with Disabilities Act provides people with disabilities with new rights in employment, telecommunications, transportation, and in the access and full utilization of public and commercial places. The Americans with Disabilities Act is the most comprehensive federal civil rights legislation enacted since 1964. Hailed by some members of Congress as a new emancipation proclamation, these new rights represent a departure from the past and a historic beginning for people with disabilities.

The author of the first draft of the Americans with Disabilities Act was Robert L. Burgdorf, Jr. A professor at the District of Columbia School of Law, he has the perspective of a member of an architectural team admiring a finished building:

Near the end of January in 1987, I sat down at a word processor in an office overlooking the National Mall on Independence Avenue in Washington, D.C. and wrote the original ADA bill that was introduced in Congress in 1988. Just a little over five years later, I am amazed at what has happened—not only was the ADA passed by a huge margin in both houses of Congress and signed by the president in an impressive ceremony on the South Lawn of the White House, but federal regulations implementing it have been issued and major portions of the Act have gone into effect. It seems a terribly short time for such a major change, truly a revolution, in the way society deals with a large class of citizens. For at its heart that is what the ADA represents—a shift in the way our society thinks about and relates to people with disabilities: a shift away from governmental charity, paternalistic helpfulness, support of dependency, and segregated services for a group considered unfortunate victims; and toward equality, integration, jobs, independence, and most importantly—*rights* for all of us individuals with disabilities.[1]

Another individual who played a key role in drafting the historic legislation is Lex Frieden, senior vice president of The Institute for Rehabilitation Research, an assistant professor at Baylor College of Medicine in Houston, and a former executive director of the National Council on Disability. Frieden, who uses a wheelchair, said: "The employment section of the ADA means that people with disabilities have the same rights as members of other minority groups and women. Title I ensures nondiscrimination in the job application process, job selection, and in job promotion. Title I is important because for the first time it establishes those rights outside the realm of the federal government, federal government-funded programs, and federal government-awarded business contracts."[2] Title I and Title II of the ADA expand employment rights to include state and local governments and covers 87 percent of America's private sector jobs.

Having made significant initial first steps with the legislation of the 1970s and 1980s, the ADA utilizes its legislative precursors but goes much further. The pillars on which the ADA rests are the achievements of nondiscrimination in hiring in the federal and federally funded sector, a free and appropriate education for all children with disabilities, a bill of rights for developmentally disabled people, and other federal legislation. But for many people with disabilities there was and is much more to accomplish.

Frank Bowe wrote eloquently about the full range of pressing civil rights issues for people with disabilities in his 1978 book, *Handicapping America*. As a deaf person, Bowe brings both his personal experience and his passion for equality and fairness to his writing:

The human and civil rights disabled Americans seek today are monumental in their simplicity. . . . Among these rights are the right to education and the right to work. . . . The right, that is, to earn a living, and live a life, to be different and to have that difference respected. . . . They do not seek the right to be equal. They are equal. What they do want is the rest of America to recognize this supremely basic fact and to act accordingly.[3]

What of course is evident is that these thoughts are central to the American experience, a history of many peoples seeking basic religious, political, and civil protections, freedoms, and rights.

Chai R. Feldblum, a visiting professor at Georgetown University Law Center, was also responsible for drafting and negotiating key provisions of the Americans with Disabilities Act. She sees the ADA mandate as assisting people with disabilities in becoming economically independent. Feldblum maintains that having a stable and fulfilling job is a fundamental part of the American dream. People with disabilities want to work and obtain jobs that meet their needs, abilities, and talents just like everyone else. In addition, people with disabilities would like to obtain promotions, and develop and advance in their careers.[4]

The Americans with Disabilities Act is a response by government to address the aspirations of people with disabilities to be equal partners in

Table 10.1

The Rights of People with Disabilities under the Americans with Disabilities Act

Employment and Job Application

1. The right not to be discriminated against on the basis of a disability in appying for employment
2. The right not to be discriminated against on the basis of being regarded as a person with a disability
3. The right to be judged on your own merits
4. The right not to be screened out of employment on the basis of a disability
5. The right to reveal to an employer a disabling condition without being discriminated against
6. The right to be tested fairly as an applicant for a job
7. The right to request and be provided with reasonable accommodation that is not an undue hardship on an employer
8. The right not to be disqualified in employment based on the inability to perform non-essential job functions
9. The right not to be limited, segregated, or classified as a person with a disability
10. The right not to be asked about a disabling condition in interviews and application forms
11. The right not to be required to undergo a medical examination before being made a job offer
12. The right for employees with disabilities to receive equal access to health and life insurance and other benefit plans
13. The right not to be discriminated against as a direct threat to safety or health, unless certain standards are met
14. The right not to be retaliated against by an employer
15. The right not to be discriminated against because of an association with disabled people
16. The right not to be discriminated against by a third party contract

Rights to Access and Use of Public Accommodations and Services

17. The right to access and full use of places of public accommodation
18. A place of public accommodation cannot have a policy that screens out or tends to screen out persons with disabilities
19. The right to access and full utilization of telecommunications
20. The right to access and full utilization of public ground transportation

SOURCE: The Americans with Disabilities Act of 1990 and the Equal Employment Opportunity Commission

American society, through employment, the utilization of public ground transportation and telecommunications, and in the enjoyment of places of public accommodation. The underlying message of the ADA is that people with disabilities have the right to earn a living, to achieve, and to prosper. The basic tenets of the ADA, the right not to be discriminated against in employment and the right to access and full utilization of places of public accommodation are a full measure of what America has historically strived to achieve for all of its citizens.

EMPLOYMENT RIGHTS

The Americans with Disabilities Act is the first federal legislation with the potential to create the change necessary in American society for people with disabilities to become equal partners and equal members of the American work force. With this new equality, people with disabilities will be able to strive, like other Americans, to "obtain jobs that meet their needs and are suited to their talents." Now a teenager who is deaf can do more than exercise the right to a free and appropriate education in the public schools. That teenager, with the assistance of a state vocational rehabilitation scholarship program, can think about acquiring a college education, obtaining skills, plan a career, look for a job, and know that there will be protections in the workplace against discrimination. In other words, once trained and educated that teenager can think about having a future, a future where a job interview will focus on ability, not on a hearing limitation.

The ADA has an umbrella-like effect on almost all employment decisions, from application to hiring, and promotions to fringe benefits. The new employment rights under the ADA are not the same as constitutional rights and liberties, such as the right to free speech or the freedom of religion. The rights of people with disabilities under the ADA are grounded in the principles of human dignity and respect for people's abilities, without regard to inconsequential personal characteristics that have no bearing on the successful and productive performance of a specific job.

In the employment rights that are presented, which went into effect on 26 July 1992, case histories from the 1980s are added to contrast with the new developments made possible by the Americans with Disabilities Act— contrasts that are often striking. With these new far-reaching employment rights also come the responsibilities and obligations of the business community affected by the new law. As Senate Minority Leader Robert J. Dole said, "It should be our obligation that people with disabilities understand their new rights and that employers and business understand the nature of their obligations."[5]

1. The Right Not to Be Discriminated Against on the Basis of a Disability in Applying for Employment

As stated in the ADA, "an employer shall not discriminate against any qualified individual with a disability because of such individual's disability in regard to application procedures, the hiring or discharge of employees, employee compensation, advancement, job training and other terms, conditions, and privileges of employment."[6] The equal employment right to secure a job, job promotion, and advance in a career without discrimination based on disability is one of the core mandates of the ADA. One of the purposes of the ADA as stated in the legislation is "to bring people with disabilities into the economic and social mainstream of American life." The ADA prohibits discrimination in all aspects of the employment relationship.

Case history: Laura Cooper graduated near the top of her law school class with exemplary credentials. Yet during her search for employment, she received more than *400 rejections* from law firms until she found a firm that was willing to look at qualifications instead of her multiple sclerosis (MS) and use of a wheelchair. Cooper remembers representatives from law firms who told her they could not hire her because of what she would do to their insurance rates, their fears of how clients would react to her, and their doubts about her ability to handle the job. Cooper became a practicing attorney for a major international law firm in San Francisco, and in 1989 she was named one of the twenty outstanding young American lawyers by the American Bar Association.[7]

Under the ADA a qualified job applicant would no longer need to tolerate interviewing and hiring practices that automatically reject a qualified candidate with a disability. In addition, under the ADA it is illegal to reject a candidate on the basis of a perception or fear that insurance rates would go up.

2. The Right Not to Be Discriminated Against on the Basis of Being Regarded as a Person with a Disability

At the very core of the Americans with Disabilities Act is the provision that it is unlawful to discriminate against people with disabilities on the basis of a disability. This protection extends to a person who may or may not have a disability but is regarded by others as a person with a disability. In the following case history a woman was discharged from her job, not because of her performance, which was good, but because she was *regarded* as having a disability.

Case history: Christopher Bell, attorney-advisor to the chairman of the EEOC, has spoken about an eccentric woman who worked in a drab university cafeteria. She had a tendency to talk to herself, but she did her work and received good reviews from her employer for fifteen years. When the university remodeled the cafeteria, she was dismissed because she was regarded as having a disability and "did not fit in with the cafeteria's new decor."[8] Under Title I of the Americans with Disabilities Act, the university would have to think twice about firing the cafeteria worker, which would violate the ADA.

3. The Right to Be Judged on Your Own Merits

The ADA provides that employees or job applicants with a disability be judged on their abilities, not on assumptions about what physical or mental limitations they may or may not have.

Example 1: A young man who has cerebral palsy is applying for a position as an engineer with a commercial real estate development company. The supervisor, who has not met the applicant, has learned that the young man has cerebral palsy and wonders whether he has the physical ability and stamina for the job. The supervisor, however, decides to go ahead with the interview. As it turns out, the applicant has all the capabilities for the job and is offered the position. The supervisor gave the young man an opportunity for an interview and in the process the applicant was judged on his own merits, not assumptions about physical limitations that he might have because of a specific type of disability.

Example 2: In the same way, a young woman who has experience as an office assistant and who has mental retardation has the right to be judged on her own merits and experience as a candidate for a similar office position. The young woman should not be judged on the assumptions or generalizations made by an employer based on the information that "she has mental retardation."

4. The Right Not to Be Screened Out of Employment on the Basis of a Disability

This right ensures that people with disabilities are not excluded from job opportunities unless they are actually unable to do the job. The exception to this provision, according to the final regulations, is when a "standard, test, or other selection criteria used by the employer is shown to be job-related for the position in question and is consistent with business necessity."[9]

According to the EEOC interpretive guidance, "Selection criteria that exclude, or tend to exclude, an individual with a disability or a class of individuals with disabilities because of their disability, but do not concern the essential functions of the job would not be consistent with business necessity."[10] An example of an unlawful employment procedure would be an employer's requesting a drivers license as a selection criteria for a job selling tickets at a movie theater. Being able to drive a car is not a function of selling tickets. The drivers license criteria would tend to screen out individuals with epilepsy, for instance, many of whom do not have a drivers license.

5. The Right to Reveal to an Employer a Disabling Condition without Being Discriminated Against

There are a number of disabilities that are called "hidden disabilities," such as a learning disability or epilepsy. In the case of epilepsy, it is often a dilemma for a person, as an applicant or employee, to reveal the condition to an employer. Physicians often recommend to their patients with epilepsy not to reveal the information to employers when applying for a position because of a negative impact on their employment prospects. There are also many people with a seizure disorder who prefer not to take the chance of being more forthcoming and open and are concerned about the reaction of an employer or potential employer. With the advent of the ADA, people with epilepsy cannot lose a job or be denied employment on the basis of a disability if they are qualified for the position.

Case history: During a congressional hearing in Boston on the ADA, a school teacher provided the following testimony:

My name is Sara Bloor, and I have epilepsy. Two years ago, I applied for a job in Newton, Massachusetts, in a position as an educator in an urban setting. I had an interview over the telephone and then I was asked to fly down to Boston for a second interview in person. At that time, I spoke to the school director, a personnel committee, and the board director.

At that time I revealed that I had epilepsy, though I knew at the time I legally did not have to share my health information with them. But I needed for them to know that at the time I could not drive. . . . At the time I was a resident of Wisconsin which has tough driving laws. My seizures were under control and I thought that in the other jobs I had, I had revealed my epilepsy. . . . And it is something I do not mind disclosing. At the end of the interview, they told me they would let me know about the job and there was no problem about the epilepsy. . . . They called me that Saturday and told me they could not hire me because of my seizures. . . . [I explained] I was seizure-free. He told me he still had not hired anyone for the position and I had gotten excellent recommendations from my references and was the person they wanted to hire. . . . He took it back to the [school] board. Ten days later they decided again they could not hire me because I had epilepsy.[11]

Sara Bloor successfully sued the school board but it took two years. A school board, as part of a local government, is covered by the employment provisions of Title I and II of the Americans with Disabilities Act. A school board that rejects a qualified individual on the basis of a disability is in violation of the ADA. If a candidate for a position feels discriminated against, under the ADA that individual may file a complaint with the EEOC. The complaint process, if settled by the EEOC, takes approximately 180 days after the complaint is filed. After this period, the individual could bring a private lawsuit in court.

6. The Right to Be Tested Fairly

A person with a disability that impairs sensory, manual, or speaking skills has the right to take an appropriate employment test that actually measures the individual's abilities. The EEOC interpretive guidance on this provision "requires that employment tests be administered to eligible applicants or employees with disabilities that impair sensory, manual, or speaking skills in formats that do not require the use of the impaired skill."[12]

The EEOC provides an example of how to administer an appropriate test in this instance. It is unlawful to administer a written employment test to an individual with dyslexia who is unable to read, if the employer is informed of the condition prior to the administration of the test. In such a case states the EEOC, "as a reasonable accommodation and in accordance with this provision, an alternative oral test should be administered to the individual."[13] (For more information on the administration of tests, see chapter 5.)

Case history 1: Joseph L. Stutts has dyslexia and was denied a heavy equipment operator job because he could not pass a written test by the employer for entering the job training program. According to the Senate Committee on Labor and Human Resources, "the written test had a disparate impact on persons with dyslexia."[14] In *Stutts v. Freeman*, the court found that the company should provide someone to read questions to Mr. Stutts to "accommodate his dyslexia."[15]

Case history 2: A young deaf man applied for a job as a custodial worker with the police department of a county government. The police department requires job applicants to take a lie detector test. The police department refused to let the young man take the lie detector test because the results would "not be accurate." The police department never allowed the applicant to take the lie detector test, and although he was qualified, he did not get the job.[16]

Under the ADA, the police department would have to provide a deaf individual with an interpreter at the time the lie detector test was administered. Not providing an alternative testing procedure would be a violation of the ADA.

7. The Right to Request and Be Provided with Reasonable Accommodation That Is Not an Undue Hardship

A reasonable accommodation, when necessary, is a means of creating a level playing field for qualified people with disabilities in the workplace.

The Senate Committee on Labor and Human Resources in its 1989 report on the ADA stated, "The committee believes strongly that reasonable accommodations should provide a meaningful equal employment opportunity. Meaningful equal employment opportunity means an opportunity to attain the same level of performance as is available to non-disabled employees having similar skills and abilities."[17]

The right for a *qualified* individual with a disability to request the use of a reasonable accommodation, which is not an undue hardship for an employer, is one of the pivotal rights contained in the Americans with Disabilities Act. The final regulations state, "It is unlawful for [an employer] to deny employment opportunities to an otherwise qualified applicant or employee with a disability based on the need of [the employer] to make reasonable accommodation to such individual's physical or mental impairments."[18] This provision requires that reasonable accommodation be made by an employer to the known physical or mental impairments of a qualified individual with a disability.

Case history: Annie Richardson (not her real name) continued to function in her position as a warehosue worker in Chicago even after multiple sclerosis (MS) made it difficult for her to get around. She used a golf cart, which she provided herself, to get from one end of the large company complex to the other. When her supervisor resigned, however, the new supervisor informed her that because "no one else used a cart," she was "not allowed to use one either." Richardson lost her job.[19]

Under Title I, companies like Richardson's are required to provide a reasonable accommodation to assist qualified workers with their jobs. People with MS have been particularly vulnerable to discrimination in the workplace because multiple sclerosis almost always has adult onset.

The National Multiple Sclerosis Society reports that a 1991 study of Brandeis University found that 91 percent of people with MS had a high school education, 33 percent had completed college, and 14 percent had completed some graduate work. While 97 percent had been employed at some time in their lives, 40 percent of those who had worked reported having lost a job because of MS.[20]

Employers who may never have considered employing a person with a disability can, as in the case of Richardson, find themselves with an employee who does have a disability. Under the ADA, the firing of Richardson would be illegal, and she would have recourse by filing a complaint with the EEOC to regain her position, lost pay, and the use of her golf cart or an alternative reasonable accommodation provided by the employer.

8. The Right Not to Be Disqualified in Employment Based on the Inability to Perform Non-Essential Job Functions

The term "essential functions" means the fundamental job duties for the employment position the individual with a disability holds as an employee or desires as an applicant. The essential functions are those job functions that an individual is able to perform, with or without reasonable accommodation. Under the ADA, an employer is not required to hire or retain an employee who is not qualified to perform the essential functions of the job. However, an employer cannot refuse to hire or terminate the employment of an individual with a disability who can perform the essential functions, but not marginal ones. An example of a marginal, non-essential job function is the answering of a shared office telephone by a qualified graphic artist who is deaf. The employer may determine that answering the telephone is non-essential as a job function of the graphic artist and can be handled by others in the office.

9. The Right Not to Be Limited, Segregated, or Classified as a Person with a Disability

The Americans with Disabilities Act prohibits an employer from limiting, segregating, or classifying job applicants or employees in a way that adversely affects equal employment opportunity status on the basis of disability.[21] According to the EEOC interpretive guidance, this regulation prohibits employers from "restricting employment opportunities on the basis of stereotypes and myths about the individual's disability."[22] Instead, the capabilities of qualified individuals with disabilities must be determined on an individualized, case-by-case basis. Employers are also prohibited from segregating qualified employees with disabilities into separate work areas or into separate lines of advancement.

The EEOC has provided these examples of employers violating this regulation:

Example 1: An employer who "limits the duties of an employee with a disability based on a presumption of what is best for that individual with such a disability or on a presumption about the abilities of an individual with such a disability."[23]

Example 2: An employer who adopts a "separate track of job promotion or progression for employees with disabilities based on a presumption that employees with disabilities are uninterested in, or incapable of, performing particular jobs."[24]

Example 3: An employer who requests "employees with disabilities to use segregated break rooms, lunch rooms, or lounges."[25]

Example 4: An employer that denies "employment to an applicant or an employee based on generalized fears about the safety of an individual with such a disability."[26]

Example 5: An employer who denies "employment to an applicant or employee based on generalized assumptions about the absenteeism rate of an individual with such a disability."[27]

Chai R. Feldblum describes this antidiscrimination provision as a "relatively straightforward application" of the ADA. Feldblum states, "An employer could not, for example, have all employees with disabilities work in a separate, segregated section of the workplace, or pay employees with disabilities on a lower pay scale for work equivalent to that performed by other employees."[28]

Case history: Janice Thomas (not her real name) has multiple sclerosis, sometimes has trouble with fatigue, and had been working for a company for six months. She was delayed in returning from a three-day business trip due to flight cancellations and was not able to get home until 2:00 A.M. Tired from her business trip, Thomas called in the next day and requested permission to stay at home. While permission was granted, when she returned to work the following day, she found that a note had been placed in her personnel file documenting her "problem with absenteeism." Due to the flu, she had missed three days of work, but other workers had missed more time. What Thomas did not understand was why she had not received a verbal warning from her supervisor, which is customary, before a note was placed in her personnel file. Thomas's supervisor agreed that the customary personnel procedure did stipulate a verbal warning before a written one, but the supervisor said she was "being tough for good reasons." The supervisor said he had previously employed another person with a disability and that "the former employee had taken advantage" of her. The supervisor said she was "not going to have the same problems with Thomas."[29]

Title VII of the Civil Rights Act of 1964 has protected people from this form of discrimination, stereotyping based on race, color, sex, religion, and national origin, for nearly thirty years. With the passage of the ADA, people with disabilities are also protected from discrimination based on classification.

10. The Right Not to Be Asked about a Disabling Condition in Interviews and on Application Forms

The reason and importance of this right is well stated in the Senate Committee on Labor and Human Resources Report on the ADA. "Historically, employment application forms and employment interviews requested information concerning an applicant's physical or mental condition. This information was often used to exclude applicants with disabilities—particularly those with so-called hidden disabilities such as epilepsy, diabetes, emotional illness, and cancer—before their ability to perform the job was even evaluated."[30]

According to the EEOC, this provision "makes clear that an employer cannot inquire as to whether an individual has a disability at the pre-offer stage of the selection process."[31] Employers cannot make inquiries about an applicant's worker's compensation status. However, employers may ask questions relating to the applicant's background and skills in order to meet the requirements of the job.

Case history: Leilia Batten, who provided testimony on the ADA to a House of Representatives subcommittee, explained how a gentleman with a history of a mental illness she knew was looking for a job. Batten said, "He had just gone to apply for a job for which he was not hired because a question on the application asked him if he ever had a psychiatric hospitalization."[32]

11. The Right Not to Be Required to Undergo a Medical Examination before Being Made a Job Offer

Under the ADA it is prohibited for an employer to require a medical examination of an applicant with a disability except under specific circumstances. An employer may request medical testing if the employer can demonstrate that such testing is job related and consistent with business necessity. An employer may make pre-employment inquiries into the ability of an applicant to perform job-related functions.

An employer may require a medical examination after making an offer of employment to an applicant and before the applicant actually begins working at the job. However, this is conditional only if the employer makes the same medical examination request of all entering employees in the same job category, regardless of disability.[33] In addition, according to Chai R. Feldblum, the results of a medical examination cannot be used by an employer to withdraw a conditional job offer from an applicant unless the results indicate that the applicant is no longer qualified to perform the specific job.[34]

12. The Right for Employees with Disabilities to Receive Equal Access to Health and Life Insurance and Other Benefit Plans

Under the same section that prohibits limiting, segregating, and classifying disabled people, the EEOC provides for the right of employed people with disabilities to be accorded equal access to health insurance. As the EEOC interpretive guidance states, "employees with disabilities must be accorded equal access to whatever health insurance coverage the employer provides to other employees. This part does not, however, affect pre-existing condition clauses included in health insurance policies offered by employers. Consequently, employers may continue to offer policies that contain such clauses, even if they adversely affect individuals with disabilities, so long as the clauses are not used as a subterfuge to evade the purposes of this part."[35]

However, an employer cannot deny a qualified individual with a disability equal access to insurance or subject a qualified individual with a disability to different terms or conditions of insurance based on a disability alone, if the disability does not pose increased risks.[36] Feldblum makes three important points on health insurance coverage under the ADA:

One, an employer may not refuse to hire a qualified individual with a disability because the employer thinks the cost of insurance will go up. Two, employers and insurance companies may continue to include pre-existing condition clauses in their health plans, even though such clauses eliminate benefits for a specified time period for people with disabilities. Three, employers and health insurance plans may limit certain medical procedures or treatments, such as limiting the amount of kidney dialysis.[37]

Case history: A 28-year-old woman with epilepsy was fired from her job at a dry cleaning shop she had for seven months because of her seizure disorder. The young woman was having blackouts once or twice a month, and she always had an aura, or warning sensation, of an impending blackout. The employer knew of the seizure disorder prior to hiring the young woman. A week before the firing, the employer was advised by the health insurer that the young woman was a "health hazard."

In addition to being an example of discrimination, this case history is an example of the correct use of the word "handicap"—a situation where the attitude of society is more handicapping than the disability itself. Under the ADA, the employer would have to show that the young woman was "a direct threat to oneself or others" in order to terminate her employment. The employer could not use the health insurer's statement as a basis for her termination. Under the ADA, an employer cannot fire an employee because the employer thinks health insurance rates will go up or as in this instance, the employer's health insurer maintains that the employee is a health hazard.[38] (For more information on health insurance, see chapter 7.)

13. The Right Not to Be Discriminated Against as a Direct Threat to Safety or Health, Unless Certain Standards Are Met

A qualified individual with a disability, such as a person who has cancer or has tested positive for HIV or who uses prescription medication to control manic-depression, has the right to apply for work or be employed in a position and not be discriminated against on the basis of a disability.

Case history: This case history is provided from the testimony before Congress on the ADA:

My name is Jerry Johnson. . . . I am also HIV positive, asymptomatic, which means I have no symptoms. As you can look at me and tell, I am still healthy, intelligent, have all my capabilities and capacity to reason and to carry on a normal decent life. On August 14, 1988, I was working for a company in the Washington, D.C. metro area when they learned of my infection and I was immediately dismissed. They told me and I quote: "Your job is no longer needed. You are more of a liability to the company." . . . We can carry on in society and we can be an asset to society.[39]

This act of employment discrimination is illegal under the ADA. In the Committee on Labor and Human Resources Report on the Americans with Disabilities Act, another example of unlawful discrimination is provided. For example, it would be unlawful to unilaterally transfer a person with an HIV infection from a job as a teacher to a job where that person has no contact with people. See, for example, *Chalk v. United States District Court*.[40] (For information on the standards for determining direct threat, see chapter 11.)

14. The Right Not to Be Retaliated Against by an Employer

Under the ADA a person with a disability is protected against retaliation from an employer because the individual made "a charge, testified, assisted, or participated in any manner in an investigation, proceeding, or hearing to enforce any provision" of the ADA. In addition, according to the EEOC final regulations, it is unlawful for an employer "to coerce, intimidate, threaten, harass or interfere with any individual" in enjoying the rights afforded individuals with disabilities.[41]

15. The Right Not to Be Discriminated Against Because of an Association with People with Disabilities

This regulation states that "it is unlawful for an [employer] to exclude or deny equal jobs or benefits to, or otherwise discriminate against, a qualified individual because of the known disability of an individual with whom the qualified individual is known to have a family, business, social or other relationship or association."[42] These are two examples of how an employer could violate this regulation.

Example 1: An applicant without a disability discloses to an employer during an interview that his wife has spina bifida and uses a wheelchair. The employer, thinking that the applicant will frequently have to take time off from work to care for his wife, turns the applicant down for employment.

Example 2: An employer discharges an employee because the employee volunteers his time after work to help people with AIDS. In both instances, according to the EEOC, the actions of the employers would be unlawful.[43] This protection derives from the Rehabilitation Act of 1973.

16. The Right Not to Be Discriminated Against by a Third Party Contract

An employer cannot enter into a contractual arrangement that has the effect of subjecting employees with disabilities to discrimination.

Example: An employer is a bank that has people with disabilities on its staff. The employer enters into a contract to have a security company provide training to all bank employees. The security company, as a third party, must ensure that its security training program for the bank is accessible to all of the bank's employees.

RIGHTS TO ACCESS AND USE OF PUBLIC ACCOMMODATIONS, TELECOMMUNICATIONS, AND PUBLIC GROUND TRANSPORTATION

The following rights have little precedent in federal law prior to the Americans with Disabilities Act. These new rights for people with disabilities to access and utilization of places of public accommodation, telecommunications, and transportation combined with the ADA's employment rights represent a new social contract between America and citizens with disabilities.

17. The Right to Access and Full Utilization of Public Accommodations

The right to the access and full use of goods and services in places of public accommodation, America's "Main Streets," is covered under Title III of the Americans with Disabilities Act, and is enforced by the Department of Justice. Many experts on the ADA agree that the employment provisions of the ADA, Title I, and the public accommodations provisions of Title III, when taken together, are the most significant and landmark civil rights sections of the Americans with Disabilities Act of 1990. A 1986 Louis Harris and Associates, Inc. poll underscored the importance of full access and use of public accommodations and services by people with disabilities:

The survey results dealing with social life and leisure experiences paint a sobering picture of an isolated and secluded population of individuals with disabilities. The large majority of people with disabilities do not go to movies, do not go to the theater, do not go to see musical performances, and do not go to sports events. A substantial minority of persons with disabilities never go to a restaurant, never go to a grocery store. . . . The extent of non-participation of individuals with disabilities in social and recreational activities is alarming.[44]

Under the ADA, places of public accommodation must not discriminate against persons with disabilities. The ADA states, "No individual shall be discriminated against on the basis of a disability in the full and equal enjoyment of the goods, services, facilities, privileges, advantages, or accommodations of any place of public accommodation by any person who owns, leases (or leases to) or operates a place of public accommodation."[45]

An interesting historical footnote to the public accommodation section of the ADA is that its origin and language can be traced to the Reconstruction era in the United States. In 1875, Congress passed "An Act to Protect All Citizens in Their Civil and Legal Rights," otherwise known as the Civil Rights Act of 1875. This nineteenth-century federal civil rights law provided citizens of all races and color with the "equal enjoyment of the accommodation and facility." Violation of the act was a misdemeanor, but the offender was directed to pay $500 in civil damages to the aggrieved party.[46]

The 1875 federal law stated in part, "That all persons within the jurisdiction of the United States shall be entitled to the full and equal enjoyment of the accommodations, advantages, facilities, and privileges of inns, public conveyances on land or water, theaters, and other places of public amusement; subject only to the conditions and limitations established by law, and applicable alike to citizens of every race and color, regardless of any previous condition of servitude."[47] The 1875 federal law was repealed eight years later due to inflamed antiblack and anti-Congress sentiment on the part of many whites vehemently opposed to the civil rights legislation.

The Civil Rights Act of 1964, enacted almost one hundred years after the 1875 law, states in part, "All persons shall be entitled to the full and equal enjoyment of the goods, services, facilities, privileges, advantages, and accommodations of any place of public accommodation, as defined in this section, without discrimination or segregation on the ground of race, color, religion, or national origin."[48]

The ADA makes these rights, incorporated in the Civil Rights Act of 1964 legislation, available to people with disabilities. Much of the ADA's legislative language is not new or revolutionary, and much of its wording can be traced through federal legislation spanning over 115 years. Most of the public accommodations section of the ADA, Title III, went into effect on 26 January 1992.

Case history: Lisa Carl, testifying before Congress on 10 May 1989, said, "When I tried to get into the Bijou Theater in Tacoma, Washington . . . the owner would not let me. She would not let me come in because of what I am. A person with cerebral palsy. I was sad for me—but more sad for her because she would not see me, only my C.P."[49]

Under the ADA, it is a violation of the law to prohibit an individual with a disability, because of the disability, from enjoying the same rights of access and utilization of places of public accommodation as all citizens, such as movie theaters, restaurants, physicians' offices, parks, dry cleaners, pharmacies, and supermarkets.

18. A Place of Public Accommodation Cannot Have a Policy That Screens Out or Tends to Screen Out Persons with Disabilities

According to Chai R. Feldblum, the ADA prohibits the managers or owners of a place of public accommodation from a policy that discriminates or tends to discriminate against the patronage of persons with disabilities. A policy of discrimination could be, for example, a restaurant that refuses to serve a person with a disability, or a nightclub that has a sign inside its window that implies that persons with disabilities are not welcome.

19. The Right to Access and Full Utilization of Telecommunications

The ADA provides the right for an estimated 24 million hearing-impaired and 2.8 million deaf people to a fully accessible and usable telephone system. Persons who are hearing or speech impaired have, under the ADA, the right to the access and full use of telecommunications relay services that operate twenty-four hours a day and that are no more expensive than functionally equivalent telephone services. Via a telephone relay system, a hearing-impaired, deaf, or speech-impaired individual sends a message by TDD to a relay operator, who simultaneously reads the message on a TDD and "voices" the message to a hearing person at the other end of the line. This right to the access and full use of telecommunications means that deaf and hearing-impaired people can communicate with hearing people at any time. A person who is hearing impaired can have a conversation with a hearing individual who is using a telephone and not a TDD. Services such as long-distance calls, collect calls, and calling card calls are part of this relay service. This section of the ADA, Title IV, goes into effect on 26 July 1993.

Example: A hearing-impaired woman who has just graduated from college and has been interviewed for a job, needs to contact her college professor, who is not hearing impaired, for a written recommendation. She places the long-distance call through the relay operator at a cost that is equivalent to standard long-distance telephone service and asks her former professor for a recommendation. The whole conversation takes place via the relay operator.

20. The Right to Access and Full Utilization of Public Ground Transportation

Under Title II of the ADA, people with disabilities have the right to access and full use of all public carriers that provide public rail or ground transportation. Persons who have mobility impairments or use wheelchairs, under the ADA, have access to public transportation, such as buses, light and rapid rail, including fixed route systems, paratransit, demand response systems, and transportation facilities. The requirements to provide paratransit services under the ADA began on 26 January 1992. People with disabilities have the right to access and use of intercity Amtrak and commuter rail by 26 July 1995, and key commuter stations must be retrofitted by 26 July 1993. Amtrak must provide one accessible car per train by 26 July 1995.

These new rights under the Americans with Disabilities Act represent not only a legal landmark for people with disabilities, they form a new direction for America and in the lives of people with disabilities and their families. New opportunities have been developed in employment. Places of public accommodation, public transportation, and telecommunications are now available for the full patronage of people with disabilities. All of these new rights can be traced to that spring day in 1964 when Hugh Gregory Gallagher was no longer satisfied with being lifted out of his wheelchair in order to get over the steps of the Library of Congress. Gallagher and 43 million other individuals with disabilities have new and expanded rights and new opportunities that provide for economic and personal independence unparalleled elsewhere in the world.

CHAPTER 11

ADA Enforcement: The Employer's Defenses and the Employee's Remedies

Compliance with the expansive provisions of the Americans with Disabilities Act is clearly the goal of the federal agencies charged with assisting the public in understanding and adhering to the new law. Indeed, people with disabilities desire independence through the ADA—the ability to work, shop, go to restaurants and movie theaters, and to have access to telecommunications, transportation, and recreation.

Much of this can be achieved through voluntary compliance by small businesses, companies, nonprofit associations, state and local governments, labor unions, employment agencies, or joint labor-management committees. Many experts agree that people with disabilities will attain independence far more quickly and comprehensively through the voluntary compliance of business and employers with the ADA than by any amount of federal agency or court-enforced compliance.

Still, disputes will inevitably arise under the ADA whether or not a public or private entity has attempted to comply with the provisions of the new law. One of the principal objectives of the ADA in mainstreaming people with disabilities into the workplace is the utilization of reasonable accommodation. In order to reasonably accommodate applicants or employees with disabilities, employers must understand the limits of their ADA obligations. In other words, employers must know how and in what circumstances they may legitimately reject an applicant or employee with a disability. Employers must be familiar with their defenses to claims of discrimination by individuals with disabilities and must realize the economic stakes if their actions are proved to be discriminatory. Furthermore, individuals with disabilities must know their rights and be familiar with the procedures for challenging an employer's actions.

Individuals with disabilities who think that they have been discriminated against as an applicant or employee need to know how to obtain information and find out what steps need to be taken to file a complaint with the Equal Employment Opportunity Commission. In addition, the Civil Rights Act of 1991, as well as other federal, state, and local laws, can work in combination with the ADA.

EMPLOYER'S DEFENSES TO CLAIMS OF DISABILITY DISCRIMINATION

Several defenses available to employers to challenge claims of discrimination based on disability are enumerated in the ADA. The EEOC regulations list some of the potential defenses available to employers and acknowledge that additional defenses, not listed in the ADA, may be utilized. Certain defenses are similar to those that have existed under the Civil Rights Act of 1964 for decades, and certain defenses derive from the Rehabilitation Act of 1973. Still other defenses that employers may utilize to challenge claims of disability discrimination are specific to the ADA. As Chai R. Feldblum has stated, "In general, the defenses allowed under the ADA comport with the basic principles underlying the law: to ensure that people with disabilities are given full and meaningful opportunities for employment, while protecting the right of employers to hire individuals who can appropriately perform the essential functions of particular jobs."[1]

Discrimination Not Based on Disability

The ADA prohibits discrimination based on disability but not on any other grounds.[2] An employer charged with disability discrimination under the ADA may use a general defense that the employer's decision to refuse to hire or fire the individual with a disability was not based on a disability, but was made for some other legitimate reason. For instance, an employer could raise this general defense if the company simply had no resources to hire another individual, disabled or not, or if the business decided to move into a different area of emphasis that was not commensurate with the disabled individual's skills.

Under this defense, the employer's reasons for the challenged employment action have nothing to do with disability and may even appear somewhat irrational (e.g., only hiring graduates of Boston College for particular jobs.)[3] To illustrate further, suppose a person with paraplegia who uses a wheelchair is denied a secretarial job because of a lack of typing speed and accuracy on a typing test. In this situation, the employer has no obligation to consider the unqualified applicant for the position unless the person was rejected due to a disability.[4]

Similarly, an employer is not required to lower employment selection standards related to essential job functions in order to conform to the qualifications of applicants with disabilities. It is a legitimate defense to an employment discrimination claim that an applicant without a disability was chosen because the nondisabled applicant was more qualified for the job in question, unless the provision of a reasonable accommodation would equalize the qualifications of both applicants. This defense will only succeed, however, if the applicant with a disability cannot show that this reason was an excuse and not the real reason for the employment decision.[5]

Undue Hardship

As previously noted, an employer is obligated to reasonably accommodate the known physical or mental limitations of a qualified applicant or employee with a disability unless the employer can demonstrate that the accommodation will impose an undue hardship on the employer's business operation. (See chapter 4 for the regulations concerning undue hardship.) The principle of undue hardship is so important to the ADA that it was not until the issuance of the final EEOC regulations that undue hardship was separated from the definition of reasonable accommodation.[6] The final regulations make clear that employers must provide reasonable accommodations to any qualified applicant or employee with a disability. If all avenues for a reasonable accommodation have been exhausted and an accommodation cannot be worked out, the employer may lawfully reject the individual with a disability and defend the rejection based on the defense of undue hardship.

It shall be a defense to a charge of discrimination, [for not making reasonable accommodation when required] that a requested or necessary accommodation would impose an undue hardship on the operation of the [employer's] business.[7]

Implications: What constitutes an undue hardship is, of course, the operative question and one in which reasonable minds may differ. An undue hardship exists when an employer is asked to provide an accommodation to a qualified applicant or employee that is *un*reasonable. An undue hardship creates for the employer, by definition, "significant difficulty or expense" in, or resulting from, the provision of a reasonable accommodation in light of several factors that must be considered in the determination. In order for employers to meet the high undue hardship standard, they must prove that the provision of an accommodation creates significant difficulty or expense. Employers must present evidence and demonstrate that the accommodation in question will, in fact, cause an undue hardship.

The flexible undue hardship standard. The standard used to determine undue hardship is flexible and courts are free to allocate weight among different factors on a case-by-case basis.[8] Whether or not an accommodation creates significant difficulty or expense is relative to the characteristics of the employer.[9] The factors to be considered when determining whether or not an accommodation creates an undue hardship include the net cost of the accommodation (the actual cost minus tax credits or deductions and other payment sources), the nature of the accommodation in question, and the effect that accommodation will have on the operation of the business. The size of the work force, the financial resources of the business involved, and, if applicable, the size and financial resources of a parent company or franchisor must also be considered when determining whether the provision of a particular accommodation creates an undue hardship.[10]

The expense of an accommodation. In determining whether the cost of an accommodation should be compared to the resources of an individual business or its parent company or franchisor, the entity that will actually incur the costs of the accommodation should be considered. For instance, if the extent of a fast food restaurant's relationship to its franchisor is the payment of an annual franchise fee, the resources of the individual restaurant should be examined when deciding whether or not a particular accommodation creates an undue hardship on the business.[11]

Courts have interpreted the flexible standard of undue hardship in slightly different ways under Section 504 of the Rehabilitation Act of 1973, the model for the employment provisions of the ADA. When deciding whether or not the business is able to reasonably absorb the costs of accommodations, courts usually compare the cost of the particular accommodation to the overall budget of the employer or business.[12] This approach tends to result in few determinations where accommodations are said to create undue hardships. As Bonnie P. Tucker and Bruce A. Goldstein, two legal experts in the disability field, have stated, "This test is unrealistic, since virtually *any* expenditure, except those made by very small businesses, could be found justifiable in relation to what would almost always be a significantly larger comparative expenditure. But the courts have not devised a logical alternative."[13] In addition, under the ADA employers must offer applicants or employees with disabilities the opportunity to pay for or provide that portion of the accommodation that is claimed to create the undue hardship.[14]

To illustrate the difficulty of proving accommodations to be undue hardships, one court decided that an annual expenditure of $6,000 for the provision of a reader to a blind government employee was not an undue hardship when compared to the government agency's $300 million administrative budget.[15] Another court found reasonable an expenditure of $6,500 out of an operating budget of $4 million to inoculate the staff of a learning center against hepatitis in order to accommodate a disabled applicant.[16] These courts may have decided these cases differently if the accommodation in question cost $6,000 but the business had a small budget or was operating on the margin of profitability.

Another approach many courts have taken under Section 504 of the

Rehabilitation Act when determining whether particular accommodations create undue hardships is to decide whether an accommodation requires "substantial additional expenditures" or "major modifications."[17] If this is the case, the accommodation will likely be ruled to be an undue hardship. Still other courts under Section 504 have decided that if an accommodation imposes a "fundamental alteration" or a "substantial modification" on the program or employer's business, that accommodation will be viewed as an undue hardship.[18]

Despite the variety of slightly different approaches to this determination, the flexible undue hardship standard is viewed by a majority of members of Congress as a successful provision of the Rehabilitation Act of 1973.[19] To be sure, businesses strive for certainty, especially when implementing new federally mandated rules, the violation of which could result in litigation. This need for certainty is not served by the relative and flexible undue hardship standard. However, when the extensive variety and degree of disabling conditions is combined with the array of different businesses and employers covered by the ADA, the merit of the flexible approach is clear.

The perception that flexibility in this determination was desirable may have resulted in the rejection by Congress of an amendment proposed during the passage of the ADA that would have created an inflexible approach. If an accommodation would have cost over 10 percent of an employee's annual salary, that accommodation would constitute an undue hardship on the employer and would not be required under the ADA.[20] This inflexible rule was rejected by Congress because it failed to take into consideration that many accommodations, such as structural modifications and assistive devices, benefit many disabled employees over time, and the costs can be amortized over a period of years.[21]

Substantial difficulty caused by an accommodation. The defense of undue hardship takes into account the financial realities of particular employers but is not merely limited to fiscal concerns. An accommodation will be found to create an undue hardship if it "would be unduly costly, extensive, substantial or disruptive, or . . . would fundamentally alter the nature or operation of the business."[22] No undue hardship exists, however, if the disruption to the employer's business is due to the fears or prejudices of other employees or patrons toward the individual's disability.[23]

A court might find undue hardship, for example, if the requested accommodation of an increase in the business' thermostat would make it too hot for other employees or customers. If an alternative reasonable accommodation could be identified, however, the employer would have to provide it. Additionally, an employer would not be able to demonstrate undue hardship if the provision of an accommodation negatively impacted the morale of other employees unless, for some reason, the accommodation affected the ability of those employees to perform their jobs.[24]

Primarily as a result of the relative undue hardship standard, an accommodation that poses an undue hardship for one employer at a particular time may not pose an undue hardship for another employer, or even for the same employer at another time.[25] Furthermore, the EEOC regulations specifically distinguish between temporary and permanent worksites when determining whether a particular accommodation creates an undue hardship on the employer. The interpretive guidance of the EEOC regulations notes that an accommodation that poses an undue hardship in a particular job setting, such as a temporary construction site, may not pose an undue hardship in another job site, such as a permanent worksite.[26]

Collective bargaining agreements. The EEOC interpretive guidance makes clear that the terms of a collective bargaining agreement may be considered when determining whether or not an accommodation is unduly disruptive to other employees or customers, or to the operation of the business. For instance, the terms of a collective bargaining agreement might be raised if an employee with three years of seniority requests, as a reasonable accommodation, reassignment to a position reserved in the agreement to employees with five years of seniority.[27]

When deciding these types of cases under Section 504 of the Rehabilitation Act of 1973, courts automatically deferred to the terms of collective bargaining agreements, which often spell out various reasonable accommodations the employer must provide for qualified individuals with disabilities. The ADA rejects this automatic approach but does view these agreements as a factor to consider when determining whether or not an accommodation will create an undue hardship. It stands to reason that if the collective bargaining agreement directly discriminates against people with disabilities (e.g., no person with AIDS will be hired for any position), both the union and the employer are subject to suit under the ADA.[28]

Intentional Discrimination: Legitimate Nondiscriminatory Reasons Defense

As a result of the enactment of the Civil Rights Act of 1991, actions brought under the ADA allow applicants or employees who claim to have been discriminated against on the basis of disability to sue for compensatory and punitive damages, in addition to equitable relief such as back pay and reinstatement.[29] Punitive damages, however, are only available when the employer has intentionally discriminated against the disabled individual, or treated the person differently, on the basis of that person's disability—also known as *disparate treatment.* For instance, an employer intentionally discriminates under the ADA if an applicant is rejected because of the appearance of the applicant's artificial arm and the effect it may have on the employer's customers. An employer also intentionally discriminates if an employee with a facial disfigurement is excluded from staff meetings because the employer does not like to look at the employee.[30] (See "Employee's Remedies" in this chapter for more discussion on punitive damages.)

As a result of the availability of compensatory and punitive damages for intentional discrimination based on disability, the number of lawsuits filed under the ADA is expected to be larger than the number contemplated when the ADA legislation was passed.[31] When an applicant or employee with a disability claims to have been intentionally discriminated against by the employer on the basis of a disability, the employer must show a "legitimate nondiscriminatory" reason for the different treatment of the employee that is unrelated to the individual's disability.[32]

It may be a defense to a charge of disparate treatment brought under [the provisions detailing prohibited disability discrimination in employment] that the challenged action is justified by a legitimate, nondiscriminatory reason.[33]

Implications: In order to establish a case claiming disparate treatment or intentional discrimination, the applicant or employee with a disability, "the claimant," must satisfy three requirements:

1. The claimant must prove to have a disability or associate with someone who has a disability.
2. The claimant must prove to have the necessary qualifications, apart from the disability to perform the particular job, with or without reasonable accommodation.
3. The claimant must prove to have been rejected for, or fired from, the job under circumstances that create an inference that the decision was based on the disability.[34]

Under disparate treatment discrimination, the employer possesses a motive or intent to discriminate against the individual with a disability that can be either explicit or implicit. The focus of the inquiry, and what must be proved, is that the employer made the employment decision or took the employment action premised on the existence of a disability. The claimant has the burden of persuasion in this phase of the case. In other words, the claimant must produce evidence and persuade the court that the claimant is a qualified individual with a disability, the employer had discriminatory intent, and due to the claimant's disability, the claimant was treated in a discriminatory manner.[35]

Legitimate nondiscriminatory reason defense. Once the individual with a disability persuades the court that the employer's decision or action was intentionally discriminatory, the employer must then produce evidence that challenges the proof that illegal discrimination occurred. The employer does not have to persuade the court that illegal discrimination did not occur but must produce and present *some* evidence that the employer's conduct was based on a legitimate nondiscriminatory reason.[36] The employer meets this obligation if the evidence the employer presents creates a factual issue that the challenged employment action may have been legitimate.

Alternatively, the employer may admit that the challenged employment action was based on disability but then assert that the claimant's disability made the claimant not "qualified" for the job. For instance, the employer might be able to show that the disability prevented the claimant from performing the essential functions of the job and that no reasonable accommodation could be agreed upon that would not create an undue hardship on the employer.[37]

Once the employer presents this evidence, the burden of proving discrimination shifts back to the claimant. If the employer produces evidence to show that there is a legitimate reason for the employment action, the individual with a disability has the opportunity to show that the "legitimate" reason offered by the employer is a pretext or an excuse for the discriminatory conduct and not the true reason for the employer's conduct.[38] If the employer produces evidence that the claimant is not qualified, an opportunity exists to show that the claimant is qualified for the job, that there is an available reasonable accommodation, and/or that the accommodation is not an undue hardship.[39]

For instance, suppose an individual who uses braces and crutches due to a neuromuscular disability works in the customer service department of a printing company. Despite good marks in all aspects of the employee's job performance, the employer abruptly fires the employee stating, "Customers are scared away because of the way you walk." The disabled individual files a charge with the EEOC and then brings a lawsuit under Title I of the ADA against the employer for intentional discrimination. In order to establish a case, the employee must produce evidence and persuade the court that the employee is a qualified individual with a disability. The employee must also produce evidence, such as witnesses who overheard the statement, and persuade the court that the reason the employee was fired was because of the employer's intent to discriminate based on the disability.

The employer must then merely produce evidence, not necessarily persuade the court, that a legitimate nondiscriminatory reason existed for the firing, such as the employee's consistently late arrival at work. An attempt by the employer to prove that the claimant is not qualified in this situation will likely be unsuccessful due to the employee's successful job performance in the past. Having offered a legitimate nondiscriminatory reason, the employee must then prove that the reason offered by the employer is a pretext for the illegal discrimination. The employee may prove this by showing that other employees consistently arrive late to work or that the employee's tardiness had never been mentioned by the employer as a problem.

There are any number of legitimate nondiscriminatory reasons for employment decisions that may be offered when the employer must produce evidence that an employment decision or action was not motivated by discrimination based on disability. An employee with a disability who has a record of poor performance, poor attendance, or is known to steal from his employer may have no claim against the employer when a negative employment decision is made. The EEOC regulations, however, specify two reasons for employers' decisions that are not considered legitimate. The fact that an individual's disability is not covered by the employer's current insurance plan, or would cause the employer's insurance premiums or worker's compensation costs to increase, is not a legitimate nondiscriminatory reason for justifying intentional discrimination against an individual with a disability.[40]

Unintentional Discrimination: Business Necessity Defense

In addition to the prohibition against intentional discrimination based on disability, known as disparate treatment, Title I of the ADA also prohibits unintentional discrimination based on disability, or *disparate impact*. Under disparate impact discrimination, employers are prohibited from using employment standards and criteria that, even when applied to job applicants and employees in a uniform manner, tend to screen out or have an adverse impact upon individuals with disabilities. These employment practices may also have a disproportionately negative impact on a class of individuals with disabilities.[41] This is not to say that employers cannot adopt appropriate job qualification standards that ensure the hiring of the most qualified applicant who can perform the job effectively and safely. Appropriate qualification standards must be related to the job in question and can involve everything from education skills, work experience, and licenses to physical and mental standards necessary for job performance and health and safety.[42] Employers may also adopt physical and mental qualifications that are necessary to perform specific jobs in such areas as transportation, construction, and law enforcement, for example. If these standards screen out people with disabilities, however, they must be job related and consistent with business necessity. The ADA requirements are designed to assure that people with disabilities are not excluded from jobs that they can perform.

Employers usually have two kinds of potentially discriminatory qualification standards, both of which under the ADA will likely be found to unintentionally discriminate against people with disabilities unless these standards are job related and necessary for the performance of essential job functions.

1. The standard excludes an entire class of individuals with disabilities (For example, a standard that states, "No person who has epilepsy, diabetes, or a heart or back condition is eligible for this job").
2. The standard measures a physical or mental ability needed to perform a job (For example, the standard states, "The person for the job must be able to lift 30 pounds for seven hours a day").[43]

Employers who have standards such as these should review them carefully. In most cases, they will not meet the requirements of the ADA. "Blanket" exclusions of this kind usually have been established because employers believe them to be necessary for health or safety reasons. Employers often use this type of standard to screen out people whom the employer fears, or assumes, may cause higher medical insurance or worker's compensation costs, or may have a higher rate of absenteeism.[44] These generalized blanket exclusions fail to take into account an assessment of a particular individual's current ability to perform a job safely and effectively and therefore violate the ADA unless they are proven to be job related and consistent with business necessity.

It may be a defense to a charge of discrimination brought under this part that a uniformly applied standard, criterion, or policy has a disparate impact on an individual with a disability or a class of individuals with disabilities that the challenged standards, criterion, or policy has been shown to be job-related and consistent with business necessity, and such performance cannot be accomplished with reasonable accommodation, as required in this part.[45]

The EEOC regulations make clear that the defense of business necessity is also available to charges of discriminatory application of selection criteria:

It may be a defense to a charge of discrimination . . . that an application of qualification standards, tests, or selection criteria that screens out or tends to screen out or otherwise denies a job or benefit to an individual with a disability has been shown to be job-related and consistent with business necessity, and such performance cannot be accomplished with reasonable accommodation, as required in this part.[46]

Implications: The process of establishing a case under disparate impact discrimination is similar to the process under disparate treatment. First, a disabled individual must prove to have a disability under the ADA definition and be qualified to perform the job in question, that is, has the requisite skill, education, and licenses. The claimant must then produce evidence and persuade the court that a uniformly applied employment practice or a group of employment practices used by the employer screened out or created a disparate impact upon that individual with a disability. The fact that the employer has no intent or motive to discriminate does not matter.[47]

When claims similar to this are brought by individuals who have been discriminated against on grounds other than disability, claimants often prove discrimination by showing a connection between a qualification standard and a low incidence of employment of minority applicants or employees. These cases frequently rely on statistical evidence to prove that objective job criteria indirectly discriminate against certain groups of people.[48] Under the ADA, statistical evidence to show a lack of minority representation in the work force due to a specific qualification standard is unnecessary. As long as a particular standard is identified that screened out the individual claimant with a disability, a disparate impact case has been established.

The theory behind this approach lies in the diversity of capabilities of people with disabilities. Often there is little or no statistical data to measure the impact of an employment practice or standard on any "class" of people with a particular disability compared to people without disabilities.[49] Throughout the ADA runs this attention to the individual and the discriminatory effects of particular practices and standards. For this reason the federal *Uniform Guidelines on Employee Selection Procedures* do not apply under the ADA to selection procedures affecting people with disabilities.[50]

The burden of proof shifts to the employer. An employer can try to prevent the claimant from establishing a disparate impact case by contradicting the claimant's facts. Once the individual with a disability has persuaded the court that a case has been established, however, the burden shifts to the employer to present evidence and persuade the court that the challenged employment practice or standard is both "job-related and consistent with business necessity." For all practical purposes, the employer admits that the qualification standard in question did discriminate against the individual with a disability but maintains that it is justified and excusable under the circumstances of the job. The employer must persuade the court, not simply produce some evidence, of this fact.

Nowhere in the ADA are the terms "job related" and "consistent with business necessity" defined. This is a result of a political compromise between the Bush administration, Congress, and disability advocates that anticipated the resolution of disputes on this issue to be decided in court. The legislative history of the ADA and the EEOC clearly states that the term "job related and consistent with business necessity" will be interpreted under the ADA as it has evolved through the case law interpreting Section 504 of the Rehabilitation Act.[51]

When is an employer's standard job related? If a qualification standard, test, or other selection criterion operates to screen out individuals or classes of individuals with disabilities, it must be a legitimate measure or qualification of the *specific* job for which it is being used. It is not enough that the standard measures qualifications for a general class of jobs. For example, a qualification standard for a secretarial job of an "ability to take shorthand dictation" is not job related if the person in the particular secretarial job actually transcribes taped dictation.[52]

The ADA allows qualification standards that measure the ability to perform both essential and marginal job functions. If the standards are job related, an employer may use these qualification standards to select and hire people who perform all job functions. It is not until an applicant cannot perform a marginal job function that the ADA requires the employer to rate the applicant solely on the ability to perform essential job functions, with or without the provision of reasonable accommodation.

For instance, suppose one of the two applicants for an administrative job has a disability that makes typing difficult. The position considers typing to be a marginal function of the job. The employer must base the hiring decision on the relative ability of each applicant to perform the essential functions of the job, with or without reasonable accommodation. An inability to type, which is a marginal function in this case, cannot be held against the applicant with a disability unless the reason for the inability to type is unrelated to the applicant's disability, that is, the individual with a disability never learned how to type. In this case, the employer is free to select the applicant who best performs all of the job functions.[53]

What does consistent with business necessity mean? As already stated, "business necessity" will be interpreted under the ADA as the term has been interpreted under the Rehabilitation Act of 1973. This means that cases that have interpreted business necessity under Title VII of the Civil Rights Act of 1964 are not directly applicable to cases brought under the ADA. This is because the defense of business necessity under the Civil Rights Act applies to discrimination against classes of people, not individuals who have been rejected due to the application of a qualification standard.[54] There is nothing in the ADA, however, that prohibits courts from looking for guidance at the business necessity cases brought under Title VII of the Civil Rights Act of 1964.[55]

An employer's qualification standard, which excludes a disabled individual because of the disability, is only consistent with business necessity under the ADA if the standard relates to the essential functions of the job. Courts that have considered this standard under the Rehabilitation Act have warned that business necessity should not be "confused with mere expediency." A disqualifying physical standard "must be directly connected with, and must substantially promote," performance of the job.[56]

Not only must the employment standard relate to the essential functions of the job in order to be consistent with business necessity, but the employer must show that there are no reasonable accommodations that will allow the individual with a disability to satisfy the selection criteria, or that the only accommodation available creates an undue hardship on the employer. In a sense, the question of whether the employer can provide an individual with a disability with a reasonable accommodation during the job selection phase is a subset of determining whether or not the selection standard is necessary to the business. For instance, an employer that requires a job interview as a job related and necessary selection criteria cannot refuse to hire a hearing-impaired applicant because the applicant could not be interviewed. The employer has an obligation to provide a reasonable accommodation, such as an interpreter.

To illustrate how qualification standards that discriminate on the basis of disability must be both job related and consistent with business necessity, suppose an employer must choose between two equally qualified job applicants, one of whom is blind. The employer decides it would be convenient, but not essential, for the employee to be able to drive in order to occasionally run errands. The employer does not hire the blind individual because the applicant does not have a license to drive. This uniformly applied criterion, having a drivers license, adversely impacts the disabled individual because of a disability. The criterion is job related but is not consistent with business necessity because driving is not an essential function of the job in question. In this situation, a charge of unintentional discrimination, brought by the blind applicant, will likely be successful.[57]

The burden of proof shifts back to the individual with a disability. Assuming the employer succeeds in persuading the court that the employment practice, or each of the employment practices in question are job related and consistent with business necessity, and that no reasonable accommodation is available, the burden of persuasion shifts back to the individual with a disability who is challenging the employer's practices. This individual must present evidence and persuade the court of one of the two following conditions:

1. The selection standard is not specifically related to the job in question.
2. Reasonable accommodations or alternative employment practices exist that equally satisfy the employer's needs but have a less discriminatory impact.[58]

In the event the claimant proves that "less restrictive alternatives" or reasonable accommodations exist that test applicants as effectively without discriminating, the challenged qualification standard will not be consistent with business necessity and the claimant will win the lawsuit.[59]

A few exceptions exist where a claimant cannot bring a disparate impact lawsuit for an employer's use of certain uniformly applied employment policies or practices. As the interpretive guidance to the EEOC regulations explains, leave policies and "no-leave" rules (e.g., no leave is allowed during the first six months of employment) cannot be challenged as unintentionally discriminatory under the disparate impact analysis.[60] An employer with a no-leave policy, however, may have to provide leave to an employee with a disability as a form of reasonable accommodation, as long as this accommodation does not create an undue hardship on the operation of the employer's business.

The Direct Threat Defense

The defense of "direct threat to the health or safety of oneself or others" has been the subject of much controversy and will likely spur significant litigation. Under Title I of the ADA, employers may use as a "qualification standard" the requirement that an individual with a disability not pose a direct threat to the health or safety of the individual or others in the workplace.[61] If an employer is able to show that as a result of a disability an employee poses a significant health or safety risk, the employer can reject the applicant or employee, unless the provision of reasonable accommodation will eliminate or reduce the risk of harm to acceptable levels.[62]

As noted in chapter 4, the EEOC expanded the original definition of direct threat to include situations where an applicant or employee poses a direct threat to the health or safety of "oneself or others," which includes the individual with a disability, other employees, and customers. Disability advocates objected to this expansion, fearing routine use of this defense by employers who retained paternalistic and stereotypical notions and attitudes toward people with disabilities. The EEOC, however, raised the degree of proof that the employer must show in order to prevail with this defense. Instead of merely proving that employing the applicant or employee with a disability would slightly increase the safety or health risk to the disabled individual or others, the employer must show that the risk is "significant" or poses a "high probability of substantial harm."[63] The EEOC states that its regulations on the direct threat defense are consistent with the legislative history and the Rehabilitation Act of 1973.[64] "Direct threat" means:

A significant risk of substantial harm to the health or safety of the individual or others that cannot be eliminated or reduced by reasonable accommodation. The determination that an individual poses a "direct threat" shall be based on an individualized assessment of the individual's present ability to safely perform the essential functions of the job. This assessment shall be based on a reasonable medical judgment that relies on the most current medical knowledge and/or on the best available objective evidence.[65]

Implications: The first point that should be understood is that an employer's direct threat standard applies to all individuals, not just to individuals with disabilities.[66] If an applicant's or employee's disability, however, poses a direct threat, the employer must provide a reasonable accommodation to reduce or eliminate the risk. If a reasonable accommodation cannot be found, the employer may refuse to hire the disabled applicant or discharge the disabled employee who poses a significant risk of substantial harm and rely on the direct threat defense.

For instance, suppose an individual who frequently and unexpectedly loses consciousness due to narcolepsy applies for a carpentry job. Essential functions of the job include the operation of dangerous equipment and power tools. If a reasonable accommodation cannot be identified that reduces the direct threat of harm to the individual with a disability or others in the workplace, the employer can legitimately reject the applicant.[67]

As previously mentioned, an employer will only prevail with the direct threat defense when, due to a disability, the applicant or employee currently poses a significant risk or high probability of substantial harm to the health or safety of the individual or others. The employer must show that the direct threat determination has been made based on a current risk of harm, not a possible future risk. Any forecast of future risk must be supported by a doctor's valid medical analysis. For example, an employer cannot reject a qualified applicant who has a mental illness based on the employer's generalized fears that stress from the position may exacerbate the mental illness in the future.[68]

A slightly increased risk, or a speculative or remote risk is insufficient.[69] For example, an employer, whose office is on the tenth floor of an office building, cannot refuse to hire an individual in a wheelchair under the direct threat defense because of the risk of harm to that individual in the event of a fire. The risk in this situation is too remote.[70] Similarly, an employer cannot assume that a person who has restricted manual dexterity due to cerebral palsy cannot work in a laboratory because of the risk of breaking sensitive equipment. This risk is based on speculation. The abilities of the particular applicant must be evaluated before a direct threat determination is made by the employer.[71] In determining whether an individual would pose a direct threat, the factors to be considered include the following:

1. The duration of the risk
2. The nature and severity of the potential harm
3. The likelihood that the potential harm will occur
4. The imminence of the potential harm[72]

Implications: In making a direct threat determination, an employer must identify a specific risk of harm that the applicant's disability creates by considering the duration of the risk, and the nature, severity, potential, and imminence of potential harm. As for the duration of the risk, suppose a school teacher has tuberculosis and with proper medication is contagious for a two-week period. Provided with a reasonable accommodation of a two-week absence from the classroom, the teacher would not pose a "direct threat." The nature and severity of the potential harm must also be considered in the direct threat determination.

The likelihood of potential harm is another important factor to consider in the direct threat determination. Because it is medically established that the HIV virus is only transmitted through entry into a person's bloodstream, there is little or no likelihood that employing an HIV-infected school teacher will result in a direct threat. Finally, the imminence of the potential harm must also be considered. If a physician's evaluation of an applicant for a heavy lifting job forecasts possible aggravation of a back condition in eight to ten years, no direct threat exists because the risk is not imminent.[73]

The direct threat determination, particularly in regard to direct threat to oneself, must be based on objective, factual evidence related to that individual's present ability to safely perform the essential functions of a job. Unfounded, patronizing assumptions and stereotypes have no place in this process. Reasonable medical judgment, based on current medical knowledge and the best available objective evidence, must be considered. Documentation from physicians, physical therapists, and rehabilitation counselors will receive substantial weight, as well as the experience and knowledge of the individual with the disability. As already noted, if the provision of reasonable accommodation can decrease the risk of the direct threat at any time throughout the process to acceptable levels, the employer must provide the accommodation and abandon the direct threat defense.[74]

When the ADA Conflicts with Other Laws

The implementation of the expansive provisions of the ADA should also be considered in relationship to federal, state, and local laws that may conflict with the new legislation. The ADA, a federal law, does not override state or local laws designed to protect public health or safety, except where these laws conflict with ADA requirements. For instance, if a state law would exclude an individual due to a safety risk, the employer must still conduct an individualized "direct threat" determination and provide reasonable accommodation to reduce the risk if possible. An employer may not simply rely on the existence of a state or local law that conflicts with the provisions of the ADA as a defense to a charge of discrimination.[75] The situation is different, however, when the ADA conflicts with other federal laws or regulations.

It may be a defense to a charge of discrimination under this part that a challenged action is required or necessitated by another federal law or regulation, or that another federal law or regulation prohibits an action (including the provision of a particular reasonable accommodation) that would otherwise be required by this part.[76]

Implications: The ADA does not override health and safety requirements that exist under other federal laws. There are several federal laws and regulations that address medical standards and safety requirements.[77] If a standard is required by another federal law, an employer must comply with it and does not have to show that the standard is job related and consistent with business necessity. For example, an applicant with a disability who is being hired to drive a vehicle in interstate commerce must meet safety requirements established by the U.S. Department of Transportation. Employers must also conform to health and safety requirements of the U.S. Occupational Safety and Health Administration (OSHA).[78] The employer may raise this obligation to other federal laws or regulations as a defense to a claim of discrimination based on disability but must attempt to provide a reasonable accommodation that would be consistent with the federal standard and less discriminatory.[79] The individual with a disability who claims to have been discriminated against may challenge the employer's defense of a conflicting federal requirement in three ways:

1. The conflict of a federal standard is a pretext, or not the real reason for the employer's action.
2. The allegedly conflicting federal standard did not require the discriminatory action.
3. There was a nondiscriminatory way to satisfy the requirements of both the ADA and the conflicting federal standard.[80]

Specific Activities Permitted under the ADA

The ADA lists specific activities that are permitted under the new law as "additional defenses" to claims of disability discrimination. These additional defenses include the specific activities allowable under voluntary medical examinations and medical inquiries made after offers of employment have been extended. (For a detailed explanation of acceptable medical inquiries and examinations, see chapter 5.)

Religious Organizations

Religious organizations are free to give preference in employment to applicants of a particular religion but are not free of the obligations imposed by Title I of the ADA.

A religious corporation, association, educational institution, or society is permitted to give preference in employment to individuals of a particular religion to perform work connected with the [activities] by that corporation, association, educational institution, or society. A religious entity may require that all applicants and employees conform to the religious tenets of such organization. However, a religious entity may not discriminate against a qualified individual, who satisfies the permitted religious criteria, because of his or her disability.[81]

Implications: Once a qualified applicant with a disability satisfies the religious organization's criteria, that the applicant believes in or conforms to the tenets of the particular religion, the religious organization cannot discriminate against the disabled individual on the basis of a disability. In other words, if two qualified applicants, one of whom has a disability, both meet the religious criteria of a religious organization, the organization is required by the ADA to consider them for employment on an equal basis. This, of course, includes the provision of reasonable accommodation, if necessary, to the qualified applicant with a disability.[82]

Alcohol and Illegal Drugs in the Workplace

An employer has some latitude in regulating the workplace to ensure that illegal drugs and alcohol are not used during the hours of employment. Employers may also comply with other federal laws and regulations regarding alcohol and illegal drug use without fear of violating the ADA.

Alcoholism. A person who is an alcoholic is considered to be an individual with a disability under the ADA whether or not the individual is currently drinking alcohol.[83] An individual who is an alcoholic is held to the same standards of job performance and conduct as other employees. The individual may be rejected or discharged from employment if the use of alcohol impairs job performance to the point where the individual is no longer qualified, that is, no longer able to perform the essential functions of the job, with or without reasonable accommodation.[84]

For instance, if an employee who is an alcoholic consistently arrives late to work, the employer can take disciplinary action against the employee based on poor job performance and conduct. The employer could not, however, treat the individual more harshly than nonalcoholic employees with the same job performance or conduct. The ADA regards an individual with an alcohol dependency or a history of alcohol dependency essentially the same as in similar provisions in the Rehabilitation Act of 1973.

Current use of illegal drugs. Current users of illegal drugs are *not* considered to be individuals with disabilities under the ADA, whether the individual is a casual user or an addict, and whether or not the illegal drug use affects the individual's job performance. An employer, therefore, can discharge or deny employment to an illegal drug user on the basis of current drug use, without fear of violating the ADA.[85] If the individual has a recognized disability, such as diabetes, and currently uses illegal drugs, the individual is still covered by the ADA, but only for disability discrimination that arises as a result of the diabetes.[86]

The illegal use of drugs includes the use, possession, or distribution of drugs that are illegal under the Controlled Substances Act. This includes the illegal use of prescription drugs that are "controlled substances."[87] Medication and experimental drugs taken under the supervision of a licensed health care professional are not considered illegal drugs. Illegal drug use is "current" when a drug test reveals that the illegal use of drugs occurred recently enough to justify an employer's reasonable belief that involvement with illegal drugs is an on-going problem.[88]

Recovering drug addicts. While current users of illegal drugs are not covered by the protections of the ADA, past drug addicts, who are no longer using drugs and are either receiving treatment or have been successfully rehabilitated, *are* considered individuals with disabilities and are covered by the ADA.[89] These individuals are covered by the ADA because there is a record of impairment, or in some cases, the individual is regarded by others as a drug addict. This is not to say that casual past users of illegal drugs are protected under the ADA as past drug addicts. In order for an individual to be "substantially limited" because of drug use, the individual must have been addicted to the drug.[90]

Allowable activities by employers. Employers can take several steps to reduce or eliminate the use of drugs and alcohol in the workplace that do not violate the ADA:

1. Prohibit the use of drugs and alcohol in the workplace.
2. Require employees to be drug-free during working hours.
3. Conduct routine tests on applicants and employees to detect the illegal use of drugs or alcohol. Drug tests are not considered medical examinations under the ADA.[91]
4. Require alcohol and illegal drug users to meet the same conduct and job performance standards as other employees.
5. Comply with other federal laws and regulations concerning the use of drugs and alcohol, including the Drug-Free Workplace Act of 1988, regulations applicable to certain types of employment, such as law enforcement positions, regulations of the Department of Transportation for airline employees, interstate motor carrier drivers and motor engineers, and regulations for safety sensitive positions established by the Department of Defense and the Nuclear Regulatory Commission.[92]

Food Handling Jobs

The ADA specifically allows the employer to apply the "direct threat" standard and the obligation for reasonable accommodation to applicants or employees who have specific infectious and communicable diseases that are transmitted through the handling of food. Under the ADA, an individual infected with these specific diseases is a person with a disability. The Secretary of the Department of Health and Human Services has published a list of these diseases, which will be updated annually.[93]

When an individual with one of the listed diseases applies for a food handling job, the employer must make a direct threat determination as described earlier in this chapter. The employer must attempt to find a reasonable accommodation that will eliminate or sufficiently reduce the direct threat of contagion. If there is an accommodation that does not create an undue hardship on the employer, the reasonable accommodation must be provided. In the event a reasonable accommodation cannot be found, the employer can refuse to hire the applicant and rely on this section of the ADA as a defense if a claim of discrimination arises.[94]

If the individual with the disabling disease is already an employee, the employer must attempt to accommodate the individual by reassigning the employee to a vacant position that does not entail the handling of food. The employer will only be required to accommodate the employee by reassignment if such a position exists, the employee is qualified for the position, and the reassignment does not create an undue hardship on the employer.[95]

Health Insurance, Life Insurance, and Other Benefit Plans

The ADA specifically permits employers to adopt or continue to provide insurance plans that comply with existing federal and state insurance requirements, even if provisions of these insurance plans negatively affect people with disabilities. Employers may provide these insurance plans only if the provisions that cause the negative effect are not used by the employer as an excuse or a subterfuge to evade the intent of the ADA.[96] In other words, the ADA does not prohibit employers from providing insurance plans that contain pre-existing condition exclusions or that limit coverage for certain procedures and treatments. Even if these restrictions negatively affect people with disabilities, they are allowable under the ADA if the restrictions are uniformly applied to all insured individuals and the restrictions are not being used to evade the purposes of the ADA.[97]

The ADA prohibition against discrimination based on disability, however, applies to the provision and administration of health insurance, life insurance, and pension plans. The ADA establishes certain protections for employees with disabilities that are important to the mandate of nondiscrimination.

1. Employees with disabilities must be given equal access and equal coverage to whatever insurance or benefit plans the employer provides.

2. An employer cannot either deny or limit coverage to an employee with a dis-

ability, based on the disability, if the disability does not pose increased insurance risks.

3. An employer cannot refuse to hire or fire an employee who is disabled or is associated with someone who is disabled because the employer's health plan does not cover the disability or because the employer's insurance or workers' compensation costs may increase.[98]

Table 11.1
Infectious and Communicable Diseases Transmitted through the Handling of Food

Infected Person Contaminates Food	Food Contaminated at Source
Hepatitis A virus	Campylobacter jejuni
Norwalk and Norwark-like viruses	Entamoeba histolytica
Salmonella typhi	Enterohemorrhagic Escherichia
coli	
Shigella species	Enterotoxigenic Escherichia coli
Staphylococcus aureus	Giardia lamblia
Streptococcus pyogenes	Nontyphoidal Salmonella
	Rotavirus
	Vibrio cholerae 01
	Yersinia enterocolitica

SOURCE: *Federal Register*, 16 August 1991, p. 40898-40899.

ENFORCEMENT OF THE ADA

The ADA does not establish its own enforcement mechanism and does not create its own remedies for individuals who prove that they have been discriminated against on the basis of disability. Instead, the ADA explicitly references and adopts the same scope of coverage of employers and the same administrative and judicial remedies that are provided under Title VII of the Civil Rights Act of 1964 for individuals discriminated against on the basis of race, color, sex, religion, age, or national origin.[99] This approach was purposefully taken to given individuals with disabilities the same rights and remedies as other protected minority groups and women.

In addition, the ADA specifically states that its provisions do not invalidate or limit the rights or remedies available under any federal or state law that provides greater or equal protection to individuals with disabilities.[100] For instance, the EEOC allows people with disabilities to file a charge of discrimination within 180 days of the discriminatory conduct. If a state or local law allows the claimant additional time to file a claim for discrimination based on disability, the EEOC will extend the filing deadline from 180 to as many as 300 days.[101]

The employment provisions of Title I of the ADA are enforced by the Equal Employment Opportunity Commission under the procedures established under the Civil Rights Act of 1964. The employment provisions for state and local governments, established under Title II of the ADA, are enforced by the Department of Justice under the Rehabilitation Act of 1973, which incorporates the same enforcement procedures that exist under the Civil Rights Act of 1964.[102] When questions arise on enforcement procedures and available remedies for disability discrimination, the Civil Rights Act of 1964 is one of the basic resources.

Filing a Charge of Disability Discrimination

An individual with a disability who claims to have been discriminated against in employment on the basis of a disability can file a claim against the employer with the Equal Employment Opportunity Commission. Since its establishment in 1964, the EEOC has implemented detailed, step-by-step procedures for the enforcement of civil rights laws.

Individuals who can file a charge. Any job applicant or employee who believes to have been discriminated against on the basis of disability in employment based on actions occurring on or after 26 July 1992 may file a charge against the employer. The EEOC calls the person filing the charge "the charging party." The "employer" is defined as any private entity with 15 or more employees (25 or more employees between 26 July 1992 and 26 July 1994), any state or local government, and any labor union, employment agency, or joint labor-management committee. An individual, whether disabled or not, may also file a charge if the individual believes to have been discriminated against because of an association with a person with a known disability. Any individual may file a charge if it is believed that retaliation has occurred as a result of challenging the employer's practices because the individual either filed a charge or informally protested. Finally, another person or organization also may file a charge on behalf of such an applicant or employee.[103]

How a charge of discrimination is filed. An individual who believes to have been discriminated against on the basis of disability should contact the nearest of fifty EEOC branch offices throughout the United States. Field offices are listed in most telephone directories under the heading "U.S. Government." The EEOC headquarters is located in Washington, D.C. A charging party has 180 days from the date of the allegedly discriminatory conduct to file a charge with the EEOC. As previously noted, this deadline can be extended to three hundred days if a state or local fair employment practices agency enforces a law prohibiting the same type of

Table 11.2
A Charge Filed under the ADA Should Contain Specific Information

1. The charging party's name, address, and telephone number (if a charge is filed on behalf of another individual, his or her identity may be kept confidential, unless required for a court action)

2. The employer's name, address, telephone number, and number of employees

3. The basis or bases of the discrimination claimed by the individual (e.g., disability, race, color, religion, sex, national origin, age or retaliation)

4. The issue or issues involved in the alleged discriminatory act(s), (e.g., hiring, promotion, wages, terms and conditions of employment, discharge)

5. Identification of the charging party's alleged disability (e.g., the physical or mental impairment and how it affects major life activities, the record of disability the employer relied upon, or how the employer regards the individual as disabled)

6. The date of the alleged discriminatory act(s)

7. Details of what allegedly happened

8. Identity of witnesses who have knowledge of alleged discriminatory act(s)

9. Any additional oral or written evidence

SOURCE: Equal Employment Opportunity Commission

discriminatory employment practice raised by the charging party. An individual may file a charge with the EEOC in person, by mail, or by telephone with verification by mail. An individual may file a single charge of discrimination on more than one basis. For instance, a woman who is blind may file a charge alleging employment discrimination on the basis of sex and disability.[104] (For the EEOC and other federal listings, see the appendix.)

Employers may not retaliate against, interfere with, intimidate, or coerce someone who files a charge of discrimination, participates in an investigation, or opposes a discriminatory practice of the employer.[105] Individuals who believe that their employer has retaliated against them in this way are free to file a charge with the EEOC, regardless of the existence of a disability.

How the EEOC processes charges of discrimination. When a disability discrimination charge is filed against an employer, the EEOC refers to the employer as the "respondent." The EEOC sends written notification within 10 days to both the charging party and the employer that a charge of

Table 11.3
Information the EEOC May Request from the Employer during the Investigation of a Disability Discrimination Charge

1. All or part of the investigation may be conducted on-site
2. Specific information on the issues raised in the charge
3. The identity of witnesses who can provide evidence about issues in the charge
4. Information about the business operation, employment process, and workplace
5. Personnel and payroll records
6. Additional oral or written evidence submitted by the employer
7. Additional information submitted by either party at any time throughout the investigation

SOURCE: Equal Employment Opportunity Commission

discrimination has been filed with the EEOC. The EEOC then investigates the charge of discrimination by reviewing the information received by the charging party and by requesting information from the employer.

The EEOC seeks to resolve the discrimination charge by conciliation and other forms of dispute resolution such as fact-finding conferences, settlement negotiations, mediation, mini-trials, and arbitration.[106] Throughout the enforcement process, the EEOC makes every effort to resolve issues through conciliation to avoid litigation, provided the legal rights of employers and people with disabilities are not compromised. The EEOC may dismiss a charge at any time throughout the investigation of the discrimination charge. This will occur if, for instance, the time deadline for filing the charge has not been satisfied or if the employer is not covered under the ADA because the definition of "covered entity" is not met.[107]

The EEOC informs the charging party and the employer of the preliminary findings of the investigation, as to whether or not discrimination occurred, the type of relief, and allows the submission of additional evidence from both parties. Once a final decision has been made, the EEOC sends both parties a "Letter of Determination," which states whether the EEOC has or has not found that discrimination has occurred.

Outcome of the EEOC investigation. If the "Letter of Determination" states that the EEOC investigation has produced no "reasonable cause" to believe that disability discrimination has occurred, the EEOC will issue a "right to sue" letter. This letter gives the individual with a disability the right to bring a lawsuit in either federal or state court alleging employment discrimination under the ADA. The EEOC is no longer a participant in the case at this point. If the investigation has shown "reasonable cause" to believe that the employer did discriminate against the charging party on the basis of disability, the EEOC will take an active role in an attempt to resolve the issue through conciliation. The full range of remedies are available to the charging party at this stage of the dispute.[108]

At all stages of the enforcement process, the EEOC will attempt to resolve the dispute without resorting to a costly lawsuit. However, if reasonable cause is found that discrimination occurred and conciliation fails to resolve the dispute, the EEOC will consider whether to initiate a lawsuit or issue a "right to sue" letter to the charging party. If the EEOC decides to litigate the case, the lawsuit will be brought in federal district court. If a "right to sue" letter is issued instead, the individual with a disability may file a private civil lawsuit, if desired, in either federal or state court within ninety days from the date of the "right to sue" letter.[109] If conciliation fails on a charge of discrimination against a state or local government, the EEOC will refer the case to the Department of Justice for consideration of litigation or issuance of a "right to sue" letter.[110]

In the event the EEOC has neither resolved nor dismissed a charge of discrimination in the first 180 days since its filing, the charging party may request, and is entitled to, a "right to sue" letter. As already noted, once this letter is issued, the charging party has ninety days to bring a civil lawsuit. In this event, the original charges that were filed with the EEOC will ordinarily be dismissed.[111]

Charges Brought under the ADA and the Rehabilitation Act

Most employers who are subject to the Rehabilitation Act of 1973, as federal fund recipients under Section 504, or as federal contractors under Section 503, are now covered by the provisions of the ADA as well. Individuals with disabilities who are discriminated against by these employers could bring a lawsuit based on both laws. In order to avoid duplication and ensure consistent standards in processing disability discrimination complaints, the EEOC and the federal agencies responsible for Section 503 and Section 504 are required by the ADA to establish coordination procedures.[112] The EEOC and the Office of Federal Contract Compliance in the Department of Labor (OFCCP) have issued a joint regulation on coordination between the ADA and Section 503 of the Rehabilitation Act.

The joint rule issued by the EEOC and the Department of Labor provides that a complaint of disability discrimination filed under Section 503 with the Department of Labor will be considered to be a charge filed simultaneously under the ADA if the complaint satisfies the requirements of the ADA.[113] In this way the individual's ADA rights are "preserved." The Department of Labor will either process these claims or refer them to the EEOC. As part of this agreement, the EEOC will refer ADA cases that fall under Section 503 to the Department of Labor when the EEOC has decided not to sue even though there is cause to believe that discrimination has occurred. Finally, where a case involves both disability discrimination and violation of the affirmative action requirements of Section 503, the EEOC will usually refer the case to the Department of Labor for processing and resolution.[114]

The Department of Justice and the Equal Employment Opportunity Commission have issued a joint rule for coordination of complaints or charges of employment discrimination based on disability subject to both the ADA and Section 504 of the Rehabilitation Act of 1973. Recipients of federal financial assistance that have the requisite number of employees under the ADA may be sued by the filing of a lawsuit with the EEOC or the agency responsible for the provision of federal funds. The joint rule stipulates that if a government agency has jurisdiction over a complaint under Section 504, it must process the complaint. If not, the complaint is referred to the EEOC for processing under Title I of the ADA. If the EEOC does not have jurisdiction under the ADA, it will refer the complaint to the Department of Justice to see if another federal agency has jurisdiction. When an agency subject to Section 504 and the EEOC both receive a dual-filed complaint or charge, it will be processed by the agency that first receives it.[115]

Filing ADA Charges versus Worker's Compensation Claims

Filing a worker's compensation claim does not prevent an injured worker from filing a charge under the ADA, assuming the injury creates a mental or physical impairment that qualifies as a disability under the new law. "Exclusivity" clauses in state workers' compensation laws bar all other civil remedies relating to an injury that has been compensated by a worker's compensation system. In other words, a worker could not recover under the workers' compensation system and then bring a private lawsuit against the employer. However, the exclusivity clauses do not prohibit a qualified individual with a disability from filing a discrimination charge with the EEOC and then filing a suit under the ADA, if issued a "right to sue" letter by the EEOC.

REMEDIES FOR THE EMPLOYEE WITH A DISABILITY

The ADA adopts the enforcement mechanisms and remedies that appear in the Civil Rights Act of 1964 for discrimination based on disability. The Civil Rights Act of 1991 amended certain provisions of the Civil Rights Act of 1964 and, thus, the ADA incorporates these amendments that relate to enforcement and remedies by reference. Simply stated, individuals with disabilities who have been discriminated against on the basis of a disability

Table 11.4
Caps on Compensatory and Punitive Damages

Number of Employees	Damages will not exceed
15-100	$ 50,000
101-200	100,000
201-500	200,000
500 or more	300,000

SOURCE: Equal Employment Opportunity Commission

under the ADA may be granted all types of "equitable" relief, such as hiring, reinstatement, promotion, back pay, front pay, reasonable accommodation, or other relief that will place them in the condition they would have been in if not for the discrimination. The ADA specifically allows attorney's fees, including expert witness fees, travel expenses, and other court costs. In other words, the person is made "whole" again.[116]

As a result of the passage of the Civil Rights Act of 1991, compensatory and punitive damages, as well as the right to demand a jury trial, are also available to individuals who have been intentionally discriminated against on the basis of disability. Compensatory damages include actual monetary losses, future monetary losses, and compensation for mental anguish and inconvenience. Compensatory damages have also recently been held to be available to individuals with disabilities who have sued for employment discrimination under Section 504 of the Rehabilitation Act of 1973.[117]

Punitive damages are also available for intentional discrimination based on disability if the employer acted with malice or reckless indifference. The total award of punitive and compensatory damages for emotional distress and future monetary loss for each individual with a disability is limited according to the size of the employer. However, federal legislation has been introduced in Congress, the Equal Remedies Act, that would eliminate these caps on compensatory and punitive damages based on fairness and equity. The damage caps currently apply to all categories of discrimination, except discrimination based on race. Punitive damages are not available against state and local governments, even if intentional discrimination against people with disabilities has occurred. In addition, no employer will be subjected to compensatory or punitive damages for failing to provide reasonable accommodation to a qualified individual with a disability if the employer can demonstrate that "good faith" efforts were made to provide reasonable accommodation.[118]

CHAPTER 12

Perspectives on the ADA

The ADA and the Person

I. King Jordan, Ph.D., President, Gallaudet University

The ADA emphasizes first and foremost, the PERSON. It is a law written to provide equal rights to individuals with disabilities. This is important to note because one of the major goals of the authors of the bill was to present a focus on what people with disabilities *can do*, not what we *cannot do*. Think about that for a minute, because it may be the single most important thing I will say. Focus on what we CAN DO. Let me show you a way to remember that. Say the word *disability*. Go ahead, say it. It is dis-ABILITY. It is not DIS-ability. The same is true of disabled. The word is dis-ABLED, not DIS-abled. Focus on ability.

Disabilities take many forms. Some of us cannot see and we therefore make use of auxiliary aids like dogs or books written in braille. Some of us cannot hear. We often use sign language interpreters or oral interpreters, telecommunication devices (TDDs) to make phone calls, and relay services to connect with phones that do not have TDDs. Some of us cannot walk and use wheelchairs to get around and ramps to give us access to buildings. The list goes on. The point here is that each of us is a unique and significant human being who wants to contribute to the society in which we live and to reap as many of the benefits from life as we can, just like everyone else. We will require some accommodations along the way. The ADA estab-

Excerpts from a speech given by I. King Jordan, Ph.D., President, Gallaudet University, at Lenoir-Rhyne College, Hickory, North Carolina, January 9, 1992.

212   Complying with the Americans with Disabilities Act

lishes by law our right to these accommodations. This is the heart of the ADA. It is a legal guarantee to equal rights for people who are disabled. Unfortunately, it is not enough. What the ADA cannot do is change attitudes toward disabled persons. American society has an inaccurate perception of Americans with disabilities.

For years we have all used such labels as "the handicapped," "the crippled," "the infirmed," and so on. These labels reinforced over and over again the notion that a person with a disability is, first and foremost, handicapped or "below par." The ADA does not use those words. I want to ask you today to throw out the word *handicapped* from your vocabulary and try to begin to erase the concept of a "handicapped person" from your mind. Practice saying to yourself, "person with a disability." Say it over and over until it makes sense. Put the person first before you note sex, race, political affiliation, or disability. Once you have it fixed in your mind, share it with your neighbors and friends. Help them to see it the same way. You can become part of our grand effort to change attitudes that implementing the ADA cannot change. That is one positive way that you can help us change society's thinking. Labels are very important. What you say about a person reveals your attitude. In turn, it affects the attitudes of your associates and co-workers, and ultimately affects the feelings of dignity and self-worth of people who are disabled.

Some years ago, I read a short story about a successful, well-known New York City businessman. One day, on his way home, he passed a destitute man sitting on the sidewalk selling pencils. Without a thought, he dropped a dollar in the man's cup and hurried on. Before he got on the train, however, he realized that he had made a mistake, what he had done was wrong. He turned around and walked back to the beggar and took several pencils from the cup. He explained, apologetically, that in his haste he had neglected to pick up his pencils and hoped the man would not be upset with him. "After all," he said, "you are a businessman just like myself. You have merchandise to sell and it is fairly priced." Then he caught the next train.

Years later at a social function, the businessman was approached by a neatly dressed salesman. The salesman stepped up to the businessman and introduced himself. "You probably don't remember me, but I will never forget you. You are the man who gave me back my self-respect. I was a 'beggar' selling pencils until you came along and told me I was a businessman."

That story hits the heart of my message about people with disabilities. We want and deserve to feel proud of who we are and what we do. We must be proud of our accomplishments, our contributions, our achievements. The ADA will make it easier for us to do this, but in a way it's kind of sad we even need the ADA. People with disabilities are good workers. We want to work! Few of us would choose to live life on welfare

I. King Jordan, Ph.D., president of Gallaudet University, is a leader for deaf people in the United States and the world. Courtesy of Gallaudet University.

if we could avoid that. We work hard! Sometimes we work harder to earn the same level of respect and recognition that our peers take for granted. We are dependable! Studies show that people with disabilities miss fewer work days and stay with the same jobs longer than those without disabilities.

In my role as president, many doors have opened for me. I have had the opportunity to serve on Justin Dart's Task Force on the Rights and Empowerment of People with Disabilities which helped ensure the enactment of the ADA. I am also a member of the President's Committee on the Employment of People with Disabilities. In these roles I have come into contact with about every disability you can think of. I have had the chance to interact with, work with, and become friends of some of the most talented, articulate, and compassionate individuals I have ever known. I have nothing but admiration for my fellow disabled colleagues and for the struggles they have overcome to win their rightful place in society. This experience has enriched my life. Many of these people with disabilities are genuine heroes. This can be both good and bad. It is good, of course, because it shows the world that people with disabilities can excel. It is bad because it allows people to continue their perception that disabled people are either heroic or pathetic. Disabled people, like people in general, cover the whole spectrum of human ability and potential.

Unfortunately, not enough people are aware of this potential. There is a large population of individuals out there with the ability and the desire to work. I consider this to be America's most overlooked national treasure. We must educate America, and then the world, regarding what they are missing by not taking advantage of this overlooked treasure! When we recognize and utilize the potential of people, instead of fearing the difference, we tap into this rich human resource. Sometimes it takes "the other guy" to draw out the potential. As a wise man once said, "A lot of people have gone further than they thought they would because someone else thought they could." I would add that someone also gave them the opportunity and encouragement to do so. The ADA will require the opportunity; we must provide the encouragement.

Workers with Mental Retardation and Title I of the Americans with Disabilities Act

Alan Abeson, Ed.D., Executive Director, The Arc

In many respects, the passage in 1990 of the Americans with Disabilities Act was the logical culmination of two decades of policy advances for American children and adults with disabilities and their families. Much of this body of law specifically or generally established new rights and opportunities along with narrowly stated freedom from discrimination.

Among the federal laws enacted during this period of time were those establishing the right of all children with disabilities to receive a free, appropriate public education (The Education of All Handicapped Children's Act of 1975 [PL 92–142], now known as IDEA, The Individuals with Disabilities Education Act), the prohibition of discrimination in any program or activity receiving federal financial assistance solely by reason of handicap (The Rehabilitation Act of 1973 [PL 93–112]), and establishing the standing of the Attorney General to sue for violations of the civil rights of persons living in institutions (Civil Rights of Institutionalized Persons Act of 1980 [PL 96–247]). While each of these statutes was extraordinarily important in its individual focus, each has also served to contribute to the developing foundation upon which the comprehensive Americans with Disabilities Act could eventually be framed, enacted, and implemented.

Although the focus of this book is on Title I of the ADA, which deals with employment, it is essential to emphasize that the statute has a much broader application. Equally important is that while some prior national policy advances have focused on specific disabilities or specific age groups, the ADA applies to all people of all ages with a disability. This fundamental requirement must be well understood so that discrimination is eliminated for all people with disabilities as established by the law.

This is a particular concern of The Arc (formerly The Association of Retarded Citizens of the United States) because, already, early in translating the law in preparation for implementation, a frequent lack of awareness of Title I (and other titles) applying to people with mental retardation has been noted. Such an omission in the employment context is not surprising in view of the historic denial of opportunities for these individuals to work. Well known and in fact motivation for the ADA was the limited chance at work given to willing workers with mental retardation. Typically, when these people have been able to achieve employment, it has been limited to entry-level, low paying, no benefits jobs involving what has traditionally been called the three "Fs", food (typically fast food restaurants), filth (janitorial jobs), and flowers (nurseries or landscaping). As a result of being limited to only these types of jobs, people with mental retardation are significantly underrepresented in the work force and so the fact that many of them can successfully perform many other kinds of jobs is not yet well known.

Also contributing to the early concern of adequately including people with mental retardation in implementing Title I is that accommodations for most of these people cannot be accomplished through the use of equipment and/or physical environmental adjustments. While some of these accommodations will assist some people with mental retardation and related disabilities, much more significant will be developing an attitude that builds upon a recognition that with proper instruction and support many people with mental retardation will be able to fulfill the "essential functions" of a wide variety of jobs.

Fortunately, eliminating discrimination against people with mental retardation as called for in Title I of the ADA is not beginning in the absence of a body of experience and know how. In fact where workers with mental retardation have been given opportunity, there now exists a solid although too brief history of capability and achievement. Today, the stories of many men and women with mental retardation obtaining and succeeding as workers are legion. For some time such tales of individual accomplishment were limited to only those individuals who remained in their community and both with and without the benefit of special education, vocational rehabilitation, and other specialized programs achieved employment success. While these workers tended to be those with mild mental retardation, in more recent years with the expansion of both traditional and newer specialized education, training, and supported programs, a whole new population of people with mental retardation with more significant mental retardation who formerly spent their time at home or day activity centers or resided in large congregate institutions have also become successfully employed.

During this time as well, employers and colleagues of these workers have begun to discover the capabilities of these people. Often, employers engaged in such hiring practices initially did so and were regarded by others as fulfilling an important societal responsibility. In other words, they were responding to some type of charitable obligation. Much to the surprise and delight of many, these people came to be regarded as outstanding employees. In the terms of many of these employers, after witnessing job performance of these individuals, they forgot about any charitable motive, and characterized hiring these people by stating it's "Just Good Business" (*Just Good Business*, The Arc, 1986).

The magnificence of Title I of the ADA for people with mental retardation is that it creates the opportunity for all employers to learn that hiring these people is in fact "Just Good Business." By preventing discrimination in all aspects of the employment process, these workers will gain the opportunity to be fairly evaluated in relation to their capabilities to fulfill a wide variety of employment responsibilities. In "The Americans with Disabilities Act At Work," a 1991 videotape produced by The Arc that presents a summary of Title I of the act through the jobs of four workers with mental retardation, the jobs depicted include a pharmacy aide in a major city hospital filling orders and delivering pharmaceutical supplies, a clerical aide in a secretarial pool of a major accounting firm, an office mail room assistant, and a general worker with an aviation company with many responsibilities, including guiding jet aircraft in and out of their assigned tarmac locations, sorting baggage, and labeling and shipping freight.

Also of crucial importance in enabling people with mental retardation to fully benefit from access to employment is for employers, personnel officers, supervisors, and future colleagues of these workers to understand that like all other employees they are each individuals. Poorly conceptualized implementation of Title I for these people would be to assume that all people who are protected by the law who are mentally retarded are the same. Like all people, they have different strengths and weaknesses, personalities, physical characteristics and above all, likes and dislikes. As with all other employees, some will learn more quickly than others and some will perform better than others. The prevailing attitude, however, must be that as is well recognized for all employees, and for all people, they are individuals.

This recognition is essential in not only hiring these workers but in providing them with the instruction and support to be effective employees. Further, as with all other employees, should their job performance merit advancement, the presence of their disability must not bar them from receiving such recognition.

In the final analysis, the straightforward purpose of the Americans with Disabilities Act for people with mental retardation is to insure that they like all other Americans have nondiscriminatory access to all that life in this nation has to offer. Appropriately, Title I provides those assurances with regard to achieving employment. This relationship between enjoying life and employment is well known. Beyond simply obtaining the financial wherewithal to live and creating opportunities for social interaction, work enables people to truly develop self-worth, knowing that they are contributing to something valued by others. Title I also recognizes, however, that in addition to benefiting workers with mental retardation, so too will American employers and productivity benefit. The Arc, as the leading national organization on behalf of children and adults with mental retardation and their families, stands ready to provide assistance to employers and the nation to assure compliance.

The Impact of Title I of the Americans with Disabilities Act on People with Multiple Sclerosis

Vice Admiral Thor Hanson, USN (Ret.),
President and CEO
Nancy Law, LSW,
Program Development Manager,
National Multiple Sclerosis Society

We at the National Multiple Sclerosis Society (NMSS) have been steadfast in our support for the Americans with Disabilities Act from the inception of this important legislation. Our staff and volunteers joined efforts with other disability groups in working for its passage. People with multiple sclerosis have experienced longstanding discrimination in employment, which makes Title I of particular importance. With the passage of the ADA, we are standing on the threshold of a new era of opportunity for people with multiple sclerosis and other disabilities.

Multiple sclerosis (MS) is a chronic, often disabling disease of the central nervous system (the brain, spinal cord, and optic nerves). Symptoms of MS are highly individual and vary in severity and duration. Approximately two thirds of those who have multiple sclerosis experience their first symptoms between the ages of twenty and forty, during their prime working years. Absolute numbers of people in the United States with the disease are difficult to obtain, as many cases go unreported. However, recent scientific estimates place the numbers of Americans with MS today at between 250,000 and 350,000. Of these, 85 percent are estimated to be of working age (16–64), and approximately two thirds of those with MS are women. Though results of studies vary, unemployment of people with MS is believed to be at least 63 percent and perhaps as high as 80 percent. Most sources agree that no more than 25 percent of people with MS are employed full time.

These figures are particularly significant as studies also show that for the most part, people with MS are well educated and possess marketable employment skills. According to a 1991 analysis by Brandeis University of selected NMSS chapters, 91 percent of those responding had a high school education, nearly a third (33 percent) had completed college, and 14 percent had at least some graduate work. Ninety-seven percent had been employed at some time in their lives. Forty percent of those who had worked reported having lost a job because of MS.

In light of such dismaying statistics, it is not surprising that people with MS and the National Multiple Sclerosis Society were tireless in their staunch support of the ADA. In looking specifically at Title I, we are hopeful that people with MS who want to work will see an end to many of the discriminatory practices in the workplace that inhibit career fulfillment. The importance of this landmark legislation is paramount to those who have experienced the helpless frustration of discrimination caused by myths and misconceptions about the ability of people with disabilities. (See Laura Cooper and Annie Richardson [not her real name], chapter 10.)

The importance of Title I as it affects employment practices can also be seen in this "real life" discrimination in the workplace incident from the NMSS Midlands Chapter:

Marion Buckley (not her real name), a department store supervisor in Omaha, was informed that she was being demoted because the management position she held would be too much responsibility for someone "with her condition" (multiple sclerosis). This demotion occurred less than three weeks after a supervisory conference during which her performance had been praised. Buckley had no recourse under the current laws in her state.

Under Title I, workers like Buckley are empowered to fight such discriminatory practices.

People with multiple sclerosis have been particularly vulnerable to discrimination in the workplace. Because MS is a condition that has an adult onset, many people newly diagnosed with MS have found themselves working for employers who would never have considered hiring a worker with MS or any other disability, and who had never learned anything about people with disabilities in the workplace. Workers newly diagnosed with MS who disclosed their conditions to employers were often confronted with unpleasant truths about their employers' views on disability. Fearing repercussions, many workers chose not to disclose, only to find themselves in the uncomfortable situation of "living a lie," struggling to conceal symptoms and difficulties from employers and co-workers.

Before the ADA, unless individuals with MS worked for a company with federal contracts, or in a state with existing civil rights legislation for people with disabilities, there was little workers with MS could do to protect their employment status. However, under the ADA, employers are obliged to work with employees, providing accommodations that may enable them to better perform a job. Equally important is the emphasis that Title I places on the employee's qualifications to perform the "essentials" of a job. Too often people with MS have lost jobs or been rejected for jobs based on their physical ability to do some extraneous job function (i.e., lifting books or boxes, writing in longhand, filing in an upper drawer).

Workers with MS have often been barred from work for which they were well qualified, not by their symptoms or disability, but by the attitudes and fears of others. People with MS report having lost jobs that they were performing adequately or well because of an employer's fears of future deterioration in their condition. Title I protects a disabled employee's right to continue to work in a job that the individual is able to perform and the right to "reasonable" accommodations to maximize efficiency.

What constitutes reasonable accommodation for an employee with multiple sclerosis? Just as MS can vary in presentation of symptoms and in severity, so will one person's need for accommodation differ dramatically from another's. It is also important to note that the need for accommodation may vary from time to time, as MS can be a disease of exacerbations and remissions. It is essential that employees with MS have opportunities to direct their own needs for accommodations within reasonable limits. This might include an enlarged computer screen or visual scanner or a unit air conditioner to counter the effects of MS-related heat intolerance.

Many accommodations for people with MS cost little or nothing. For example, an office close to the rest room can help a person with bladder problems. An afternoon rest period can maximize productivity for a person with MS who has symptoms of fatigue. It is important for employer and employee to work cooperatively and creatively to find solutions to problems of symptom management in the workplace. Success in forming a mutually beneficial employer-employee partnership is integrally related to a mindset of commitment to "making it work." The importance of this mindset is illustrated in the NMSS publication, *Inside MS*:

Jim Barry, a marketing specialist from Westchester County, New York, lost two jobs because of MS-related vision problems. However, the NYNEX corporation was not only willing to give Jim a chance to work, the company provided him with a Xerox Kurzweil personal reader (that scans writing and speaks the text), a large-screen monitor and a computer with a voice synthesizer that accepts spoken commands.

Accommodation makes a difference. Jim Barry is a productive and valued employee.

The National Multiple Sclerosis Society (NMSS) was founded in 1946, and has grown to become one of the largest voluntary health organizations in the country. Through its 140 chapters and branches, it serves all 50 states. The NMSS is committed to support the implementation of the ADA and has launched a campaign to emphasize employment of people with MS as a major program initiative for 1992. Employers and people with MS are welcome to call local NMSS chapters, or the national information line at 1–800-LEARN MS for information and assistance.

Appendix: Federal and National Association Resources

FEDERAL AGENCIES THAT ENFORCE THE ADA

[For Title II of the ADA]
U.S. Department of Justice
Civil Rights Division
Coordination and Review Section
P.O. Box 66118
Washington, DC 20035–6118
(202) 307–2222 Voice/TDD   ADA Hotline (202) 514–0301 Voice
(202) 514–0383 TDD

[For Title III of the ADA]
U.S. Department of Justice
Civil Rights Division
Public Access Section
P.O. Box 66738
Washington, DC 20035–6738
(202) 434–9300 Voice/TDD   ADA Hotline (202) 514–0301 Voice
(202) 514–0383 TDD

Equal Employment Opportunity Commission (EEOC)
1801 K Street, N.W.
Washington, DC 20507
(202) 634–6922   (800) USA-EEOC

U.S. Department of Transportation
400 7th St., S.W.
Washington, DC 20590
(202) 366–9305 Voice or (202) 755–7687 TDD

Federal Communications Commission
1919 M Street, N.W.
Washington, DC 20554
(202) 632–7260 Voice or (202) 632–6999 TDD

FEDERAL AGENCIES PROVIDING
TECHNICAL ASSISTANCE

President's Committee on Employment of People with Disabilities (PCEPD)
1331 F St., N.W.
Third Floor
Washington, DC 20004
(202) 376–6200 Voice or (202) 653–5050 TDD
ADA Technical Assistance: (202) 3786–6200 Voice
(202) 376–6205 TDD

Job Accommodation Network (JAN)
P.O. Box 468
Morgantown, WV 26505
(800) ADA-WORK   (800) 526–7234 Voice/TDD

Architectural and Transportation Barriers Compliance Board
1111 18th Street, N.W., Suite 501
Washington, DC 20036–3894
(800) USA-ABLE   (202) 653–7834

National Council on Disability
800 Independence Ave., S.W. Suite 814
Washington, DC 20581
(202) 267–3846 Voice   (202) 267–3232 TDD

Small Business Administration
1441 L Street, N.W.
Washington, DC 20014
(202) 653–6822

National Rehabilitation Information Center (NARIC)
8455 Colesville Road, Suite 935
Silver Spring, MD 20910–3319
(800) 346–2742   (301) 588–9284

Department of Commerce
14th Street and Constitution Ave., N.W.
Washington, DC 20230
(202) 377–2000

National AIDS Clearinghouse
P.O. Box 6003
Rockville, MD 20849–6003
(800) 455–5231

Federal Information Relay Service
Office of the Assistant Regional Administrator
7th and D Streets, S.W.
Washington, DC 20407
(800) 877–8339   (202) 708–9300   both are Voice/TDD

Regional Disability and Business Accommodation Centers

Region I (Connecticut, Maine, Massachusetts, New Hampshire, Rhode Island, and Vermont)
New England Disability and Business Technical Assistance Center
145 Newberry St.
Portland, ME 04101
(207) 874–6535 Voice/TDD

Region II (New Jersey, New York, Puerto Rico, and the Virgin Islands)
Northeast Disability and Business Technical Assistance Center
354 South Broad Street
Trenton, NJ 08608
(609) 392–4004 Voice   (609) 392–7044 TDD

Region III (Delaware, Maryland, Pennsylvania, Virginia, Washington, D.C., and West Virginia)
Mid-Atlantic Disability and Business Technical Assistance Center
2111 Wilson Boulevard Suite 400
Arlington, VA 22201
(703) 525–3268 Voice/TDD

Region IV (Alabama, Florida, Georgia, Kentucky, Mississippi, North Carolina, South Carolina, and Tennessee)
Southeast Disability and Business Technical Assistance Center
1776 Peachtree Street
Suite 310 North
Atlanta, GA 30309
(404) 888–0022 Voice   (404) 888–9007 TDD

Region V (Illinois, Indiana, Michigan, Minnesota, Ohio, and Wisconsin)
Greater Lakes Disability and Business Technical Assistance Center
1640 West Roosevelt Road (M/C 627)
Chicago, IL 60608
(312) 413–1407 Voice   (312) 413–0453 TDD

Region VI (Arkansas, Louisiana, New Mexico, Oklahoma, and Texas)
Southwest Disability and Business Technical Assistance Center
2323 South Shepherd Blvd., Suite 1000
Houston, TX 77019
(713) 520–0232 Voice   (713) 520–5136 TDD

Region VII (Iowa, Kansas, Missouri, and Nebraska)
Great Plains Disability and Business Technical Assistance Center
4816 Santana Dr.
Columbia, MO 65203
(314) 882–3600 Voice/TDD

Region VIII (Colorado, Montana, North Dakota, South Dakota, Utah, and Wyoming)
Rocky Mountain Disability and Business Technical Assistance Center
3630 Sinton Road, Suite 103

Colorado Springs, CO 80907–5072
(719) 444–0252 Voice   (719) 444–0268 TDD

Region IX (Arizona, California, Hawaii, Nevada, and the Pacific Basin)
Pacific Coast Disability and Business Technical Assistance Center
440 Grand Avenue, Suite 500
Oakland, CA 94610
(510) 465–7884 Voice   (510) 465–3172 TDD

Region X (Alaska, Idaho, Oregon, and Washington)
Northwest Disability and Business Technical Assistance Center
605 Woodview Dr.
Lacey, WA 98503
(206) 438–3168 Voice   (206) 438–3167 TDD

NATIONAL ASSOCIATIONS

ABLEDATA, Adaptive Equipment Department
Newington Children's Hospital
181 E. Cedar Street
Newington, CT 06111
(800) 344–5405   (202) 667–5405

American Academy of Physical Medicine and Rehabilitation
122 South Michigan Ave.
Suite 1300
Chicago, IL 60603
(312) 922–9366

American Amputee Foundation, Inc.
P.O. Box 250218
Little Rock, AR 72225
(501) 666–2523

American Bar Association
1800 M St., N.W.
Washington, DC 20036
(202) 331–2200

American Cancer Society
National Office
1599 Clifton Road, NE
Atlanta, GA 30329
(800) ACS–2345

American Diabetes Association, Inc.
National Center
1660 Duke St.
Alexandria, VA 22314
(800) 232–3472

American Foundation for the Blind
15 West 16th Street

New York, NY 10011
(800) 232–5463   (212) 620–2000

American Heart Association
National Office
730 Greenville Avenue
Dallas, TX 75231
(214) 373–6300

American Institute of Architects
c/o Information Center
1735 New York Avenue, N.W.
Washington, DC 20006
(202) 626–7493

American Paralysis Association
500 Morris Avenue
Springfield, NJ 07081
(800) 225–0292   (201) 379–2690 (in NJ)

American Parkinson Disease Association
60 Bay Street
New York, NY 10301
(800) 223–2732   (718) 981–8001

American Red Cross
National Headquarters
Office of HIV/AIDS Education
17th and D Streets, N.W.
Washington, DC 20006
(202) 434–4059

American Speech-Language-Hearing Association
10801 Rockville Pike
Rockville, MD 20852
(800) 638–8255 Voice   (301) 897–0157 TDD

AT&T National Special Needs Center
2001 Route 46
Suite 310
Parsippany, NJ 07054
(800) 233–1222 Voice   (800) 833–3232 TDD

Apple Office of Special Education Programs
Apple Computer
20525 Mariani Avenue
Cupertino, CA 95014
(408) 973–6484

The Arc (formerly the Association for Retarded Citizens of the United States)
500 East Border Street
Suite 300
Arlington, TX 76010
(817) 261–6003

Arthritis Foundation
1314 Spring Street, N.W.

Atlanta, GA 30309
(404) 872–7100

Barrier Free Environments, Inc.
P.O. Box 30634
Water Garden
Highway 70 West
Raleigh, NC 27622
(919) 782–7823 Voice/TDD

Building Owners and Managers Association International
1201 New York Ave., N.W.
Suite 300
Washington, DC 20005
(202) 408–2684

Council of Better Business Bureaus' Foundation
4200 Wilson Blvd. Suite 800
Arlington, VA 22203–1804
(703) 276–0100

Disabled American Veterans
807 Maine Ave., S.W.
Washington, DC 20024
(202) 554–3501

Disability Rights Education and Defense Fund (DREDF)
2212 Sixth St.
Berkeley, CA 94710
ADA Hotline: (800) 466–4ADA Voice/TDD

The Dole Foundation for Employment of People with Disabilities
1819 H Street, N.W. Suite 850
Washington, DC 20006
(202) 457–0318 Voice/TDD

Epilepsy Foundation of America
4351 Garden City Drive
Landover, MD 20785
(301) 459–3700   (800) 332–1000 (patient information and referral)

IBM National Support Center for Persons with Disabilities
P.O. Box 2150
Atlanta, GA 30055
(800) 426–2133 Voice   (800) 284–9482 TDD

Job Opportunities for the Blind (JOB)
1800 Johnson Street
Baltimore, MD 21230
(301) 659–9314

Joseph P. Kennedy, Jr. Foundation
1350 New York Ave., N.W.
Suite 500

Washington, DC 20005
(202) 393–1250

Mainstream, Inc.
1200 15th Street, N.W.
Washington, DC 20005
(202) 898–1400

National Alliance of Business
1201 New York Ave., N.W.
Washington, DC 20005
(202) 289–2905 Voice   (202) 289–2977 TDD

National Alliance for the Mentally Ill (NAMI)
2101 Wilson Boulevard, Suite 302
Arlington, VA 22201
(800) 524-NAMI   (703) 524–7600

National Association of Developmental Disabilities Councils
1234 Massachusetts Ave., N.W. Suite 103
Washington, DC 20005
(202) 347–1234

National Association of Protection and Advocacy Systems
900 2nd St., N.E.
Suite 211
Washington, DC 20002
(202) 408–9518 Voice (202) 408–9521 TDD

National Center for Access Unlimited
155 North Wacker Drive
Suite 315
Chicago, IL 60606
(312) 368–0380 Voice   (312) 368–0179 TDD

National Center for Law and Deafness
Gallaudet University
800 Florida Avenue, N.E.
Washington, DC 20002
(202) 651–5000 Voice   (202) 651–5052 TDD

National Center for Learning Disabilities
99 Park Avenue
New York, NY 10016
(212) 687–7211

National Easter Seal Society
70 East Lake Street, 15th Floor
Chicago, IL 60601
(312) 726–6200 Voice   (312) 726–4258 TDD

National Head Injury Foundation, Inc.
1140 Connecticut Avenue, N.W., Suite 812
Washington, D.C. 20036
(202) 296–6443

National Leadership Coalition on AIDS
1730 M Street, N.W.
Suite 905
Washington, DC 20036
(202) 429–0930

National Multiple Sclerosis Society
810 Seventh Avenue
New York, NY 10017
(800) 624–8236   (212) 986–3240

National Organization on Disability
910 16th Street, N.W. Suite 600
Washington, DC 20006
(202) 293–5960 Voice   (202) 293–5968 TDD
(800) 248-ABLE

National Rehabilitation Association
1910 Association Drive
Suite 205
Reston, VA 22091–1502
(703) 715–9090 Voice   (703) 715–9209 TDD

Paralyzed Veterans of America (PVA)
801 Eighteenth Street, N.W.
Washington, DC 20006
(202) 872–1300

Spina Bifida Association of America
1700 Rockville Pike
Suite 250
Rockville, MD 20852
(800) 621–3141   (301) 770–7222

Tourette Syndrome Association
42–40 Bell Blvd.
Bayside, NY 11361
(718) 224–2999

United Cerebral Palsy Associations, Inc.
1522 K Street, N.W.
Suite 1112
Washington, DC 20005
(800) USA–5UCP   (202) 842–1266 Voice/TDD

Notes

CHAPTER 1

1. National Park Service, Robert C. Ferris, ed., *Signers of the Declaration* (Washington, D.C.: Government Printing Office, 1973), 79–81.

2. Harris E. Starr, ed., *Dictionary of American Biography* (New York: Charles Scribner's Sons, 1949), 29.

3. Justin Dart, Jr., interview, March 1992.

4. National Council on Disability, *Toward Independence* (Washington, D.C.: Government Printing Office, February 1986).

5. Ibid.

6. Louis Harris and Associates, Inc., *ICD Survey of Disabled Americans; Bringing Disabled Americans into the Mainstream: A Nationwide Survey of 1,000 Disabled People* (New York: Louis Harris and Associates, Inc., 1986), 47–49.

7. Don Fersh, "National Rehabilitation Month, Solid Support at National, State Level," *Journal of Rehabilitation*, January/February/March 1980.

8. Louis Harris and Associates, Inc., 1986.

9. Senate Committee on Labor and Human Resources, *The Americans with Disabilities Act of 1989* (Washington, D.C.: Government Printing Office, 30 August 1989), Report 101–116, 17.

10. Ibid.

11. Ibid., 2.

12. *The Americans with Disabilities Act of 1990*, PL 101–336, enacted 26 July 1990, 104 STAT. 327, 42USC 12101, Sec. 2 Findings and Purposes.

13. Ibid.

14. President's Committee on Employment of People with Disabilities, *Worklife* (Washington, D.C.: Government Printing Office, Summer 1990), Vol. 3, No. 2, 18.

15. Ibid., 18.

16. *Worklife*, Vol. 3, No. 3, Fall 1990, 12.

17. Ibid., 20.

18. Ibid., 14.

19. Ibid., 20.

20. Ibid., 21.

21. William H. Kolberg, correspondence, October 1991.

22. *Legislative History*, 1991, Vol. 3, 2249.

23. *Worklife*, Vol. 3, No. 3, Fall 1990, 23.

24. James Brady, Jr., interview, July 1990.

25. *Legislative History*, 1991, Vol. 3, 1870.

26. Paul G. Hearne, correspondence, 13 January 1992.

27. National Institutes of Health, *Report of the Task Force on Medical Reha-bilitation Research* (Bethesda, Md., 1990), 5.

28. National Institutes of Medicine, *Disability in America: Toward a National Agenda for Prevention*, Washington, D.C., 1991, 1:1.

29. Ibid.

30. Sylvia Walker, "Toward Economic Opportunity and Independence: A Goal for Minority Persons with Disabilities," *Building Bridges to Independence*, Sylvia Walker, et. al. (Washington, D.C.: Government Printing Office, 1988), 196.

31. Frank Bowe, *Black Adults with Disabilities*, President's Committee on Employment of People with Disabilities, 1985, 3.

32. *The Americans with Disabilities Act of 1989*, 2 August 1989, 22.

33. Ibid.

34. *Report of the Task Force*, 23–35.

35. Equal Employment Opportunity Commission and U.S. Department of Justice, *Americans with Disabilities Act Handbook* (Washington, D.C.: Government Printing Office, October 1991), I–47, 48.

36. National Mental Health Association, "ADA: Americans with Disabilities Act of 1990," (Alexandria, Va., 1990), 15.

37. Chai R. Feldblum, interview, November 1990, and Christopher Bell, interview, February 1991.

38. *Legislative History*, Vol. 1, 107.

39. Louis Harris and Associates, Inc., *ICD Survey of Disabled Americans*, 1986, 31–35.

40. Bureau of the Census, *Labor Force Status and Other Characteristics of Persons with a Work Disability: 1981 to 1988* (Washington, D.C.: Government Printing Office, July 1989), 1–7.

41. Louis Harris and Associates, Inc., *The ICD Survey II: Employing Disabled Americans, A National Survey of 920 Employers* (New York, March 1987), 7–90.

42. Ibid., 45–48.

43. Ibid., 45.

44. Ibid., 23.

45. Bureau of National Affairs, Inc., *The Civil Rights Act of 1964* (Washington, D.C.: BNA Inc., 1964), vii.

46. Ibid., 1.

47. Ibid., 177.

48. Tom Gray, Small Business Administration, interview, September 1991.

49. Ibid.

50. Howard Moses, EEOC, interview, 7 November 1991.

51. Tom Gray, interview, September 1991.

52. Ibid.

53. Ibid.

54. Ibid.

55. "Diversity at Work," *USA Today*, 26 August 1991.

56. E. I. du Pont de Nemours and Company, "*Equal to the Task II*, 1990 Du Pont Survey of Employment with Disabilities." (Wilmington, Del., 1990), 1–23.

57. *Worklife*, Fall 1991, 6.

58. Sylvia Walker, *Building Bridges to Independence*, 187.

59. Gopal Pati, interview, June 1990.

60. *Legislative History*, Vol. 1, 319.

61. Ibid.

62. Wendell Johnson, *People in Quandaries* (New York: Harper & Row, 1946), 24.

63. *U.S. News and World Report*, 3 March 1980.

64. David Wallechinsky and Irving Wallace, *The People's Almanac* (New York: Doubleday and Company, 1975), 300.

65. Joseph T. Shipley, *Dictionary of Word Origins* (New York: The Philosophical Library, 1945), 52–53.

66. *The Americans with Disabilities Act of 1989*, 45.

67. Kevin R. Hopkins and Susan L. Nestleroth, "Willing and Able," *Businessweek*, 28 October 1991, 1–38.

68. Fact sheet, The Arc, 1991.

69. *Worklife*, Fall 1990, 17.

70. *Businessweek*, 1–38.

71. Senator Tom Harkin, press release, 26 July 1990.

72. *Worklife*, Vol. 3, No. 3, Fall 1990, 22.

73. Ibid.

74. *Building Bridges to Independence*, 184–207.

75. *The Americans with Disabilities Act of 1989*, 51.

76. *Worklife*, Fall 1990, 20.

77. *Building Bridges to Independence*, 193.

78. *Businessweek*, 35–36.

CHAPTER 2

1. *The Americans with Disabilities Act of 1990*, PL 101–336, 26 July 1990, Title III, IV.

2. Tom Gray, Small Business Administration, interview, August 1991.

3. *ADA*, PL 101–336, Title I, Section 101.

4. Ibid., Title II, and Title III, Section 301.

5. Ibid., Title III, Section 302, 304.

6. Ibid.

7. Ibid.

8. Ibid., Title III, Section 302.

9. Ibid., Title III, Section 301(9).

10. Ibid., Title III, Section 301(7).

11. Equal Employment Opportunity Commission and U.S. Department of Justice, *Americans with Disabilities Act Handbook* (Washington, D.C.: Government Printing Office, October 1991), Appendix G, 1–3.

12. *The Americans with Disabilities Act of 1990*, Title II, Section 401.

13. Ibid., Title V, Section 506.

14. Mark Nagler, *Perspectives on Disability* (Palo Alto, Calif.: Health Markets Research, 1990), Evan J. Kemp, Jr., "Foreward," (*sic*), vii-x.

15. Ibid.

16. *ADA*, PL 101–336, Section 2.

17. Ibid.

18. House Committee on Education and Labor, *Legislative History of the Americans with Disabilities Act* (Washington, D.C.: Government Printing Office, 1991), Vol. 1, 253.

19. Committee on Labor and Human Resources, *The Americans with Disabilities Act of 1989*, 15–18.

20. Louis Harris, statement at a press conference held by the National Organization on Disability, 11 September 1991.

21. Ibid.

22. Edwin S. Newman, *Civil Liberty and Civil Rights* (Dobbs Ferry, N.Y.: Oceana Publications, 1967), 67.

23. *Americans with Disabilities Act of 1990*, Section 3.

24. Howard Moses, EEOC, interview, 7 November 1991.

25. Ibid.

26. *ADA Handbook*, I–37.

27. Ibid., III–12, 39.

CHAPTER 3

1. Robert L. Burgdorf, Jr., and Christopher Bell, "Eliminating Discrimination Against Physically and Mentally Handicapped Persons: A Statutory Blueprint," *Mental and Physical Disability Law Reporter*, Vol. 8, No. 1, January/February 1984, 64–75.

2. Nell C. Carney, "Seventy Years of Hope, Seventy Years of Success," *Journal of Rehabilitation*, October/November/December 1990, 6–10.

3. Hugh G. Gallagher, interview, March 1991.

4. Stephen L. Percy, *Disability, Civil Rights, and Public Policy* (Tuscaloosa: University of Alabama Press, 1989), 44–63.

5. Ibid., 47.

6. Ibid., 53.

7. Ibid., 58.

8. Julia Lawlor, *USA Today*, "Employers Still Perplexed by Disabilities Act," 27 March 1991.

9. Ibid., 62.

10. *The Rehabilitation Act of 1973*, Section 504.

11. Bureau of National Affairs, Inc., *The Civil Rights Act of 1964* (Washington, D.C.: BNA Inc., 1964), 97.

12. Burgdorf and Bell, 71.

13. Ibid.

14. Rep. Steny H. Hoyer, speech on the Americans with Disabilities Act of 1990, House of Representatives, *Congressional Record*, 13 June 1990, E 1913–1921.

15. Ibid.

16. *The Civil Rights Act of 1991.*

17. Christopher Bell, EEOC, interview, December 1991.

18. Senate Committee on Labor and Human Resources, *The Americans with Disabilities Act of 1989* (Washington, D.C.: Government Printing Office, 30 August 1989), Report 101–116.

19. National Council on Disability, *Toward Independence* (Washington, D.C.: Government Printing Office, February 1986), 18–26.

20. Senator Tom Harkin, press release, 26 July 1990.

21. *The Labor Lawyer*, court decisions. ,

22. Julia Lawlor, *USA Today*, 27 March 1991.

23. *The Americans with Disabilities Act Handbook*, 1–47.

24. Louis Harris and Associates, Inc., *ICD Survey of Disabled Americans; Bringing Disabled Americans into the Mainstream; A Nationwide Survey of 1,000 Disabled People* (New York, 1986), 23.

25. Equal Employment Opportunities Commission, *A Technical Assistance Manual on the Employment Provisions of the Americans with Disabilities Act* (Washington, D.C.: Government Printing Office, January 1992), Vol. I, 23.

26. Stephen L. Percy, *Disability, Civil Rights, and Public Policy*, 53.

27. Frank Bowe, *Rehabilitating America* (New York: Harper & Row, 1980), 63.

28. Burgdorf and Bell, *Mental and Physical Disability Law Reporter*, 72.

29. *Americans with Disabilities Act of 1990*, Section 2 (b).

30. *Legislative History*, Vol. 2, 321.

31. Mark Nagler, *Perspectives on Disability* (Palo Alto, Calif.: Health Markets Research, 1990), Evan J. Kemp, Jr., "Foreward," (*sic*), vii-x.

32. Ibid.

CHAPTER 4

1. Equal Employment Opportunities Commission, "Equal Employment Opportunity for Individuals with Disabilities: Final Rule," *Federal Register* (Washington, D.C.: Government Printing Office, 26 July 1991), 29 CFR 1630, 35726–35753.

2. Equal Employment Opportunities Commission, "Equal Employment Opportunity for Individuals with Disabilities; Notice of Proposed Rulemaking," *Federal Register* (Washington, D.C.: Government Printing Office), 29 CFR Part 1630, 8578–8603.

3. Ibid., 8578.

4. Committee on Education and Labor, *Legislative History*, 1991.

5. Christopher G. Bell, interview, October 1991.

6. *Americans with Disabilities Act, Legislative History*, Sec. 106.

7. Equal Employment Opportunity Commission, "Final Rule," *Federal Register*, 35736.

8. *Americans with Disabilities Act of 1990*, PL 101–36, 104 STAT. 330.

9. *Federal Register*, 35745.

10. Bonnie P. Tucker, "The EEOC's Safety Defense Under Title I of the ADA: Valid or Invalid?" 2 *Disability Compliance Bulletin*, 5 (Horsham, Pa.: LRP Publications, 16 October 1991), 4.

11. *ADA*, PL 101–336, 104 STAT. 330.

12. *Federal Register*, 35741.

13. Ibid., 35735.

14. Ibid.

15. Ibid., 35741.

16. Ibid., 35735.

17. Department of Justice Legal Opinion (1989).

18. *Federal Register*, 35735.

19. Ibid.

20. Ibid., 35740, 35741.

21. Ibid.

22. Chai R. Feldblum, "The Americans with Disabilities Act: Definition of Disability," *The Labor Lawyer* 7, no. 11 (Washington, D.C.: 1991) 1–26.

23. *Federal Register*, 35741.

24. Ibid., 35735.

25. Ibid.

26. Ibid.

27. Ibid.

28. *School Board of Nassau County v. Arline*, 480 US 273 (1987).

29. Feldblum, 7 *The Labor Lawyer* 11, 16.

30. Ibid.

31. *Arline*, 480 US at 284.

32. *ADA*, 101–336, 104 STAT. 331.

33. *Federal Register*, 35744.

34. Feldblum, 7 *The Labor Lawyer* 11, 18–26.

35. *Federal Register*, 35736.

36. Ibid., 35735.

37. Ibid.

38. Ibid., 35743.

39. Russel H. Gardner and Carolyn J. Campanella, "The Undue Hardship Defense to the Reasonable Accommodation Requirement of the Americans with Disabilities Act of 1990," 7 *The Labor Lawyer* 37 (Washington, D.C.: 1991) 50; Timothy Noah and Albert R. Karr, "What New Civil Rights Law Will Mean," *Wall Street Journal*, 4 November 1991, Sec. B10.

40. *Federal Register*, 35735, 35736.

41. Ibid.

42. Ibid., 35729.

43. Ibid., 35744.

44. Ibid.

45. Ibid.

46. Ibid., 35736.

47. Ibid.

48. Ibid., 35745.

CHAPTER 5

1. *The Americans with Disabilities Act*, PL 101–336, enacted 26 July 1990, 104 STAT. 329, Sec. 102(a).

2. Equal Employment Opportunities Commission, "Equal Employment Opportunity for Individuals with Disabilities; Final Rule," *Federal Register* (Washington, D.C.: Government Printing Office, 26 July 1991), 29 CFR 1630, 35726–35753.

3. *ADA*, PL 101–336, 104 STAT. 332, Sec. 102(b).

4. *Federal Register*, 26 July 1991, 35747.

5. Commerce Clearing House, Inc., *Commerce Clearing House's Explanation of the Americans with Disabilities Act of 1990* (Chicago: CCH Editorial Staff Publication, 5 June 1991), 1–39.

6. *Federal Register*, 35737.

7. Ibid.

8. Ibid., 35750.

9. Ibid., 35737.

10. Ibid., 35750.

11. Christopher G. Bell, EEOC, interview, September 1991.

12. Equal Employment Opportunity Commission and U.S. Department of Justice, *Americans with Disabilities Act Handbook* (Washington, D.C.: Government Printing Office, October 1991), I–71.

13. *Federal Register*, 35750.

14. Ibid., 35737.

15. Commerce Clearing House, 29–30.

16. *Federal Register*, 35737.

17. Ibid., 35749.

18. Commerce Clearing House, 30.

19. Ibid.

20. *Federal Register*, 35737.

21. Commerce Clearing House, 30.

22. *ADA Handbook*, I–73, 75.

23. Ibid., I–73, 74.

24. Ibid.

25. *Federal Register*, 35750, 35751.

26. Ibid., 35732.

27. Commerce Clearing House, 31.

28. *Federal Register*, 35750, 35751.

29. Ibid.

30. Ibid., 35751.

31. Ibid.

32. *ADA Handbook*, I–75.

33. Commerce Clearing House, 32.

34. *ADA*, PL 101–336, 104 STAT. 336, Sec. 102(c)(3)(C).

35. *Federal Register*, 35738.

36. Commerce Clearing House, 32.

37. *Federal Register*, 35751.

38. Ibid., 35732.

39. *ADA Handbook*, I–74, 75.

40. Ibid.

41. *Federal Register*, 35751.

42. Ibid.

43. *ADA Handbook*, I–75.
44. *Federal Register*, 35738.
45. Ibid., 35751.
46. Ibid.
47. Ibid., 35755.

CHAPTER 6

1. Equal Employment Opportunity Commission and U.S. Department of Justice, *Americans with Disabilities Act Handbook* (Washington, D.C.: Government Printing Office, October 1991), III–46.
2. Ibid.
3. Ibid., III–47.
4. Ibid., III–52.
5. Ibid., III–57.
6. Ibid., III–41.
7. Ibid.
8. Ibid., III–65.
9. Ibid., III–111, 117.
10. Ibid., III–111, 112, 119.
11. Ibid., III–128, 129.
12. Ibid., III–128–131.
13. Ibid., III–134.
14. Ibid., III–141.
15. Ibid., III–71.
16. Ibid., III–74, 75.
17. Ibid.
18. Ibid.
19. Ibid., III–78.
20. Ibid.
21. Ibid., III–85.
22. Ibid., III–93.
23. Ibid., III–156.
24. H.R. Rep. No. 485, 101st Cong., 2d Sess., Part 4, 64 (1990).
25. *ADA Handbook*, III–156, 157.
26. Ibid., III–158, 159.
27. Ibid., III–160, 161.
28. Ibid., III–165.
29. Equal Employment Opportunities Commission, "Equal Employment Opportunities for People with Disabilities; Final Rule," *Federal Register* (Washington, D.C.: Government Printing Office, 26 July 1991), 29 CFR 1630, 35751.
30. *ADA*, PL 101–336, 104 STAT. 330, 337.
31. Ibid.
32. *ADA Handbook*, II–26.
33. Ibid., II–46.
34. Ibid., II–27.
35. Ibid., II–56.
36. Ibid., II–63.

37. Ibid., II–64.
38. Ibid., II–56.
39. Ibid., II–57–60.
40. Ibid.
41. Ibid., II–60.
42. Ibid., II–60–62.
43. Ibid.
44. Ibid., II–54.
45. Ibid., II–30.
46. Ibid.
47. Ibid., II–30, 31.
48. Ibid., II–11, 12.

CHAPTER 7

1. Kevin R. Hopkins and Susan L. Nestleroth, "Willing and Able," *Businessweek*, 28 October 1991, 35.

2. Jane West, ed., *The Americans with Disabilities Act: From Policy to Practice* (New York: Milbank Memorial Fund, 1991), 111–128.

3. Senator Tom Harkin, press release, 26 July 1990.

4. Hopkins and Nestleroth, *Businessweek*, 6.

5. Ibid.

6. Susan R. Meisinger, Society for Human Resource Management, correspondence, November 1991.

7. Ibid.

8. Tom Gray, Small Business Administration, interview, August 1991.

9. The number of nonprofit associations was provided by the American Society of Association Executives.

10. Committee on Labor and Human Resources, *The Americans with Disabilities Act of 1989*, 26.

11. Ibid.

12. Ibid.

13. Equal Employment Opportunity Commission and U.S. Department of Justice, *Americans with Disabilities Act Handbook* (Washington, D.C.: Government Printing Office, October 1991) I–1.

14. *ADA*, PL 101–336, Section 102(a).

15. Ibid., Section 101(8).

16. Ibid., Section 101(9).

17. Committee on Education and Labor, *Legislative History of the Americans with Disabilities Act*, Report 101–485, 15 May 1990, Vol. 1, 344.

18. *ADA Handbook*, I–38–40.

19. Ibid.

20. Ibid., I–41.

21. Mark Nagler, *Perspectives on Disability* (Palo Alto, Calif.: Health Markets Research, 1990), Evan J. Kemp, Jr., "Foreward," (*sic*), viii-x.

22. Ibid.

23. EEOC, "The Americans with Disabilities Act: Your Rights as an Employer," 5.

24. *Perspectives on Disability*, viii-x.

25. Ibid.

26. Ibid.

27. *ADA Handbook*, I–71–75.

28. Ibid.

29. Ibid.

30. Ibid.

31. Ibid., I–38–40.

32. Ibid., I–47.

33. Ibid., I–53.

34. *The Americans with Disabilities Act of 1990*, PL 101–336, Section 101(2).

35. Joyce Couch Cole and Ruth Bragman, "Exploratory Investigations of the Information Desired by Employers When Hiring People with Disabilities," *Journal of Applied Rehabilitation Counseling*, 14:4 (Winter 1983), 38–40.

36. Claudia H. Deutsch, "Mastering the Language of Disability," *New York Times*, 10 February 1991.

37. *Businessweek*, 19.

38. W. John Moore, "On the Case," *National Journal*, 2 March 1991, 501–507.

39. Ibid.

40. *ADA Handbook*, I–86–87.

41. Lex Frieden, interview, September 1991.

42. Ibid.

43. Ibid.

44. Steven A. Holmes, "U.S. Rules Will Let Employers Reject Disabled Over Safety Issues," *New York Times*, 23 July 1991.

45. Ibid.

46. Karen Ball, "Disabled Group Calls New EEOC Job Rule Paternalistic Thinking," Associated Press, 22 July 1991.

47. *ADA Handbook*, I–47–48.

48. Bureau of National Affairs, Inc., "Current Developments," No. 144, Washington, D.C., 26 July 1991.

49. *ADA Handbook*, I–11.

50. "U.S. Rules Will Let Employers Reject Disabled Over Safety Issues," *New York Times*, 23 July 1991.

51. Ibid.

52. Ibid.

53. *ADA Handbook*, I–85–86.

54. Ibid., III–3.

55. Ibid.

56. Ibid.

57. Ibid.

58. Ibid.

CHAPTER 8

1. Kevin R. Hopkins and Susan L. Nestleroth, "Willing and Able," *Businessweek*, 28 October 1991, 19.

2. Mary Voboril, "Father's Vision Pushed Leader in Rights for Disabled," *Austin American Statesman*, 17 September 1991.

3. Judy E. Pickens, Patricia Walsh Rao, and Linda Cook Roberts, *Without Bias: A Guidebook to Nondiscriminatory Communication* (San Francisco, Calif.: International Association of Business Communicators, 1977), 1–73.

4. Mark Nagler, *Perspectives on Disability* (Palo Alto, Calif.: Health Markets Research, 1990), Evan J. Kemp, Jr., "Foreward," (*sic*), vii-x.

5. *Legal Report*, Society for Human Resource Management, Winter 1990.

6. *Perspectives on Disability*, vii-x.

7. James Mueller, *The Workplace Workbook: An Illustrated Guide to Job Accommodation and Assistive Technology* (Washington, D.C.: The Dole Foundation, 1990), 3–107.

8. National Center for Medical Rehabilitation Research, National Institutes of Health, "The Scope of Physical Disability in America," June 1991.

9. W. Allen Hauser and Dale C. Hesdorffer, *Facts About Epilepsy* (Landover, Md.: Epilepsy Foundation of America, 1990), 13.

10. *Legal Rights of Persons with Epilepsy* (Landover, Md.: Epilepsy Foundation of America, 1991).

11. Hauser and Hesdorffer, *Facts About Epilepsy*, 13.

12. National Institute of Neurological and Communicative Disorders and Stroke, "Epilepsy: Hope Through Research," Bethesda, Md., July 1981.

13. Hauser and Hesdorffer, *Facts About Epilepsy*, 9.

14. Peter Van Haver Beke, Epilepsy Foundation of America, telephone interview, March 1992.

15. Alan Abeson, correspondence, October 1991.

16. "Fact Sheet," The Arc, 1991.

17. Alan Abeson, correspondence, November 1991.

18. "Fact Sheet," The Arc, 1991.

19. National Center for Medical Rehabilitation Research.

20. Jane Meredith Adams, "Employing the Seriously Mentally Ill," *The Washington Post*, 13 May 1991.

21. Milt Freudenheim, "New Law to Bring Wider Job Rights for the Mentally Ill," *The New York Times*, 23 September 1991.

22. Clifford W. Beers, *A Mind That Found Itself: An Autobiography* (Garden City, N.Y.: Doubleday & Company, 1908), 208.

23. Patty Duke and Gloria Hochman, *A Brilliant Madness: Living with Manic-Depressive Illness* (New York: Bantam Books, 1992), 153–185.

24. Sally Wise, United Cerebral Palsy Associations, Inc., telephone interview, October 1991.

25. Jane M. Healy, *Your Child's Growing Mind* (New York: Doubleday, 1987), 153–185.

26. Jane West, ed., *The Americans with Disabilities Act: From Policy to Practice* (New York: Milbank Memorial Fund, 1991), 85–86.

27. Wade Lambert, "Discrimination Afflicts People with HIV," *Wall Street Journal*, 19 November 1991.

28. Ibid.

29. Jim Graham, Whitman-Walker Clinic, telephone interview, November 1991.

30. Centers for Disease Control and Prevention, "What You Should Know About AIDS," 1988.

31. Lambert, *Wall Street Journal*.

32. Rosalind Brannigan, National Leadership Coalition on AIDS, telephone interview, October 1991.

33. Charles J. Nau, Esq., "The ADA and HIV: What Employers Need to Know Now." (Washington, D.C.: National Leadership Coalition on AIDS, 1991).

34. Examples of AIDS education in the worksite setting can be found in Alan Emery, *The Workplace Profiles Project: Common Features and Profiles of HIV/ AIDS in the Workplace Programs* (Washington, D.C.: National Leadership Coalition on AIDS, 1991).

35. Bernard Posner, National Council on Disability, interview, April 1992.

36. Ibid.

CHAPTER 9

1. Equal Employment Opportunity Commission and U.S. Department of Justice, *Americans with Disabilities Act Handbook*, October 1991, I–41.

2. Richard C. Douglas, President's Committee on Employment of People with Disabilities, correspondence, March 1992.

3. *ADA Handbook*, I–41.

4. Ibid.

5. Ibid., II–51.

6. Ibid., III–71.

7. Ibid., III–34–37.

8. Committee on Labor and Human Resources, *The Americans with Disabilities Act of 1989*, 3 January 1989, 31.

9. *ADA Handbook*, I–42.

10. Committee on Labor and Human Resources, *The Americans with Disabilities Act of 1989*, 31.

11. *ADA Handbook*, III–21.

12. "Employment and Accommodation of Individuals with Disabilities," *Daily Labor Report* (Washington, D.C.: Bureau of National Affairs, Inc., 3 June 1991), C–1–8.

13. *ADA Handbook*, III–22.

14. *The Americans with Disabilities Act of 1989*, 31.

15. *ADA Handbook*, III–22, 23.

16. *The Americans with Disabilities Act of 1989*, 32.

17. *ADA Handbook*, I–43.

18. Ibid.

19. Ibid., III–29.

20. Ibid.

21. Equal Employment Opportunity Commission, *A Technical Assistance Manual on the Employment Provisions (Title I) of the Americans with Disabilities Act* (Washington, D.C.: Government Printing Office, January 1992), 5–75.

22. *Achieving Physical and Communication Accessibility* (Chicago: National Center for Access Unlimited, August 1991), 19.

23. Ibid.

24. Ibid.

25. *ADA Handbook*, I–41.

26. Frank Bowe, "It's *Just* a Telephone?" *The Disability Rag*, March/April 1991, 29–30.

27. *Legislative History*, Vol. 1, 307.

28. Ibid., 308.

29. Jane West, ed., *The Americans with Disabilities Act: From Policy to Practice* (New York: Milbank Memorial Fund, 1991), 313–332.

30. EEOC, "The Americans with Disabilities Act: Your Responsibilities as an Employer," 1991, available in braille, large print, audiotape, and electronic file on computer disk.

31. Ibid.

32. Ibid.

33. Ibid.

34. Equal Employment Opportunity Commission, "Final Rule," *Federal Register*, 26 July 1991, 29 CFR Part 1630, 35726–35753.

35. Ibid.

36. Richard C. Douglas, correspondence, March 1992.

CHAPTER 10

1. Robert L. Burgdorf, Jr., correspondence, October 1991.

2. *The Americans with Disabilities Act of 1990*, PL 101–336, Title I.

3. Frank Bowe, *Handicapping America: Barriers to Disabled People* (New York: Harper & Row, 1978), 185–187.

4. Jane West, ed., *The Americans with Disabilities Act: From Policy to Practice* (New York: Milbank Memorial Fund, 1991), 81–107.

5. *Worklife*, Vol. 3, No. 2, Summer 1990, 23.

6. Committee on Labor and Human Resources, *The Americans with Disabilities Act of 1989*, 37.

7. Equal Employment Opportunity Commission and U.S. Department of Justice, *The Americans with Disabilities Handbook* (October 1991), I–51.

8. Ibid., I–17.

9. "Assessing the Impact of the New Disabilities Act," *San Francisco Recorder*, 27 March 1991.

10. *ADA Handbook*, I–66.

11. Ibid.

12. Ibid., I–67.

13. Ibid.

14. *The Americans with Disabilities Act of 1989*, 34.

15. Ibid., 34.

16. Marc Charmatz, The National Center for Law and Deafness, Gallaudet University, correspondence, January 1992.

17. *The Americans with Disabilities Act of 1989*, 35.

18. *ADA Handbook*, I–64.

19. Ibid.

20. Ibid., I–53.

21. Ibid.

22. Ibid.
23. Ibid.
24. Ibid.
25. Ibid.
26. Ibid.
27. West, *The ADA: From Policy to Practice*, 91.
28. Ibid.
29. Nancy Law, National Multiple Sclerosis Society, correspondence, November 1991.
30. *The Americans with Disabilities Act of 1989*, 39.
31. *ADA Handbook*, 70.
32. *Legislative History*, Vol. 2, 1206.
33. *ADA Handbook*, I–73.
34. West, *The ADA: From Policy to Practice*, 99.
35. *ADA Handbook*, I–53.
36. Ibid., I–87.
37. West, *The ADA: From Policy to Practice*, 101.
38. Cynthia Lehman, Epilepsy Foundation of America, correspondence, November 1991.
39. *The Americans with Disabilities Act of 1989*, 34.
40. *ADA Handbook*, I–69.
41. Ibid., I–58.
42. Ibid.
43. National Council on Disability, *Implications for Federal Policy of the 1986 Harris Survey of Americans with Disabilities*, 37.
44. *Legislative History*, Vol. 1, 307.
45. Edwin S. Newman, *Civil Liberty and Civil Rights* (Dobbs Ferry, N.Y.: Oceana Publications, 1967), 66.
46. Henry Steele Commager, *Documents of American History* (New York: Appleton-Century-Crofts, 1968), 536.
47. Bureau of National Affairs, Inc., *The Civil Rights Act of 1964* (Washington, D.C.: BNA Inc., 1964), 105.
48. Henry Steele Commager, 536.
49. West, ed., *The ADA: From Policy to Practice*, 340.

CHAPTER 11

1. Jane West, ed., *The Americans with Disabilities Act: From Policy to Practice* (New York: Milbank Memorial Fund, 1991), 104.
2. Ibid., 102.
3. Ibid.
4. Equal Employment Opportunity Commission, *A Technical Assistance Manual on the Employment Provisions (Title I) of the Americans with Disabilities Act* (Washington, D.C.: Government Printing Office, January 1992), V–18.
5. Chai R. Feldblum, *Americans with Disabilities Act Selected Employment Requirements* (Washington, D.C.: Georgetown University Law Center, 1991), 23.
6. Equal Employment Opportunities Commission, "Equal Employment Opportunity for Individuals with Disabilities, Final Rule," *Federal Register* (Wash-

ington, D.C.: Government Printing Office, 26 July 1991), 29 CFR 1630, 35726–35753, 35729.

7. Ibid., 35738.

8. Bonnie P. Tucker and Bruce A. Goldstein, *Legal Rights of Persons with Disabilities: An Analysis of Federal Law* (Worsham, Pa.: LPR Publications, 1991), 5:6.

9. West, ed., *The ADA: From Policy to Practice*, 94.

10. EEOC, *Federal Register*, 35736.

11. Equal Employment Opportunity Commission and U.S. Department of Justice, *Americans with Disabilities Act Handbook* (Washington, D.C.: Government Printing Office, October 1991), I–45.

12. See, e.g., *Nelson v. Thornburgh*, 567 F.Supp. 369 (E.D.Pa. 1983).

13. Tucker and Goldstein, *Legal Rights of Persons with Disabilities*, 5:6.

14. *Federal Register*, 35752.

15. *Nelson*, 567 F.Supp. 369 (1983).

16. *Kohl v. Woodhaven Learning Center*, 672 F.Supp. 1226 (W.D.Mo. 1987).

17. *Duquette v. Dupuis*, 582 F.Supp. 1365 (D.N.H. 1984).

18. *Southeastern Community College v. Davis*, 442 U.S. 397, 99 S.Ct. 2361 (1979).

19. Rep. Steny H. Hoyer, *Congressional Record*, Extensions of Remarks (Washington, D.C.: Government Printing Office, 13 June 1990), E–1915.

20. Ibid.

21. Ibid.

22. *Federal Register*, 35744.

23. Ibid., 35752.

24. *ADA Handbook*, I–79, 80.

25. Ibid.

26. *Federal Register*, 35752.

27. West, ed., *The ADA: From Policy to Practice*, 36.

28. Ibid.

29. Timothy Noah and Albert R. Karr, "What New Civil Rights Law Will Mean," *Wall Street Journal*, 4 November 1991, sec. B10.

30. *Federal Register*, 35751.

31. Noah and Karr, *Wall Street Journal*, 4 November 1991, sec. B10.

32. *ADA Handbook*, I–77.

33. *Federal Register*, 35738.

34. West, ed., *The ADA: From Policy to Practice*, 102.

35. United States Commission on Civil Rights, *Report of the United States Commission on Civil Rights on the Civil Rights Act of 1990* (Washington, D.C.: Government Printing Office, July 1990), 18.

36. Ibid., 19.

37. West, ed., *The ADA: From Policy to Practice*, 103.

38. *Report on the Civil Rights Act of 1990*, 19.

39. West, ed., *The ADA: From Policy to Practice*, 103.

40. *Federal Register*, 35751.

41. Ibid.

42. EEOC, *ADA Technical Assistance Manual*, IV–5.

43. Ibid., IV–6.

44. Ibid.

45. *Federal Register*, 35738.

46. Ibid.

47. *Report on the Civil Rights Act of 1990*, 17.

48. Ibid., 18.

49. *ADA Technical Assistance Manual*, IV–4.

50. Ibid.

51. *Federal Register*, 35749.

52. *ADA Technical Assistance Manual*, IV–2.

53. Ibid., IV–3.

54. Ibid.

55. Chai R. Feldblum, interview, January 1992.

56. West, ed., *The ADA: From Policy to Practice*, 24; and *Bentivegena v. United States Department of Labor*, 694 F.2d 619, 622 (1982).

57. *Federal Register*, 35751.

58. *Report on the Civil Rights Act of 1990*, 19.

59. Chai R. Feldblum, interview, January 1992.

60. *Federal Register*, 35752.

61. Ibid., 35738.

62. Ibid., 35745.

63. Ibid., 35745, 35737.

64. Ibid., 35730.

65. Ibid., 35736.

66. *ADA Handbook*, I–47.

67. Ibid.

68. *Federal Register*, 35745.

69. *ADA Technical Assistance Manual*, IV–9.

70. Chairman Evan J. Kemp, Jr., EEOC, interview, November 1991.

71. *ADA Technical Assistance Manual*, IV–10.

72. *Federal Register*, 35736.

73. *ADA Technical Assistance Manual*, IV–11.

74. Ibid., IV–14.

75. Ibid., 17.

76. *Federal Register*, 35738.

77. Ibid., 35752.

78. *ADA Technical Assistance Manual*, IV–16.

79. Ibid.

80. *Federal Register*, 35752.

81. Ibid., 35738.

82. Ibid., 35752.

83. Christopher G. Bell, EEOC, interview, February 1992.

84. *ADA Technical Assistance Manual*, VIII–1.

85. Ibid., VIII–2.

86. Feldblum, *Americans with Disabilities Act Selected Employment Requirements*, 15.

87. *ADA Technical Assistance Manual*, VIII–2.

88. Ibid.

89. *The Americans with Disabilities Act of 1990*, PL 101–336, 104 STAT. 330, 377.

90. *ADA Technical Assistance Manual*, VIII–4.

91. *Federal Register*, 35739.

92. *ADA Technical Assistance Manual*, VIII–8.

93. *Federal Register*, 35753.

94. *ADA Technical Assistance Manual*, IV–15.

95. *Federal Register*, 35753.

96. Ibid., 35739.

97. *ADA Technical Assistance Manual*, VII–9.

98. Ibid.

99. *ADA: From Policy to Practice*, 104.

100. *ADA*, PL 101–336, Sec 501(b).

101. EEOC, "The Americans with Disabilities Act: Your Employment Rights as an Individual with a Disability," 1991, 5.

102. U.S. Department of Justice, "Nondiscrimination on the Basis of Disability in State and Local Government Services; Final Rule," *Federal Register* (Washington, D.C.: Government Printing Office, 26 July 1991), 28 CFR Part 35, 35694–35723, 35713.

103. *ADA Technical Assistance Manual*, X–1.

104. Ibid., X–4.

105. *ADA*, PL 101–336, Sec. 503(a) & (b).

106. Ibid., Sec. 513.

107. *ADA Technical Assistance Manual*, X–6, 7.

108. Christopher Bell, interview, February 1992.

109. *ADA Technical Assistance Manual*, X–7.

110. Ibid., X–5.

111. Christopher Bell, interview, February 1992.

112. *ADA*, PL 101–336, Sec. 107(b).

113. *ADA Technical Assistance Manual*, X–8.

114. Ibid.

115. 28 C.F.R. Part 37, Department of Justice, 1992.

116. Ibid.

117. *Tanberg v. Weld County Sheriff*, DC Colo., No. 91-B–248, 18 March 1992.

118. *Civil Rights Act of 1991*.

Select Bibliography

American Red Cross. *HIV/AIDS Education Catalog* and "Workplace HIV/AIDS Instructor's Manual" and "HIV/AIDS Instructor's Manual" (also in Spanish), Washington, 1991.

Emery, Alan. *The Workplace Profiles Project: Common Features and Profiles of HIV/AIDS in the Workplace Programs*. National Leadership Coalition on AIDS, Washington, 1991.

Epilepsy Foundation of America. *Legal Rights of Persons with Epilepsy*. Landover, Md., 1991.

Equal Employment Opportunity Commission and U.S. Department of Justice. *Americans with Disabilities Act Handbook*. Washington: Government Printing Office, October 1991.

Equal Employment Opportunity Commission. *A Technical Assistance Manual on the Employment Provisions of the Americans with Disabilities Act*, Vols. I, II. Washington: Government Printing Office, January 1992.

Gallagher, Hugh G. *FDR's Splendid Deception*. New York: Dodd, Mead, 1985.

———. *Betrayed: Patients, Physicians, and the License to Kill in the Third Reich*. New York: H. Holt, 1990.

House Committee on Education and Labor. *Legislative History of the Americans with Disabilities Act*, Vols. I, II, III. Washington: Government Printing Office, 1991.

Mueller, James. *The Workplace Workbook: An Illustrated Guide to Job Accommodation and Assistive Technology*. Washington: The Dole Foundation for Employment of People with Disabilities, 1990.

National Alliance of Business. *The ADA Sourcebook*. Washington, 1992.

National Council on Disability. *Toward Independence*. Washington: Government Printing Office, February 1986.

National Center for Access Unlimited. *Achieving Physical and Communication Accessibility and Readily Achievable Checklist: A Survey for Accessibility*. Chicago, August 1991.

National Easter Seal Society. "The Americans with Disabilities Act Resource Guide." Chicago, 1991.

National Institutes of Health. *Report of the Task Force on Medical Rehabilitation Research*. Bethesda, Md., 1990.

Nau, Charles J., Esq. "The ADA and HIV: What Employers Need to Know Now."
    National Leadership Council on AIDS, Washington, 1991.
Senate Committee on Labor and Human Resources. *The Americans with Disabilities Act of 1989*. Washington: Government Printing Office, 30 August 1989,
    Rep. 101–116.
West, Jane, ed. *The Americans with Disabilities Act: From Policy to Practice*. New
    York: Milbank Memorial Fund, 1991.

Index

About the Authors

DON FERSH is a medical writer in Washington, D.C., and former public affairs project director for the President's Committee on Employment of People with Disabilities, the National Rehabilitation Association, and NIH's National Center for Medical Rehabilitation Research. Mr. Fersh has contributed articles to the *Washington Post*, wrote *Heart in Government* for the American Heart Association in 1984 and, more recently, is the senior editor of *The Alcohol Fact Book* for the U.S. Department of Health and Human Services (1993).

PETER W. THOMAS, ESQ. is an attorney with the Washington, D.C. law firm of White, Verville, Fulton, and Saner. Mr. Thomas is the General Counsel of the American State of the Art Prosthetic Association, an advisory board member of the NIH's National Center for Medical Rehabilitation Research, and Legislative Director of the Amputee Coalition of America.